BUYING A HOME IN ITALY

by

David Hampshire

& Mary Jane Cryan

SURVIVAL BOOKS • LONDON • ENGLAND

First published 1999

Survival Books Limited, Suite C, Third Floor
Standbrook House, 2-5 Old Bond Street
London W1X 3TB, United Kingdom
☎ (44) 171-493 4244, Fax (44) 171-491 0605
E-mail: survivalbooks@computronx.com
Internet: computronx.com/survivalbooks

British Library Cataloguing in Publication Data
A CIP record for this book is available from the British Library
ISBN 0 9519804 7 5

Printed and bound in Great Britain by Page Bros. (Norwich) Ltd., Mile Cross Lane,
Norwich, Norfolk NR6 6SA, UK.

ACKNOWLEDGEMENTS

My sincere thanks to all those who contributed to the successful publication of this book, in particular the many people who provided information and took the time and trouble to read and comment on the many draft versions. I would especially like to thank including Ron & Pat Scarborough, Karen Verheul (proof-reader), Fulvio Ferri, the staff of *Ville e Casali* magazine, Luciano D'Alessandro, Gianni Bernabò Di Negro, Joe Laredo and Dave Walkiden for their help and everyone else who contributed in any way whom I have omitted to mention. Also a special thank you to Jim Watson (☎ UK 01788-813609) for the superb illustrations, cartoons and cover.

By the same publisher:

Buying a Home Abroad
Buying a Home in Florida
Buying a Home in France
Buying a Home in Ireland
Buying a Home in Portugal
Buying a Home in Spain
Living and Working in America
Living and Working in Australia
Living and Working in Britain
Living and Working in France
Living and Working in New Zealand
Living and Working in Spain
Living and Working in Switzerland

What Readers and Reviewers Have Said About Survival Books

When you buy a model plane for your child, a video recorder, or some new computer gizmo, you get with it a leaflet or booklet pleading 'Read Me First', or bearing large friendly letters or bold type saying '**IMPORTANT** - follow the instructions carefully'. This book should be similarly supplied to all those entering France with anything more durable than a 5-day return ticket. — It is worth reading even if you are just visiting briefly, or if you have lived here for years and feel totally knowledgeable and secure. But if you need to find out how France works then it is indispensable. Native French people probably have a less thorough understanding of how their country functions. — Where it is most essential, the book is most up to the minute.

Living France

We would like to congratulate you on this work: it is really super! We hand it out to our expatriates and they read it with great interest and pleasure.

ICI (Switzerland) AG

Rarely has a 'survival guide' contained such useful advice — This book dispels doubts for first-time travellers, yet is also useful for seasoned globetrotters — In a word, if you're planning to move to the US or go there for a long-term stay, then buy this book both for general reading and as a ready-reference.

American Citizens Abroad

It's everything you always wanted to ask but didn't for fear of the contemptuous put down — The best English-language guide — Its pages are stuffed with practical information on everyday subjects and are designed to compliment the traditional guidebook.

Swiss News

A complete revelation to me — I found it both enlightening and interesting, not to mention amusing.

Carole Clark

Let's say it at once. David Hampshire's Living and Working in France is the best handbook ever produced for visitors and foreign residents in this country; indeed, my discussion with locals showed that it has much to teach even those born and bred in l'Hexagone— It is Hampshire's meticulous detail which lifts his work way beyond the range of other books with similar titles. Often you think of a supplementary question and search for the answer in vain. With Hampshire this is rarely the case. — He writes with great clarity (and gives French equivalents of all key terms), a touch of humor and a ready eye for the odd (and often illuminating) fact. — This book is absolutely indispensable.

The Riviera Reporter

The ultimate reference book — Every conceivable subject imaginable is exhaustively explained in simple terms — An excellent introduction to fully enjoy all that this fine country has to offer and save time and money in the process.

American Club of Zurich

What Readers and Reviewers Have Said About Survival Books

What a great work, wealth of useful information, well-balanced wording and accuracy in details. My compliments!

Thomas Müller

This handbook has all the practical information one needs to set up home in the UK — The sheer volume of information is almost daunting — Highly recommended for anyone moving to the UK.

American Citizens Abroad

A very good book which has answered so many questions and even some I hadn't thought of — I would certainly recommend it.

Brian Fairman

A mine of information — I might have avoided some embarrassments and frights if I had read it prior to my first Swiss encounters — Deserves an honoured place on any newcomer's bookshelf.

English Teachers Association, Switzerland

Covers just about all the things you want to know on the subject — In answer to the desert island question about the one how-to book on France, this book would be it — Almost 500 pages of solid accurate reading — This book is about enjoyment as much as survival.

The Recorder

It's so funny — I love it and definitely need a copy of my own — Thanks very much for having written such a humorous and helpful book.

Heidi Guiliani

A must for all foreigners coming to Switzerland.

Antoinette O' Donoghue

A comprehensive guide to all things French, written in a highly readable and amusing style, for anyone planning to live, work or retire in France.

The Times

A concise, thorough account of the Do's and DONT's for a foreigner in Switzerland —Crammed with useful information and lightened with humorous quips which make the facts more readable.

American Citizens Abroad

Covers every conceivable question that might be asked concerning everyday life — I know of no other book that could take the place of this one.

France in Print

Hats off to Living and Working in Switzerland!

Ronnie Almeida

CONTENTS

5. ARRIVAL & SETTLING IN 201

APPENDICES 211

INDEX 233

SUGGESTIONS 237

ORDER FORM 240

IMPORTANT NOTE

Readers should note that the laws and regulations for buying property in Italy aren't the same as in other countries and are also liable to change periodically. I **cannot recommend too strongly that you check with an official and reliable source (not always the same) and take expert legal advice before paying any money or signing any legal documents. Don't, however, believe everything you're told or read, even, dare I say it, herein!**

To help you obtain further information and verify data with official sources, useful addresses and references to other sources of information have been included in all chapters and in appendices A and B. Important points have been emphasised throughout the book **in bold print**, some of which it would be expensive or foolish to disregard. **Ignore them at your peril or cost.** Unless specifically stated, the reference to any company, organisation, product or publication in this book *doesn't* constitute an endorsement or recommendation. Any reference to any place or person (living or dead) is purely coincidental.

AUTHOR'S NOTES

- All prices are shown in Italian lire (Lit.) unless otherwise noted. Prices quoted should be taken as estimates only, although they were mostly correct when going to print and fortunately don't usually change overnight. Although prices are sometimes quoted exclusive of value added tax (VAT) in Italy, most prices are quoted inclusive of tax, which is the method used when quoting prices in this book unless otherwise stated.

- His/he/him/man/men (etc.) also mean her/she/her/woman/women (no offence ladies!). This is done simply to make life easier for both the reader and, in particular, the author, and **isn't** intended to be sexist.

- The Italian translation of many key words and phrases is shown in brackets in *italics*.

- Warnings and important points are shown in **bold** type.

- Frequent references are made throughout this book to the European Union (EU), which comprises Austria, Belgium, Denmark, Finland, France, Germany, Greece, Ireland, Italy, Luxembourg, the Netherlands, Portugal, Spain, Sweden and the United Kingdom. The European Economic Area (EEA) includes the EU countries plus Iceland, Liechtenstein and Norway.

- Lists of Useful Addresses and Further Reading are contained in **Appendices A** and **B** respectively.

- For those unfamiliar with the metric system of weights and measures, Imperial conversion tables are shown in **Appendix C**.

- A **Service Directory** containing the names and addresses of companies and organisations doing business in Italy is contained in **Appendix D**.

- A map of the regions of Italy is included in **Appendix E** and a map showing the major cities and geographical features is on page 6.

- A list of property, mortgage and other terms used in this book is included in the glossary in **Appendix F**.

INTRODUCTION

If you're planning to buy a home in Italy or even just thinking about it — this is THE BOOK for you! Whether you want a *palazzo*, farmhouse, cottage or apartment, a holiday or permanent home, this book will help make your dreams come true. The aim of *Buying a Home in Italy* is to provide you with the information necessary to help you choose the most favourable location and the most appropriate home **to satisfy your individual requirements.** Most important of all it will help you avoid the pitfalls and risks associated with buying a home in Italy, which for most people is one of the largest financial transactions they will undertake during their lifetimes.

You may already own a home in your home country; however, buying a home in Italy (or in any foreign country) is a different matter altogether. One of the most common mistakes many people make when buying a home in Italy is to assume that the laws and purchase procedures are the same as in their home country. **This is almost certainly not true!** Buying property in Italy is generally safe, particularly when compared with certain other countries. However, if you don't follow the rules provided for your protection, a purchase can result in serious financial losses as many people have discovered to their cost.

Before buying a home in Italy you need to ask yourself *exactly* why you want to buy a home there? Is your primary concern a good long-term investment or do you wish to work or retire there? Where and what can you afford to buy? Do you plan to let your home to offset the running costs? What about property, capital gains and inheritance taxes? *Buying a Home in Italy* will help you answer these and many other questions. It won't, however, tell you where to live and what to buy or whether, having made your decision, you will be happy – that part is up to you!

For many people, buying a home in Italy has previously been a case of pot luck. However, with a copy of *Buying a Home in Italy* to hand you will have a wealth of priceless information at your fingertips. Information derived from a variety of sources, both official and unofficial, not least the hard won personal experiences of the author, his friends, colleagues and acquaintances. This book doesn't, however, contain all the answers (most of us don't even know the right questions to ask). What it *will* do is reduce the risk of making an expensive mistake that you may bitterly regret later and help you make informed decisions and calculated judgements, instead of costly mistakes and uneducated guesses (forewarned is forearmed!). **Most important of all, it will help you save money and repay your investment many times over.**

The world-wide recession in the early '90s caused an upheaval in world property markets, during which many so-called 'gilt-edged' property investments went to the wall. However, property remains one of the best long-term investments and it's certainly one of the most pleasurable. Buying a home in Italy is a wonderful way to make new friends, broaden your horizons and revitalise your life – and it provides a welcome bolt-hole to recuperate from the stresses and strains of modern life. I trust this book will help you avoid the pitfalls and smooth your way to many happy years in your new home in Italy, secure in the knowledge that you have made the right decision.

Buana Fortuna!

David Hampshire
December 1998

1.

WHY ITALY ?

Italy is one of the most beautiful countries in Europe, possibly the most attractive of all, with more than its fair share of ravishing landscapes and stunning towns. It's a country of huge variety, offering something for everyone: magnificent beaches for sun-worshippers; beautiful unspoiled countryside for the greens; a wealth of magnificent ancient cities and towns for history enthusiasts (virtually every town is a history book of battles and religious milestones); an abundance of mountains and seas for sports lovers; vibrant night-life for the jet set; fine wines for oenophiles and superb cuisine for gourmets; a profusion of culture, art and serious music for art lovers; and tranquillity for the stressed. Few other countries in the world offer such an exhilarating mixture of culture and climate, history and tradition, sophistication and style. When buying property in Italy you aren't buying simply a home, but a lifestyle. As a location for a holiday, retirement or permanent home, Italy has few rivals and in addition to the wide choice of properties and generally good value for money, it offers a fine climate for most of the year, particularly in the south.

There are many excellent reasons for buying a home in Italy, although it's important not to be under any illusions about what you can expect from a home there. The first and most important question you need to ask yourself is *exactly* why do you want to buy a home in Italy? For example, are you seeking a holiday or a retirement home? If you're seeking a second home, will it be mainly used for long weekends or lengthier stays? Do you plan to let it to offset some of the mortgage and running costs? How important is the property income? Are you primarily looking for a sound investment or do you plan to work or start a business in Italy? Often buyers have a variety of reasons for buying a home in Italy, for example many people buy a holiday home with a view to living there permanently or semi-permanently when they retire. If this is the case, there are many more factors to take into account than if you're 'simply' buying a holiday home that you will occupy for a few weeks a year only (when it may be wiser not to buy at all!). If, on the other hand, you plan to work or start a business in Italy, you will be faced with a whole different set of criteria.

Can you really afford to buy a home in Italy? What of the future? Is your income secure and protected against inflation and currency fluctuations? In the '80s, many foreigners purchased holiday homes in Italy by taking out second mortgages on their family homes and stretching their financial resources to the limits. Not surprisingly, when the recession struck in the '90s many people had their homes repossessed or were forced to sell at a huge loss when they were unable to maintain the mortgage payments. (Although this wasn't such a big problem in Italy as it was in some other countries, as it has traditionally been more difficult to raise a loan to buy a second home there.) Buying a home abroad can be a good long-term investment, although in recent years many people have had their fingers burnt in the volatile property market in many countries, including some parts of Italy.

Property values in most regions of Italy increase at an average of less than 5 per cent a year or in line with inflation, although in some fashionable resorts and regions (such as the Italian lakes, the Italian Riviera and Tuscany) prices rise faster than average, which is usually reflected in much higher purchase prices. There's generally a stable property market in most of Italy (barring recessions), which acts as a discouragement to speculators wishing to make a fast buck. You also need to recover the high costs associated with buying a home in Italy when you sell. **You shouldn't expect to make a fast profit when buying property in Italy, but should look upon**

it as an investment in your family's future happiness, rather than merely in financial terms.
There are both advantages and disadvantages to buying a home in Italy, although for most people the benefits far outweigh the drawbacks. Among the many advantages of buying a home in Italy are guaranteed summer sunshine; good value for money (providing you avoid the most fashionable areas), particularly if you want a country house with a large plot of land; the solidity and spaciousness òf rural homes; unparalleled design and a huge variety of architectural styles; stable property market; safe purchase procedure (providing you aren't reckless); integrity of (most) licensed real estate agents and notaries; the availability of superb food and excellent wines at reasonable prices; relatively easy and inexpensive to get to (at least for most western Europeans); good rental possibilities (in many areas); excellent local tradesmen and services; a gentler, slower pace of life in rural areas; the warmth and bonhomie of Italian people; the timeless splendour of Italy on your doorstep; and, last but not least, a quality of life unsurpassed in virtually any other country.

There are of course a few drawbacks, not least the high purchase costs associated with buying property; unexpected renovation and restoration costs (if you don't do your homework); the risk of overpaying for a home and being unable to sell it and recoup your investment; the possibility of over-stretching your finances (e.g. by taking on too large a mortgage) and being unable to maintain the payments; the relatively high crime rate in some areas; the threat of severe storms and earthquakes in some areas; overcrowding in popular tourist areas; traffic congestion in most towns and cities; overbearing bureaucracy (which was invented to prevent Italians having paradise on earth!); an unstable national government (56 since 1945!); the relatively high running costs of a home compared with some other countries and the heavy workload associated with owning a large home and garden; high taxes for residents and an increasing cost of living; and the expense of getting to and from Italy if you own a holiday home there and don't live in a nearby country or a country with good air links.

Unless you know exactly what you're looking for and where, it's advisable to rent a property for a period until you're more familiar with an area. As when making any major financial decision, it isn't advisable to be in too much of a hurry. Many people make expensive (even catastrophic) errors when buying homes in Italy, usually because they do insufficient research and are in too much of a hurry, often setting themselves ridiculous deadlines (such as buying a home during a long weekend break or a week's holiday). Not surprisingly, most people wouldn't dream of acting so rashly when buying a property in their home country! It isn't uncommon for buyers to regret their decision after some time and wish they had purchased a different type of property in a different region (or even in a different country).

Before deciding to buy a home in Italy, it's advisable to do extensive research and read a number of books especially written for those planning to live or work there (like this one!). It also helps to study specialist property magazines and newspapers (see **Appendix A** for a list), and to visit overseas property exhibitions such as those organised by Outbound Publishing in Britain (see **Appendix D**). **Bear in mind that the cost of investing in a few books or magazines (and other research) is tiny compared with the expense of making a big mistake.** Finally, don't believe everything you read (even herein)!

This chapter provides information about permits and visas, retirement, working, buying a business, communications (e.g. telephone), getting to Italy and getting around, particularly by car.

DO YOU NEED A PERMIT OR VISA?

Before making any plans to buy a home in Italy, you must ensure that you will be permitted to use the property when you wish and for whatever purpose you have in mind, and whether you will need a visa or residence permit. While foreigners are freely permitted to buy property in Italy, most aren't permitted to remain longer than three months a year without an appropriate permit or visa. If there's a possibility that you or a family member may wish to work or live permanently in Italy, you should enquire whether this will be possible before making any plans to buy a home there. Bear in mind that Italy is a *very, very* bureaucratic country, among the worst in the western world (if not the worst), and despite the fact that it's a member of the European Union (EU) the documentation necessary (even for EU nationals) to work or live there is pernicious. The 'rules' can vary depending on the region, city or town, and you must sometimes wait months to obtain a residence or work visa.

Citizens of many EU countries can visit Italy with a national identity card, while all others require a full passport. EU nationals and visitors from a number of other countries don't require visas (see below). However, a non-EU national (*extracomunitari*) usually requires a visa to come to Italy to work, study or retire (Some North Americans seem to think that they can travel to Italy to work there without any thought of permits or visas – which certainly isn't true!). All foreigners need a permit to stay (*permesso di soggiorno*) in Italy for longer than three months and non-EU nationals may need a visa to enter Italy, either as a visitor or for any other purpose. Visas may be valid for a single entry only or for multiple entries within a limited period. A visa is stamped in your passport, which must be valid for at least 60 days *after* the date you plan to leave Italy.

All those wishing to remain in Italy for longer than three months must apply at the local police headquarters (*questura*) for a permit to stay (*permesso di soggiorno*) within eight days of their arrival (which can take up to three months to obtain). The *permesso* testifies that you're permitted to live in the country and not that you're a resident. Once you have your *permesso* you can apply for a residence permit (*certificato di residenza*), which is necessary if you spend longer than 183 days a year in Italy. Right of residence (*il diritto di soggiorno*) entails registering at the registry office (*ufficio anagrafe*) in your local community (*comune*) and obtaining a residence certificate (*certificato di residenza*).

While in Italy, you should always carry your passport, stay or residence permit (if you have one), which serves as an identity card (*carta d'identità*) that all Italians must carry by law. Foreign residents can obtain an identity card from their local registry office. You can be asked to produce your identification papers at any time by the Italian police or other officials and if you don't have them you can be taken to a police station and interrogated. Immigration is an inflammatory issue in northern Italy and in recent years the country has been flooded with refugees from Africa, Eastern Europe (particularly Albania and the former Yugoslavia) and Asia. Permit infringements are taken seriously by the authorities and there are penalties for breaches of regulations, including fines and even deportation for flagrant abuses.

Visitors

Visitors can remain in Italy for a maximum of 90 days at a time. Visitors from EU countries plus Andorra, Canada, Cyprus, the Czech Republic, Hungary, Iceland, Japan, Malta, Monaco, New Zealand, Norway, Singapore, Slovakia, South Korea, Switzerland and the USA *don't* require a visa for stays of up to 90 days. All other nationalities need a visa to visit Italy. Italian immigration authorities may require non-EU visitors to produce a return ticket and proof of accommodation, health insurance and financial resources. If you wish to stay longer than three months, you must obtain an extension from the local police. Note that when you stay with friends in Italy (rather than, for example, at a hotel or campsite) for longer than three days you're officially required to register with the local police, although few short-stay visitors comply with this.

EU nationals who visit Italy to seek employment or start a business have three months in which to find a job or apply for permit to stay (*permesso di soggiorno*), although if they haven't found employment or have insufficient funds, the application will be refused. However, if your passport hasn't been stamped (which is unlikely, particularly for EU nationals), the authorities have no way of knowing when you entered the country, therefore the system is 'flexible'. If you enter Italy for any reason other than as a visitor, you should have your passport stamped, although this should happen automatically as you need a visa if you're a non-EU national. If you're a non-EU national, it isn't possible to enter Italy as a tourist and change your status to that of an employee, student or resident, and you must return to your country of residence and apply for a visa.

RETIREMENT

Retired and non-active EU nationals don't require a visa before moving to Italy, but an application for a permit to stay (*permesso di soggiorno*) must be made within eight days of your arrival. Non-EU nationals require a residence visa (*visto per dimora*) to live in Italy for longer than three months and should make a visa application at an Italian consulate abroad around four or five months before their planned departure date. All non-employed residents must provide proof that they have an adequate income or financial resources to live in Italy without working. The minimum amount necessary is equivalent to around Lit. 600,000 per month (excluding rent or mortgage payments) for each adult member of a family (although you're unlikely to be able to live on this!). All foreign residents (including EU residents) who don't qualify for medical treatment under the national health service (*Servizio Sanitario Nazionale/SSN*), must have private health insurance and must be able to support themselves without resorting to state funds. EU nationals in receipt of a state pension are usually eligible for medical treatment under SSN, but require proof of receipt of an old age pension.

WORKING

If there's a possibility that you or any family members may wish to work in Italy, you must ensure that it will be possible before buying a home. If you don't qualify to live and work in Italy by birthright, family relationship or as a national of a European Union (EU) or EEA (European Economic Area) country, obtaining a work permit may be difficult or impossible. If you're a national of an EU member country, you don't require official approval to live or work in Italy, although you still require a stay or residence permit. EU nationals who visit Italy with the intention of finding a job must apply at a local police station for a permit (*ricevuta di segnalazione di siggiorno*) within eight days which entitles them to remain in Italy for three months while looking for a job.

When you have found work, you must take the *ricevuta* together with a letter from your employer confirming your employment to the police station to obtain a permit to stay (*permesso di soggiorno*). You must also apply for a work permit (*permesso di lavoro*), which is valid only for as long as you're employed and is available to both residents and non-residents. Non-EU nationals also require a workers' registration card (*libretto di lavoro*) from the provincial inspectorate of work (*Inspettorato Provinciale del Lavoro*), which is valid for ten years. It's a work card that all citizens and residents of Italy need in order to be legally employed, and serves as an employment record.

Italy has had a virtual freeze on the employment of non-EU nationals for many years, which has been strengthened in recent years due to the high unemployment rate (around 12 per cent). Work permits for non-EU nationals must be obtained outside Italy, where an application for work authorisation (*autorizzazione al lavoro*) must be made at your local Italian embassy. The employment of non-EU nationals must be approved by the Italian labour authorities, who can propose the employment of an EU national in place of a foreigner (although this is rare). Note that there's no way to convert a tourist visa into a work visa and therefore if you're a non-EU national and need a visa to work in Italy, you *must* obtain it before your arrival in the country. There's nothing to stop you visiting Italy as a tourist in order to find a job, but you cannot work without going home and applying for a work visa (which can take months to obtain). For this reason, many people work illegally in Italy, which has a huge black economy (*economia nera/sommersa*).

Before moving to Italy to work, you should dispassionately examine your motives and credentials. What kind of work can you realistically expect to find in Italy? What are your qualifications and experience? Are they recognised in Italy? How good is your Italian? Unless your Italian is fluent, you won't be competing on equal terms with Italians (you won't anyway, but that's a different matter!). Most Italian employers aren't interested in employing anyone without, at the very least, an adequate working knowledge of Italian. Are there any jobs in your profession or trade in the area where you wish to live? The answers to these and many other questions can be quite disheartening, but it's better to ask them *before* moving to Italy rather than afterwards. While hoping for the best, you should plan for the worst case scenario and have a contingency plan and sufficient funds to last until you're established.

Many people turn to self-employment (see below) or start a business to make a living, although this path is strewn with pitfalls for the newcomer. **Many foreigners don't do sufficient homework before moving to Italy.** If you're planning to start a business in Italy, you must also do battle with the notoriously obstructive Italian bureaucracy (*buona fortuna!*). **Note that it's difficult for non-EU nationals to obtain a residence permit to work as self-employed in Italy.**

SELF-EMPLOYMENT

If you're an EU-national or a permanent resident with a *certificato di residenza* you can work as self-employed (*lavora in proprio*) or as a sole trader (*commerciante in proprio*) in Italy. If you wish to work as self-employed in a profession or start a freelance business in Italy, you must meet certain legal requirements and register with the appropriate organisations, e.g. the local chamber of commerce (*camera di commercio*). Note that a *permesso di soggiorno* doesn't automatically allow you to work as self-employed and it will need to be changed to a *permesso di soggiorno per lavoro autonomo* (how easy this is depends on your nationality and status).

Under Italian law, a self-employed person must have an official status and it's illegal to simply hang up a sign and start business. Members of some professions and trades must have certain qualifications and certificates recognised in Italy. **You should <u>never</u> be tempted to start work before you're registered as there are harsh penalties, which may include a large fine, confiscation of machinery or tools, deportation and a ban from entering Italy for a number of years.**

As a self-employed person you don't have the protection of a limited company should your business fail, although there are certain tax advantages. It may be advantageous to operate as a limited company, for example a *Società a Responsabilità Limitata (Srl)* or *Società per Azioni (SpA)*. Always obtain professional advice before deciding whether to operate as a sole trader or form a company, as it has far-reaching social security, tax and other consequences.

STARTING A BUSINESS

The bureaucracy associated with starting a business (*azienda*) in Italy is horrendous and rates among the most pernicious in the world. Italy is a red tape jungle and Italian civil servants (*impiegati*) can be inordinately obstructive, endlessly recycling bits of paper to create 'employment' for themselves. For foreigners the red tape is almost impenetrable, particularly if you don't speak Italian, and you will be inundated with official documents and must be able to understand them. It's only when you come up against the full force of Italian bureaucracy that you understand what it *really* means to be a foreigner! You should expect to spend most of your time battling with civil servants when establishing a new business. However, despite the red tape, Italy is traditionally a land of small companies (there are over three million each employing less than 50 people) and individual traders, where the culture and economic philosophy actually encourages and even nurtures the creation of small businesses.

Before undertaking any business transactions in Italy, it's important to obtain legal advice to ensure that you're operating within the law. There are severe penalties for anyone who ignores the regulations and legal requirements. It's also important to obtain legal advice before establishing a limited company in Italy. Businesses must usually register for value added tax. Non-EU nationals require a special licence to start a business in Italy and no commitments should be made until permission has been granted. Among the best sources of help and information are local chambers of commerce and town halls (*municipio*).

Generally speaking you shouldn't consider running a business in Italy in a field in which you don't have previous experience (excluding 'businesses' such as bed and breakfast, where experience isn't really necessary). It's often advisable to work for someone else in the same line of business in order to gain experience, rather than jump in at the deep end. Always thoroughly investigate an existing or proposed business before investing any money. **As any expert can tell you, Italy isn't a country for amateur entrepreneurs, particularly amateurs who don't speak fluent Italian!** Many small businesses in Italy exist on a shoe-string and certainly aren't what would be considered thriving enterprises. As in many countries, most people are self-employed for the lifestyle and freedom it affords (no clocks or bosses!), rather than the financial rewards. It's important to keep your plans small and manageable and stay well within your budget, rather than undertaking some *grandioso* scheme.

International accountants such as Price Waterhouse and Ernst & Young have offices throughout Italy, and are an invaluable source of information (in English) on subjects such as forming a company, company law, taxation and social security. Many countries maintain chambers of commerce in Italy, which are an invaluable source of information and assistance.

Buying an Existing Business: It's much easier to buy an existing business in Italy than start a new one and it's also less of a risk. The paperwork for taking over an existing business is also simpler, although still complex. Note, however, that buying a business that's a going concern is difficult as the Italians aren't in a habit of buying and selling businesses, which are usually passed down from generation to generation. If you plan to buy a business, obtain an independent valuation (or two) and employ an accountant (*commercialista*) to audit the books. **Never sign anything that you don't understand 110 per cent and even if you think you understand it, you should still obtain unbiased professional advice, e.g. from local experts such as banks and accountants, before buying a business.** In fact it's best not to start a business until you have the infrastructure established including an accountant, lawyer and banking facilities. There are various ways to set up a small business and it's essential to obtain professional advice regarding the best method of establishing and registering a business in Italy, which can dramatically affect your tax position. It's important to employ an accountant to do your books.

Starting a New Business: Most people are far too optimistic about the prospects for a new business in Italy and over-estimate income levels (it often takes years to make a profit). Be realistic or even pessimistic when estimating your income and overestimate the costs and underestimate the revenue (then reduce it by 50 per cent!). While hoping for the best, you should plan for the worst and have sufficient funds to last until you're established (under-funding is the major cause of business failures). New projects are rarely, if ever, completed within budget and you need to ensure that you have sufficient working capital and can survive until a business takes off. Italian banks are extremely wary of lending to new businesses, particularly businesses run by foreigners (would you trust a foreigner?), and it's almost impossible for foreigners to obtain finance in Italy. If you wish to borrow money to buy property or for a business venture in Italy, you should carefully consider where and in what currency to raise the necessary finance.

Location: Choosing the location for a business is even more important than the location for a home. Depending on the type of business, you may need access to *autostrade* and rail links, or to be located in a popular tourist area or near local attractions. Local plans regarding communications, industry and major building developments, e.g. housing complexes and new shopping centres, may also be important. Plans regarding new *autostrade* and rail links are normally available from local town halls.

Employees: Hiring employees shouldn't be taken lightly in Italy and must be taken into account *before* starting a business. You must enter into a contract under Italian labour law and employees enjoy extensive rights. It's also *very* expensive to hire employees, as in addition to salaries you must pay an additional around 50 per cent in social security contributions, a 13th month's salary and five weeks paid annual holiday.

Type of Business: The most common businesses operated by foreigners in Italy include holiday accommodation (e.g. bed & breakfast, apartments, cottages and chalets); caravan and camping sites; building and allied trades; farming; catering (e.g. bars, cafés and restaurants); hotels; shops; franchises; estate agencies; translation bureaux; language schools; landscape gardening; and holiday and sports centres (e.g. tennis, golf, water sports and horse-riding). The majority of businesses established by foreigners are linked to the leisure and catering industries, followed by property investment and development.

Companies: Companies cannot be purchased 'off the shelf' in Italy and it usually takes a number of months to establish a company. Incorporating a company in Italy takes longer and is more expensive and more complicated than in many other European countries (those bureaucrats again!). There are many different kinds of 'limited companies' or business entities in Italy and choosing the right one is important. The most common types of companies in Italy are a *Società a Responsibilità Limitata (Srl)* and a *Società per Azioni (SpA)* with a minimum share capitalisation of Lit. 20 and 200 million respectively. **Always obtain professional legal advice regarding the advantages and disadvantages of different limited companies.**

Grants: Many different grants and incentives are available for new businesses in Italy, particularly in rural areas and the south of the country. Grants include EU subsidies, central government grants, regional development grants, redeployment grants, and grants from provinces and local communities. Grants include assistance to buy buildings and equipment (or the provision of low-cost business premises), subsidies for job creation and tax incentives. Contact Italian chambers of commerce and embassies for information (see **Appendix A**).

Wealth Warning: Whatever people may tell you, working for yourself isn't easy and requires a lot of hard work (self-employed people generally work much longer hours than employees); a sizeable investment and sufficient operating funds (most new businesses fail due to a lack of capital); good organisation (e.g. bookkeeping and planning); excellent customer relations; and a measure of luck (although generally the harder you work, the more 'luck' you will have). Don't be seduced by the apparent laid-back way of life in Italy – if you want to be a success in business you cannot play at it. Bear in mind that some two-thirds of all new businesses fail within three to five years and that the self-employed enjoy far fewer social security benefits than employees.

KEEPING IN TOUCH

Telephone

The Italian telephone service is operated by Telecom Italia (TI), which was privatised in October 1997. Since this date competition has been introduced and users can now choose their provider for long-distance and international calls. Services have been much improved in recent years, during which the telephone network has been updated and exchanges digitalised and automated. However, Italy still has some way to go to match the USA, Britain and many other countries for choice, service and economy. The country also has a national mobile telephone service (see below), encompassing the most populous regions of the country. Emergency telephone numbers are listed at the front of all telephone directories.

Installation: When moving into a new home in Italy with a telephone line, you will need to have the account transferred to your name. It's cheaper to take over (*subentro*) the previous tenant's or owner's number and have the account transferred to your name (although you may receive calls from his friends and relatives!). Note, however, that if you do this you also become responsible for any outstanding bills, therefore check that they have been paid. To have a line reconnected and a new number assigned you should ring Telecom on 187 and tell them that you want a phone line connected. They will tell you which office you must go to in order to sign a contract. You must take with you your permit to stay (*permesso di soggiorno*) and passport, plus a photocopy of each.

If you're planning to move into a property without an existing telephone line, you will need to have one installed (*nuovo impianto*). Note that installation charges in rural areas can be prohibitive if you're home is located a long way from the nearest connection point. It previously took as long as three months to have a phone installed, but in most areas it now takes up to ten days. No deposit is usually payable providing you pay your bills by direct debit from a bank account. The cost of installation will appear on your first bill. Note that if you wish to cancel (*disdetta*) your service, you must give 15 days notice.

When you have a private phone you're entitled to a free copy of the local provincial telephone directory (*elenco*) white and yellow pages (*pagine gialle*), plus a booklet entitled *Tutto Città* containing local maps, useful telephone numbers and

addresses, and postal codes. A copy of new directories is delivered annually to all subscribers. Directories for other provinces can be purchased for a nominal sum. English yellow pages for Bologna, Florence, Milan, Rome and Venice are also available in one directory (☎ 06-474 0861).

Using the Telephone: Using the telephone in Italy is much the same as in any other country. In recent years the domestic system has been in a constant state of change, during which telephone codes and numbers have changed with alarming regularity. If a telephone number is due to change the new number will often be listed in brackets (preceded by the word *prenderà*) after the existing number in the telephone directory. When a number has changed, you will hear a message (in Italian) informing you of this and possible giving you the new number. Area codes (*prefissi*) in Italy begin with 0 and have up to four digits, followed by a four to eight digit subscriber number. Since December 1998, when making a domestic call (even local calls with the same area code) you must dial the area code. A booklet (*tutto telefono*) containing all area codes is published by Telecom Italia and available from bookshops.

There are a range of special numbers in Italy which are assigned different colours. Green numbers (*numeri verdi*) start with 167 and are 'freephone' numbers (although you're charged one or more units for each freephone call you make!). Blue numbers (*numeri azzurri*) are to report child abuse, pink numbers (*numeri rosa*) to report abuse of women and violet numbers (*numeri viola*) to report any other kind of abuse. Red numbers (*numeri rossi*) are to obtain prenatal advice and orange numbers (*numeri arancioni*) are for general psychiatric counselling. Blue numbers (*numero blu*) are numbers you call most frequently, including your internet connection, for which there's a discount (you receive a 50 per cent discount on calls to your Internet provider for a flat fee of Lit. 10,000 per month).

In Italy you dial 112 for the national police (*Carabinieri*), 113 for local police (*polizia*), 115 for the fire service (*vigili del fuoco*), 116 for a highway emergency (*soccorso stradale ACI*) and 118 for a sanitary emergency (*emergenza sanitaria*), which includes gas leaks. Calls to the *carabinieri*, and fire and gas emergencies are free, and you can still make calls to these services if a telephone is cut off for non-payment. Other useful service numbers include domestic reverse charge (10), domestic directory enquiries (12), international reverse charge (15), international operator (170), international directory enquiries (176) and to report a line fault (182). Note that local operators usually speak only Italian, although a translation service is available on 170. There's a charge for calls to directory enquiries.

Extra Services: Telecom provides a range of custom and optional telephone services. To take advantage of them your telephone must be connected to a digital exchange and you must have a touch-tone telephone. Custom calling or optional services can be ordered individually or as part of a package and include call waiting (*avviso di chiamata*), call forwarding (*trasferimento di chiamata*), a three-way conversation (*conversazione a tre*) and a block on outgoing calls (*autodisabilitazione*). Other services include one that takes a message from a caller when your line is engaged and automatically calls you back with the message when your line is free.

Costs: Telephone charges in Italy include line charges; telephone and other equipment rentals; credit card calls; and general call charges. The monthly line rental or service charge (*abbonnamento*) is Lit. 32,600 per month. Telephone costs are continually being reduced by Telecom Italia in the wake of increasing competition, although they are still among the highest in Europe. There are four rate periods for domestic calls: peak (8.30am to 1pm Monday to Friday); ordinary (8 to 8.30am and 1 to 6.30pm Monday to Friday and 8am to 1pm on Saturdays; reduced (6.30 to 10pm on Monday to Friday, 1 to 10pm on Saturday and 8am to 10pm on Sundays and public holidays); and economy (cheap rate) from 10pm to 8am daily. During the peak rate, one unit (*scatto*) is equal to two minutes, which increases to six minutes during the economy rate. There are discounts on the numbers you call most (*numero blu*), which can include your internet connection. The cheap rate is from 10pm to 8am daily in Europe and from 11pm to 8am for most intercontinental calls, during which there's a 30 per cent reduction. You can check the cost of a call (in units) by dialling *#40 before making a call and again after making a call.

International Calls: It's possible to make direct IDD (International Direct Dialling) calls to most countries from both private and public telephones. A full list of country codes is shown in the information pages of white pages, plus area codes for main cities and tariffs. To make an international call you must first dial 00 to obtain an international line. When you hear the new (international) tone, dial the country code, the area code (*without* the first zero) and the subscriber's number. When making an international call to Italy, dial the international access code followed by 39 for Italy, then the area code <u>including</u> the initial 0 and the subscriber's number. A call to Rome from the UK, for example, would begin 00-39-06. You can make reverse charge/collect (*chiamata a carico del destinatario* or *chiamata collect*) and person-to-person (*con preavviso*) calls from any phone by dialling 172 followed by the country code, which connects you to an operator in the country you're calling. To obtain an English-speaking operator from one of the three major US telephone companies you call AT&T USADIRECT (☎ 800-874 4000), MCI Call USA (☎ 800-444 4444) or Sprint Express (☎ 800-793 1153).

Callback Companies: An increasing number of expatriates (and many Italians) make use of callback services provided by companies such as Rapid Link, Via Venezia 14/B, 80021 Afragola (NA) (☎ 048-4102404, e-mail: pp10013 @cybernet.it), American Phone Network, US 19 North, Suite 225, Clearwater, FL 33763 (☎ 813-726-5719, e-mail: afn@pobox.com) and Phone Anywhere, Gueteramtstr. 7, D-69115, Heidelberg, Germany (☎ 49-6221-13390, e-mail: panyge@pobox.com), whereby you call a special number and can make international calls over leased lines for up to 50 per cent less than Telecom Italia's rates.

Bills: Telecom Italia usually bills its customers every two months (although you can arrange to be billed monthly) and allows you two weeks to pay your bill (*conto*). Call costs are calculated on the number of units (*scatti*) you use and bills include value added tax (IVA) at 20 per cent. If you're connected to a digital exchange you can request an itemised bill (*documentazione traffico teleselettivo*), for which there's no additional charge. An itemised bill lists all calls with the date and time, the number called, the duration and the charge, and is particularly useful if you let a second home in Italy or lend it to your friends (although you may be wiser to remove your phone altogether!).

Bills can be paid at Telecom offices or at post offices and banks (when a surcharge is payable). You can also pay your telephone bill by direct debit (*domiziliazione*) from a bank or post office account or have payments spread throughout the year. These last two methods are recommended if you spend a lot of time away from home or own a holiday home, as they will ensure that you won't be disconnected for non-payment. If you're a non-resident, you can have bills sent to an address outside Italy. **Note that it's important to check your bills for accuracy and to keep a record of all payments.** Bills can be wildly inaccurate (usually in Telecom's favour); you can use a metering device (*indicatore di conteggio*) to check your usage if you suspect over-charging. Note that if you're late paying a bill you may be disconnected, although if six consecutive bills have been paid on time there's no penalty if a subsequent payment is received a few days late (how generous!).

Payphones: There are numerous public payphones throughout Italy, although it isn't unusual for them to be out of order (*guasto*). Phones accept coins, tokens (*gettóni*), phonecards or credit cards, or a combination of these. Coin payphones accept 100, 200 and 500 lire coins or Lit. 200 tokens available from post offices, tobacconists and news kiosks. Lit. 200 is the minimum that can be inserted, which is the cost of a local call. Phones that accept only tokens are rare nowadays, although some are still in use. Instructions are provided in English and other languages. Most payphones can receive calls (the number is displayed). When a payphone can be used for long distance and international calls, it's indicated by *teleselezione*. Phones that accept phonecards (*carta/schede telefoniche*) are common in cities and towns. Phonecards are available in values of 5,000, 10,000 and 15,000 lire and can be purchased from bars, news stands, tobacconists and other outlets, and from dispensing machines at airports and main railway stations. To activate a phonecard you tear off the perforated tab at the corner and insert it in the slot provided. The value (or outstanding credit) of a card is displayed when it's inserted and spent cards can be replaced mid-way through a call.

Public phones are also provided in bars and restaurants (*telefono/cabina a scatti*) where you're charged according to the number of units you use. Businesses with payphones are denoted by a round yellow sign on the outside of the building showing a telephone dial. Note that hotels and restaurants are no longer permitted to add a surcharge to telephone calls made on their premises (hurrah)! Some phones accept Telecom credit cards (where calls can also be billed to your home phone if you're a Telecom subscriber) and international credit cards, and their are fax phones in airports and at other locations. You can also make calls from telephone (*telefoni*) offices, where you're assigned a booth and pay after making a call.

Mobile Phones: Mobile phones (*telefonino*) are very popular in Italy where no self-respecting romeo or yuppy would be seen dead without one (they are also considered a vital accessory in a country where the telephone system has traditionally been so unreliable). The number of mobile phones in Italy is around 13 million (around 30 per cent of the population has one, only exceeded in Europe by Scandinavia), three-quarters of which are on contract, with the remainder having pre-paid cards (which are increasing in popularity). The main companies are TIM, a subsidiary of Telecom Italia, with some ten million customers, and Omnitel with around three million. Both operators offer a wide range of tariffs and have digital networks which allow GSM phones to used throughout Europe and the world. Note that mobile phones mustn't be used when driving unless you have a hands-free (*viva voce*) device.

Internet 'Telephone' Services: The success of the Internet is built on the ability to gather information from computers around the world by connecting to a nearby service for the cost of a local telephone call. If you have correspondents or friends who are connected to the Internet, you can make international 'calls' for the price of a local telephone call to your Internet provider, which may even be free. Once on the Internet there are no other charges, no matter how much distance is covered or time is spent on-line. Internet users can buy software from companies such as Vodaltec and Quarterdeck (costing around Lit. 150,000) that effectively turns their personal computer into a voice-based telephone (both parties must have compatible computer software). You also need a sound card, speakers, a microphone and a modem, and access to a local Internet provider (costing around Lit. 30,000 a month). While the quality of communication isn't as good as using a telephone (it's similar to using a CB radio) and you need to arrange call times in advance, making international 'calls' costs virtually nothing. The Internet is also useful for sending and receiving electronic mail (e-mail).

Fax: There has been a huge increase in the use of fax (facsimile) machines in the last decade in Italy, helped by lower prices, the proliferation of callback phone services (see above), and the failings (and frequent strikes) of the Italian post office (a fax is handy for sending letters, order forms, etc.). Fax machines can be purchased from Telecom Italia and a wide variety of other companies and shops. Shop around for the best price. Before bringing a fax machine to Italy, check that it will work there (i.e. is *compatibile*) or that it can be modified. Note, however, that getting a fax machine repaired in Italy may be impossible unless the same machine is sold there. Faxes can also be sent (and received) at post offices and from private fax offices (e.g. *cartolerie*) throughout Italy. Domestic faxes cost around Lit. 3,000 for the first page and Lit. 2,000 for subsequent pages, plus Lit. 50 a second for the actual call. International faxes are around Lit. 6,000 for the first page and Lit. 4,000 for subsequent pages, plus Lit. 100 per second for the call.

Mail Services

The Italian post office (*Poste Italiane*, although officially named the *Poste, Telegrafi e Telefono (PTT)* and identified by a 'PT' sign) has hardly been re-organised since the 19th century – and it shows! As with anything to do with civil servants in Italy, the postal system (you cannot call it a 'service') is positively Neanderthal and is easily the worst in Western Europe (and possibly the whole of Europe). Nothing of value should be entrusted to the Italian post office and all valuable mail (i.e. anything other than junk mail) should be either registered (*raccomandate*) or sent via a private courier company. It's said that the post office throws away all unregistered mail, although this is probably an exaggeration. The (independent) Vatican post office in St. Peter's square is the most efficient and reliable in Italy as it sends all its international mail to Switzerland!

Business hours for most post offices (*posta* or *ufficio postale*) are from 8am to 6pm from Monday to Friday, and from 8am until noon on Saturday and the last day of the month. Main post offices in major cities may remain open until between 7 and 8pm. Note, however, that business hours in rural towns and villages may be more limited. In addition to the usual postal services, post offices provide a bill-paying service for utility bills (electricity, gas and telephone) and certain taxes (e.g. road and TV tax). Bills must be paid in cash (via *conto corrente postale*) and there's a surcharge of around Lit. 1,200 for each one paid. Main post offices provide typewriters for writing telegrams, stationery shops, a parcel wrapping service and a fax (send/receive) service.

Postal rates are complicated and postal clerks often make mistakes; a rate card (*tariffario postale*) can be purchased from bookshops (only a post office that doesn't actually want you to post any mail would charge for this!). Letters up to 20g cost Lit. 850 to EU countries (Lit. 900 to the rest of Europe), Lit. 1,300 to North America, and Lit. 2000 to Australia and New Zealand. Affix a blue airmail sticker to airmail letters or write 'Via Aerea' in the top left-hand corner of the envelope. Aerogrammes cost Lit. 850 to any country and can be purchased only from post offices. Letters can be sent express for a surcharge of Lit. 3,000 and registered mail (*raccomandato*) costs Lit. 3,400 (in addition to the mail cost). Note that there's no guarantee that express mail will arrive any earlier than ordinary post. Insurance (*assicurata*) is recommended for important and valuable letters and parcels (the cost depends on the weight). You may need to go to a special parcel post office to send a parcel. Stamps (*francobolli*) can be purchased from tobacconists (*tabacchi*) shown by a large 'T' sign.

Airmail letters take up to ten days to the UK (the slowest service in Europe), 15 days to the USA and two to three weeks to Australia. Postcards can take even longer as they are low priority (send them in an envelope if you want them to arrive sooner). Local mail takes at least three days to arrive (next day delivery doesn't exist in Italy unless you pay extra for express) and domestic mail to remote areas of Italy can take up to two weeks! Normal mail boxes are red and in cities there are different boxes (or slots) for local mail (*per la città*), other destinations (*altre destinazioni*) and air mail (*via aerea*). There are also orange boxes for express mail and blue boxes for international mail in major cities. The international postal identification for Italian postal or zip codes (*codice postale*) is 'I', which is placed before the code (although its use isn't mandatory). Italy uses an obligatory five-digit postcode which is written before the town. Poste restante (*fermo posta*) mail can be addressed to the main post office in any town, from where it can be collected on payment of a small fee.

Telegrams (*telegramma*) can be sent from post offices and *telegrafo* offices (open all night) and some hotels. They can also be dictated over the phone by dialling 186. Information about all postal services can be obtained by phoning 160.

Courier Services: Express mail and courier services are provided by the post office, Italian railways and airlines, and international courier companies such as DHL, Federal Express and UPS. Companies such as Skymail offer a reliable alternative to the post office, including mail forwarding, remail (where mail is collected locally and sent to a major city in the country of destination, from where it's delivered by the local post office), mailbox, magazine subscriptions (USA) and catalog shopping (USA). Look under *corrieri* in the yellow pages or *recapito pacchi, plichi e lettere* (delivery of letters and small packages – usually local, e.g. within a city). The Swiss post office provides an excellent international mail service for Italian companies (and the Vatican post office). One of the most economical ways to send urgent international letters or parcels is via the post office's EMS (express mail service) serving around 160 countries (one of the Italian post office's few quality services). However, from Italy this service is only available at around 80 post offices in major cities.

GETTING THERE

Although it isn't so important if you're planning to live permanently in Italy and stay put, one of the major considerations when buying a holiday home is the cost of getting to and from Italy. How long will it take you to get to a home in Italy, taking into account journeys to and from airports, ports and railway stations? How frequent are flights, ferries or trains at the time(s) of year when you plan to travel? Are direct flights or trains available? Is it feasible to travel by car? What is the cost of travel from your home country to the region where you're planning to buy a home in Italy? Are off-season discounts or inexpensive charter flights available? If a long journey is involved, you should bear in mind that it may take you a day or two to recover, e.g. from jet-lag after a long flight. Obviously the travelling time and cost of travel to a home in Italy will be more critical if you're planning to spend frequent long weekends there rather than a few lengthier visits.

By Air: There are direct international scheduled and charter flights to all major cities in Italy (e.g. there are direct flights from the UK to around 20 Italian cities) and many other towns are served by domestic flights. International airlines serving Italy (apart from Alitalia) include Air Canada, Air France, American Airlines, British Airways, Canadian Airlines, Continental Airlines, Delta Airlines, Iberia, Icelandair, KLM, Lufthansa, Northwest Airlines, Sabena, SAS, Swissair, TWA and US Airways. The Italian national carrier is Alitalia, which is state owned and has it's main hub at Rome's Fiumicino airport. It's renowned as one of Europe's least efficient national carriers, plagued by strikes, over-manning and restrictive practices, although it's due to be privatised soon which should eventually see things improve. Not surprisingly, Alitalia dominates the busy and lucrative Milan-Rome route.

Italy has international airports in Rome (Leonardo da Vinci, better know as Fiumicino, and Ciampino, which serves mainly charter flights), Milan (Linate for domestic and European flights, and Malpensa for intercontinental flights), Bologna, Catania (Sicily), Genoa, Olbia (Sardinia), Naples, Pisa, Palermo (Sicily), Turin and Venice. However, the lack of sufficient major international airports in the north of the country sometimes forces travellers to take connecting flights to Italy from Zurich, Paris, Frankfurt or London. This has been eased with the opening of Milan's Malpensa 2000 airport in 1998, although its first few weeks of operation were total chaos. It has also been plagued by controversy as the Italian government forced all foreign intercontinental flights to use the new airport, while the old Linate airport was mainly used by Alitalia and Air One (also Italian) domestic flights from Rome. In the short term at least, using Malpensa will be a major disadvantage for airlines as it's 53km/33mi from Milan (Linate is just 10km/6mi from the city centre) and the train link isn't scheduled to open until summer 1999.

There are usually several direct flights a day from London Heathrow to Bologna, Florence, Genoa, Milan, Naples, Pisa, Rome, Turin and Venice and there are also scheduled and charter flights from London Gatwick and other UK airports to various Italian cities (including Palermo). Normal scheduled fares to Rome are around £250 single and £500 return. Apex and chartered fares are much cheaper and cost from around £100 return to Milan or Rome and an additional £10 to £20 to Pisa or Naples. The vast majority of flights go to Milan or Rome, although there's usually at least one a day to Bologna, Naples, Pisa and Turin. There are also flights from Manchester to Milan and Rome and Meridiana fly from London to Olbia (Sardinia) and to Cagliari (Sardinia) via Florence.

Several airlines fly direct to Italy from the USA including Alitalia, Delta and TWA, although scheduled fares are expensive. Alitalia offer the widest choice of direct flights from the US including daily flights from Boston, Chicago, Los Angeles, New York and Miami to both Milan and Rome. Delta fly daily from Chicago, Los Angeles and New York to Rome, and TWA fly daily from Chicago and Los Angeles via New York to Milan and Rome. Most European airlines fly via their European base to Italy, rather than direct. The cheapest return fares from the USA are around

$650 from New York to Rome rising to $750 during the shoulder season and to $950 during the peak season; add around $100 for flights from Chicago and Miami and $200 from Los Angeles. Charter flights are available from the US to Italy, but aren't such a good option as they are in Europe as scheduled airlines can often beat the prices with special offers, and offer more convenience and fewer restrictions. Flights take around eight hours from New York to Milan or Rome. From Canada, both Alitalia and Air Canada have direct flights to Rome and Milan from Toronto and Montreal.

By Train: There are direct trains to Italy from many major European cities and countries including Austria, France, Spain and Switzerland. Note that some international services run at night only and daytime journeys may involve a change of train. If you take a fast train such as the French TGV or Italy's ETR, journey times are much reduced, e.g. Lyon-Milan five hours (with a stop in Turin), Paris-Turin 5.5 hours and Paris-Milan 6 hours 40 minutes. You can travel to Italy from London by train via Paris (where a change of trains is necessary) and southern France or through Belgium, Germany and Switzerland. However, it's expensive compared with charter flights and takes much longer. It costs around £90 single and £140 return from London to Milan, £110 single and £180 return to Rome; and £200 return to Sicily. Travel times from London are around 20 hours to Milan, 24 hours to Rome and 42 hours to Sicily. If you're *very* wealthy you can even take the Orient Express from Paris to Venice, which operates twice weekly from mid-March to mid-November and also travels on to Florence and Rome around ten times a year.

Motorail: Motorail is a European network of special trains, generally overnight, carrying passengers and their cars or motorbikes over distances of up to 1,500km (900mi). Caravans cannot be taken on car trains. Motorail trains with sleeping cars operate on various routes including Boulogne-Bologna; Boulogne-Rome; Boulogne-Alessandria; Boulogne-Leghorn; Boulogne-Lille-Milan; Brussels-Milan; Dusseldorf-Cologne-Milan-Genoa; Dusseldorf-Cologne-Bolzano; Hamburg-Hanover-Verona; Munich-Rimini; Paris-Milan; 'S Hertogenbosch-Domodossola-Genoa-Milan; 'S Hertogenbosch-Chiasso-Milan; and Vienna-Venice. A wide range of sleeping accommodation is available. Trains don't run every day and on most routes operate during peak months only. Note, however, that car trains certainly aren't a cheap option and if you have the time (and inclination) it's much cheaper to drive to Italy.

By Sea: Regular international car and passenger ferry services operate between Italy and various countries including Albania, Croatia, Egypt, France (Corsica), Greece, Israel, Malta, Tunisia and Turkey. Ticket prices are usually reasonable but vary depending on the time of year and are (naturally) most expensive during summer. Note that some services operate during the summer only and services are severely curtailed during the winter on most routes.

By Road: You can also travel to Italy by bus and there are direct services from all neighbouring countries and from the UK, e.g. London to Bologna, Florence, Milan, Rome and Turin. London to Milan (with Eurolines or Eurobus) takes around 24 hours and Rome 33 hours, with return fares around £120 and £140 respectively. There's a 10 per cent reduction for students and fares are around half price for children. Many people prefer to drive to Italy, which saves you the expense of renting a car on arrival. If you're driving from the UK, bear in mind that it's almost 1,100km (ca. 700mi) from Calais to Milan (taking some 11 hours) and a further around 300km (200mi) to Florence.

GETTING AROUND BY PUBLIC TRANSPORT

Public transport (*mezzi pubblici*) services in Italy vary considerably depending on where you live. Public transport is generally good to excellent in Italian cities, most of which have efficient local bus and rail services, supplemented by a *metrò* (underground railway) system (in Milan, Naples and Rome) and trams in some cities. Italian railways (*Ferrovie dello Stato/FS*) provide a good and occasionally fast service, particularly between cities served by ETR 450 *Pendolino* trains. It's a relaxing way to travel in Italy, particularly if you have plenty of time to enjoy the relatively slow local trains that criss-cross the country. FS offer a range of special tickets and passes for commuters and travellers who book in advance. Most major cities have fully integrated public transport systems, where the same ticket is valid for buses, trams and the *metrò*.

On the negative side, services are often poorly organised (timetables are usually works of fiction) and are beset by frequent strikes, delays and breakdowns. Bus and rail services are poor or non-existent in rural areas and it's generally essential to have your own transport if you live in the country (most Italians prefer to use their cars for long-distance journeys, rather than fly or use high-speed trains).

Bus: Italy has extensive inter-city and urban bus services and, in fact, has more buses than any other European country. The main long-distance, inter-city companies include SITA (nation-wide), Autostradale (northern Italy) and Lazzi (central Italy), while each province usually has its own coach company. Note that when they aren't driving, most Italians prefer trains when travelling long-distance, which are inexpensive and usually faster than buses. However, when travelling relative short distances, buses can be more direct and faster than local trains. There are generally good connections between inter-city buses and trains, and terminals are usually located close to train stations.

There are excellent bus services in the major cities, some of which also have trams or trolley buses. In cities you usually purchase a ticket (*biglietti*) before boarding a bus, which are sold at tobacconists (*tabacchi*), newspaper kiosks, bars (there's usually a *biglietti* sign), campsite shops and hotel reception desks. A wide range of season and special tickets are available in the major cities. Private bus services are often confusing and uncoordinated, and in cities often leave from different locations rather than a central bus station. Services can also be fragmented, localised and sometimes *very* slow. There are bus lanes in many cities, although Italy's anarchistic motorists also tend to use them (illegally), which defeats the object. In stark contrast to the cities, buses in rural areas are few and far between, and the scant services that exist are usually designed to meet the needs of schoolchildren, workers, and housewives on market days. This means that buses usually run early and late in the day with little or nothing in between, and services may cease altogether during the long summer school holiday period (July to August).

Rail: The Italian railway network covers some 25,000km (ca. 15,000mi) and reaches even the remotest areas (although there are few lines in Alpine regions due to the hilly terrain). It's operated by state rail (*Ferrovie dello Stato/FS*), which has been partially privatised in recent years, although it's still heavily subsidised by the state. There are also a number of privately operated lines in Italy. Although generally slow, overcrowded and not very reliable, FS operates one of the best value for money railways in Western Europe and services have improved in recent years with faster trains and better reliability. FS operates a complicated ticket system, whereby fares are calculated according to class, distance and type of train. Most trains have first and second class carriages, although some fast trains are first class only and some suburban trains second class only. Most long-distance trains travel overnight, when first and second class sleeping cars and second class *couchettes* (in a communal cabin) are usually available.

A wide variety of special tickets are available including season tickets and special tickets for tourists. Those aged over 60 can buy a 'silver card' (*carta d'argento*) for Lit. 40,000 a year and receive a 20 per cent discount on all tickets. Travelling by train is generally faster, more comfortable and relaxing than travelling by bus or coach, and in some cases trains are faster than air travel when the time taken to get to and from airports is included. Fast intercity train services are the most reliable and the cheapest way to get around Italy (much cheaper than renting a car and paying road tolls). Train information is available from FS Informa (☎ 01478-88088), although it can be difficult to get through.

Air: Italy has a number of airlines providing domestic services including Aero Transporti Italiani (ATI), a subsidiary of Alitalia, Aermediterranea, Air Dolimiti, Air One, Air Sicilia, Alitalia, Alisarda, Aligiulia, Alpi Eagles, Azurra, Meridiana, Minerva and Transavio. There's an extensive domestic air network in Italy, which has over 100 domestic/international airports including Alghero, Ancona, Bari, Bergamo, Bologna, Brindisi, Cagliari, Catania, Florence, Genoa, Lamezia-Terme, Lampedusa, Milan, Naples, Olbia, Palermo, Pantelleria, Parma, Perugia, Pescara, Pisa, Reggio di Calabria, Rimini, Rome, Sassari, Trapani, Trieste, Treviso, Turin, Venice and Verona. Some 40 Italian airports are served from Rome and most domestic flights are under an hour. However, travelling by air within Italy is expensive, although discounts are available, notably for evening and night flights. Private air taxi services also operate from many Italian airports.

Ferries: Italy has a well-developed network of ferries (*traghetti*) and hydrofoils (*aliscafi*), although services are usually severely curtailed outside the summer months. Regular services connect the mainland with Italy's many islands including Villa San Giovanni to Sicily; Civitavecchia and Livorno to Sardinia; Naples to the islands of Capri, Ischia and Sorrento; and various points on the mainland to the Aeolian, Pontine, Tremeti and Lipari islands. Regular car ferry services also link Naples to Reggio di Calabra and Genoa, Sardinia, Naples and Sicily. Ferries and hydrofoils also operate between towns on the lakes of Como, Garda and Maggiore. Restaurant, bar and recreation facilities such as cinemas are provided on the larger, long-haul ferries, where passengers can choose between a cabin (first or second class) and an airline-type, reclining armchair (*poltrona*). Italy's major ferry operator is Tirrenia.

Taxis: Taxis (*tassì* or *taxi*) in Italy are various colours including black, green, white and yellow (the most common colour) and must be picked up from taxi stands or booked by telephone. They don't usually cruise the streets waiting for someone to hail them (although you can get a taxi this way). Taxis are plentiful at airports and train stations, and radio taxes usually respond quickly when called. Taxis usually have meters, although you need to make sure that a driver uses it, and if there's no meter, agree the fare in advance. Make sure you aren't given the grand (roundabout) tour! Taxis are relatively expensive in Italy, where even a short ride in Rome costs around Lit. 10,000. There are surcharges (posted inside taxis) for trips to airports, at night, on public holidays and for luggage. Drivers also expect a 10 to 15 per cent tip.

DRIVING

Like motorists in all countries, the Italians have their own idiosyncrasies and customs, many of which are peculiar to a particular city or region. The personalities of most Italians (as with all Latins) change the moment they get behind the wheel of a car, when even the most placid person can become an aggressive, impatient and intolerant homicidal maniac with an unshakeable conviction in his own immortality. The Italians revere racing drivers (particularly those that drive for Ferrari – even Germans!) and the country has a long, proud record of grand prix and sports car racing (although nowadays the *Mille Miglia* is run daily on Italy's roads). However, although some Italian drivers are lunatics, they aren't as bad as their reputation may suggest and most are actually good drivers.

Nevertheless, one thing that most have in common is an inability to know when to slow down and they are notorious for their impatience. The shortest measurement of time in Italy is said to be the period between the traffic lights changing to green and the driver behind you beeping his horn. That's when they have bothered to stop at all, as in Italy a red light (when working) is simply a sign to take care rather than stop, and many drivers just drive through them (particularly in Naples). Driving in Italy is the survival of the fittest and it isn't a place for faint hearts and foreigners who don't know where they are going. Not surprisingly, Italy has one of the highest road accident tolls in the European Union, although the death rate (around 7,000 a year) is 'relatively' low considering the number of accidents. Poor discipline (road rules are optional to Italians), lack of enforcement, inadequate road laws and the Italians' frenetic driving style all combine to create havoc. There are also some 12 million cars in Italy over ten years of age, many which are in poor condition.

Once they've discarded their 'learner' plates, the majority of Italian drivers are assailed by an uncontrollable urge to drive everywhere at maximum speed and they are among the world's most pathologically aggressive drivers. Italians have a passion for fast cars and abhor driving slowly and slow drivers (particularly foreigners). Like all Latins, few things have any impact on slowing down Italian drivers, short of a substantial brick wall. Italians have little respect for traffic rules, particularly those concerned with parking (in cities, a car is a device used to create parking spaces).

Italian drivers wear their dents with pride and there are many (many) dented cars in Italy. What makes driving in Italy even more of a lottery is that for many months of the year Italian roads are liberally sprinkled with assorted foreigners, whose driving habits vary from exemplary to suicidal and include many (such as the British) who don't even know which side of the road to drive on!

When not overtaking, Italian drivers may sit a few metres (centimetres) from your bumper trying to push you along irrespective of traffic density, road and weather conditions, or the prevailing speed limit (speed of itself doesn't kill, but driving at any speed, legal or illegal, can be lethal under the wrong conditions). The Italians are among Europe's worst tailgaters and there's no solution, short of moving out of their way or stopping, which is often impossible. Always try to leave a large gap between your vehicle and the one in front. This isn't just to give you more time to stop should the vehicles in front decide to get together, but also to give the inevitable tailgater behind you more time to stop. **The closer the car behind you, the further you should be from the vehicle in front.** On *autostrade* and trunk roads, you must keep a safe distance from the vehicle in front and you can be fined for not doing so. Avoid the fast (overtaking) lane on *autostrade* unless you're prepared to drive at least 200kph (ca. 125mph); Italians generally drive very fast and often bumper to bumper (they want to get their money's worth from the high tolls).

Driving in Italian cities is a nightmare and is best avoided. Traffic congestion and pollution in Italian cities is among the worst in Europe and consequently a pass is now required to enter many historical city centres (*centro storico*), which is available only to residents and local businesses. Some cities (such as Milan) have introduced a system whereby only vehicles whose registration plate ends in an even number may enter the city on even dates and vehicles with an odd number on odd dates. In some cities, only vehicles with a catalyser (*marmitta catalitica*) running on lead-free petrol can enter the city centre. Rome passed a 'blue face' (*fascia blu*) law in recent years banning most vehicles from the city centre, which now allows people to breathe something remotely resembling fresh air.

If you drive in winter in northern Italy when snow and ice are commonplace – **take it easy!** In bad conditions you will notice that most Italian drivers slow down considerably and even the habitual tailgaters leave a larger gap than usual. Even a light snowfall can be treacherous, particularly on an icy road. When road conditions are bad, you should allow two to three times longer than usual to reach your destination (if you're wise, you'll stay at home). Note that many mountain passes are closed in winter (check with the Automobil Club d'Italia/ACI).

Don't be too discouraged by the road hogs and tail-gaters. Driving in Italy can be a pleasant experience (cities excepted), particularly when using secondary country roads, which are relatively traffic-free most of the time. If you come from a country where traffic drives on the left, most people quickly get used to driving on the 'wrong' side of the road. Just take it easy at first and bear in mind that there are other foreigners around just as confused as you are!

Italian Roads: Italian roads are generally good and the country has an excellent motorway (*autostrada*) network. Italy has a network of around 6,000km (3,700mi) of *autostrade,* most of which are toll (*pedaggio*) roads, although there are some 1,000km (620mi) of free expressways (*superstrade*) around cities. The main north-south route is the *Autostrada del Sole* from Milan to Reggio di Calabria (designated the A1 from Milan to Naples and the A3 from Naples to Reggio di Calabria, which is toll-free). Although you may need to take out a second mortgage to drive on them, *autostrade* are Italy's safest roads (you cannot get hit by an Italian overtaking on a blind bend).

Autostrade tolls depends on the horsepower (*cavalli fiscali*) of your car or the wheel-base and number of axles (usually the former), and the particular company operating the toll. The rate per kilometre varies but is usually around Lit. 100 per km. Tolls can be paid in lire and most major currencies including sterling, French and Swiss francs, Austrian schillings, Deutschmarks and US dollars. Note that you usually receive a poor rate of exchange, so you're better off paying in *lire*. Credit cards aren't usually accepted. On most *autostrade* you collect a card when you start your journey and pay when you leave the *autostrada*, while on certain stretches there are fixed charges which you pay when you start your journey.

Some companies offer season tickets at reduced rates and you can also buy a Viacard (like a telephone card) at some *autostrade* tolls, bars, restaurants and certain banks (costing from Lit. 50,000 or Lit. 90,000), which makes paying tolls easier and faster as you can use reserved lanes. Alternatively you can obtain a Telepass which requires a sensor to be installed in your car that records the distance you travel on toll roads when you pass through special Telepass gates. You're then billed by direct debit from a bank account. Viacards and Telepasses aren't available on all *autostrade*. It's usually well worth paying the tolls on a long journey, rather than travelling on toll-free highways, as your journey will be much quicker and more relaxing. Note that you aren't permitted to stop on the hard shoulder of a motorway unless there's an emergency and you can be fined over Lit. 100,000 for doing so .

Italy also has a number of toll tunnels including Mont Blanc and Frejus between Italy and France respectively, both 11km (ca. 7mi) in length, and the Gran San Bernadino linking Italy and Switzerland. The fee is from around Lit. 25,000 one way for a small car (up to 2.3m between axles). Note that many mountain road passes are closed in winter (road conditions can be obtained 24 hours a day by calling 06-4477). State roads (*strade statali*), shown on maps as 'SS', are often multi-lane, dual carriageway roads, and although slower than *autostrade*, they have no tolls. Provincial roads (*strade provinciali*), shown on maps as 'SP', vary considerably in quality and may be little more than rough tracks in some areas. The lowest grade are comune roads (*strade comunali*), which are roads maintained by local comunes (e.g. towns). *Autostrade*, *strade statali* and most *strade provinciali* are numbered, while other roads aren't.

Dial the emergency number (113) to report an accident or breakdown. On *autostrade* there are emergency phones every 2km (1.25mi), some of which have separate buttons for breakdowns (indicated by a spanner) and injuries (indicated by a red cross). Simply press the appropriate button and wait for help to arrive.

Importing a car: It's usually cheaper to buy a car abroad and import it into Italy as they are expensive due to the high taxes. On the other hand, the weakness of the lire in recent years has made Italy one of the cheapest places to buy cars in the EU, although this is only of value if you're planning to export a vehicle. A car can be imported from another EU country without paying any taxes (e.g. VAT or import duty), providing tax was paid in the former EU country and it has been owned and used for at least six months in that country prior to importation. Note that this is a one-time concession. A vehicle's documentation no longer needs to be authenticated and legalised.

A car must be imported within your first six months as a resident. If you import a car temporarily, you're given a customs receipt (*bolletta doganale*) and can drive it on foreign registration plates for up to one year if you're a non-resident. However, if you become a resident it must be imported permanently and registered (*immatricolare*) in Italy (registration must be requested within ten days of taking up residence). It's illegal for non-residents to buy and operate a car in Italy (unless it's for export). Before a car can be registered it must pass an inspection (*collaudo*), when the owner must be on hand. It's best to have the inspection and paperwork done by an agent (*agenzie pratiche auto*) who specialises in paperwork for cars, who will charge around Lit. 250,000. Keep your Italian registration certificate (*libretto*) and insurance certificate in your car with the receipt for road tax.

Buying or selling a car: You need a residence certificate (*certificato di residenza*) and a tax number (*codice fiscale*) to buy a car. Non-residents can only purchase a vehicle from a manufacturer and must export it within a year of its purchase. If you have provisional residence, you will be given special 'tourist' registration plates with the letters 'EE' (*Escursionisti Esteri*) on them. Plates are valid as long as you own a car and they belong to the car not the owner, i.e. you cannot transfer them to another vehicle. If you purchase a second-hand car that isn't registered in the province where you're resident, you must have it re-registered, which is expensive. You must pay a fee to transfer ownership (*passaggio di proprietà*) of around Lit. 200,000, which is done by a notary. You may have to wait months for your car registration papers, although you can obtain interim documents (*foglio sostitutivo*) which must be renewed every three months. Car maintenance tests were introduced in recent years, which are now required after four years for new cars and thereafter every two years. In addition, cars must be tested for emissions annually (which costs Lit. 15,000) after which (providing it passes) you receive a *bollino blu* on your windscreen.

When selling a car in Italy, many people simply put a 'for sale' sign (*vendesi*) in the window and park it in a prominent place. A garage must have a proxy (*procura*) to sell a car for you. The change of ownership is called *trapasso* and costs around Lit. 650,000 or some Lit. 750,000 to 800,000 if it's done by the Automobil Club d'Italia (ACI) or an agent. You have ten days to notify the authorities of a change of owner of a vehicle. The necessary papers for the transfer of ownership are drawn up at an ACI office or in a car salesroom and registration plates (*foglio di circolazione*) are issued by the provincial *motorizazzione civile*.

Road Tax: Road or car tax (*la tassa di circolazione* or simply *auto bollo*) in Italy depends on the horsepower (*cavallo*) of your car and whether it runs on petrol or diesel, and can be very high for some vehicles. You can find out the cost from ACI offices and from charts posted in post offices or from the January edition of the *Quattroruote* car magazine. Before buying a second-hand car in Italy, make sure that the road tax payments are up-to-date, otherwise you will be liable for any back payments when you renew it. Road tax is required even when a car isn't being used on public roads. The *bollo di circolazione* need no longer be displayed on windscreens. For most drivers, road tax expires on 31st December and you have one month (until 31st January) to renew it.

You must carry all your documents when driving in Italy, i.e. driving licence, car registration document, insurance certificate and certificate of roadworthiness. If you're stopped by the police without them, you can be fined on the spot.

Driving Licences: The minimum age for driving in Italy is 18 for a motor car or motorcycle over 125cc and 14 for a motorcycle (moped) up to 50cc. A foreigner who's resident in Italy can drive there for one year with his foreign licence. Non-EU nationals also generally require a translation or an international driving permit issued in their home country. A translation can be obtained in Italy from offices of the

Automobil Club d'Italia (ACI). During this period, and before obtaining a residence permit (*certificatio di residenza*), you must swap your foreign licence for an Italian licence (*patente*), if possible, or take an Italian driving test. If you live in Italy for one year without obtaining an Italian licence, you must take an Italian driving test.

Driving licences can be converted from all EU countries, Algeria, Brazil, Bulgaria, Colombia, Costa Rica, Croatia, Cuba, Cyprus, Egypt, Haiti, Hungary, Honduras, Iran, Israel, Japan, Korea, Libya, Malaysia, Malta, Mauritius, Monaco, Morocco, Nicaragua, Norway, Oman, Panama, Philippines, San Marino, Saudi Arabia, Singapore, Slovenia, Sri Lanka, Sudan, Switzerland, Syria, Thailand, Tunisia, Turkey, United Arab Emirates and Vietnam. Note that this list doesn't include Australia, Canada, New Zealand or the USA (except for diplomatic personnel in the case of Canada and the USA).

As of July 1996, all EU (pink) driving licences (i.e. with a multi-lingual cover) have been recognised in all EU countries irrespective of the length of your stay (officially an old green UK driving licence is valid only with a translation). However, in Italy an EU licence must be 'convalidated' at your local provisional motor registry (*ufficio motorizzazione*) or an ACI office, where it's stamped to acknowledge that you're now living in Italy. For non-EU nationals, conversion of a foreign licence to an Italian one is necessary and costs around Lit. 300,000 (perhaps they are personally signed by Michelangelo?) and takes around four months. You will also require a medical certificate. Note that, as with anything to do with officialdom in Italy, the procedure is highly complicated and takes eons to complete. If you need to take a driving test, the written section must be taken in Italian and can be difficult for foreigners, many of whom fail a number of times. You can employ an agent who carries out *pratiche auto* to do the required paperwork for you.

An Italian licence is valid for a maximum of ten years if you're aged under 50, five years above the age of 50 and three years if you're over 70. At the end of the licence validity period you must pass a medical examination and if you're elderly a medical certificate from your doctor may be required stating that you don't suffer from a medical condition which could affect your driving. If you're aged over 80 it can be difficult to obtain a driving licence. The driving licence is to be changed in 1999 to a pink plastic credit card format, which will contain the EU logo in the top left-hand corner with an 'I' (for Italy) in the middle and a photograph of the driver. Note that you must carry your licence (and other car papers) with you at all times when driving in Italy. If you wear spectacles or contact lenses, you must carry a (spare) pair in a vehicle.

Car Insurance: All motor vehicles plus trailers and semi-trailers must be insured for third party liability (*responsabilità civile*) when entering Italy. However, it isn't mandatory for cars insured in most European countries to have an international insurance 'green' card. Vehicles insured in an EU country, the Czech Republic, Hungary, Liechtenstein, Norway, the Slovak Republic and Switzerland are automatically covered for third party liability in Italy. The categories of car insurance available in Italy include third party, which is the minimum required by law; third party fire and theft (also called part comprehensive in some countries); collision (which pays for damage to your car in an accident); and comprehensive (*casco*), which includes non-collision damage to a vehicle, such as falling rocks or vandalism). Bear in mind that the compulsory minimum insurance limits are lower than in many other EU countries. Fully comprehensive insurance doesn't provide the same cover as in many other countries and doesn't include injuries to passengers. If you have fully comprehensive insurance and plan to drive outside Italy, you should obtain a green card (*carta verde*) from your insurance company. Note that the car and not the driver is insured in Italy, although cover for the driver (*conducente anomino*) can be taken out as a supplement.

Insurance is available from many sources including direct insurance companies and brokers. Shop around (you can do this via the Internet at www.diagramma.it) as rates vary considerably; if you find a low premium, it's wise to check that important benefits haven't been excluded. Insurance premiums are high in Italy, which is a reflection of the high accident rate and the large number of stolen cars. Premiums vary considerably depending on a range of factors including the type of insurance, the vehicle, your age and accident record, and where you live. Insurance policies in Italy are generally valid from one to ten years and must be cancelled 30 to 90 days before the renewal date (otherwise it's automatically expended for a further period). Note that Italian insurance companies can be very slow to pay out in the event of accidents (other than minor accidents) and many people don't bother to claim for minor accidents (which would affect their no-claims discount) or even get them repaired. Bear in mind that your insurance card must be displayed behind your vehicle's windscreen.

Car Crime: Most European countries have a problem with car crime, i.e. thefts of and from cars, and Italy is certainly no exception. Foreign-registered vehicles are popular targets. If you drive anything other than a worthless heap you should have theft insurance, which includes your car stereo and personal belongings. New vehicles should be fitted with an alarm, an engine immobiliser of the rolling code variety (the best system) or another anti-theft device, plus a visible deterrent, such as a steering or gear stick lock. It's particularly important to protect your car if you own a model that's desirable to professional car thieves, e.g. most new sports and executive models, which are often stolen by crooks to order. Vehicles should also be garaged whenever possible.

Few cars are fitted with deadlocks and most can be broken into in seconds by a competent thief. However, even the best security system won't usually prevent someone from breaking into your car and may not stop your car from being stolen, but it will at least make it more difficult and may persuade a thief to look for an easier target. Radios, tape and CD players attract thieves like bees to a honey pot in Italian cities and resort towns. If you buy an expensive stereo system, you should buy one with a removable unit or with a removable (face-off) control panel (called a *frontalino*) that you can pop into a pocket or bag. However, never forget to remove it (and your mobile telephone), even when parking for a few minutes. Some manufacturers provide stereo systems that won't work when they're removed from their original vehicles or are inoperable without a security code (although this isn't a lot of use if the thief doesn't know this!).

Windows are often broken to steal contents and can be replaced while you wait in major cities (in Italy, BMW stands for 'break my window'). When leaving your car unattended, store any valuables (including clothes) in the boot (trunk) or preferably take them with you. Note, however, that storing valuables in the boot isn't foolproof, as when a car is empty a thief may be tempted to force open the boot with a crowbar. It isn't advisable to leave your original car papers in your car (which may help a thief dispose of it). When parking overnight or when it's dark, it's advisable to park in a secure overnight car park or garage, or at least in a well-lit area. If possible, avoid parking in insecure long-term car parks, as they are favourite hunting grounds for car thieves. Service stations on the *autostrade* are favourite haunts for thieves who can clean out your car in a few minutes and make a fast getaway; when stopping here try to park your car where you can keep an eye on it. When driving in cities keep your doors locked and your windows partly or fully closed and store valuables and bags on the floor (not on seats).

Highway piracy (possibly armed) is becoming an increasing problem in some European countries, including Italy, where foreign drivers are often the targets. Gangs deliberately bump or ram cars to get drivers to stop, usually late at night when there's little traffic about. Thieves may also pose as a policeman and try to get you to stop by flashing a 'badge' or setting up bogus road blocks. In the worst cases thieves take not just the car and its contents, but even the clothes their victims are wearing. Travelling at night in some areas (particularly in the far south of Italy) can be hazardous due to armed highwaymen and should be avoided if possible.

General Road Rules

The following general road rules may help you adjust to driving in Italy. Don't, however, expect other motorists to adhere to them (most Italian drivers invent their own 'rules', which are liable to change from day to day).

- You may already be aware that the Italians drive on the right-hand side of the road (when not driving in the middle!). It saves confusion if you do likewise. If you aren't used to driving on the right, take it easy until you're accustomed to it. Be particularly alert when leaving lay-bys, T-junctions, one-way streets, petrol stations and car parks, as it's easy to lapse into driving on the left. It's helpful to display a reminder (e.g. 'Think Right!') on your car's dashboard.

- In towns you may be faced with a bewildering array of signs, traffic lights, road markings, etc. If you're ever in doubt about who has priority, give way to trams, buses and all traffic coming from your RIGHT. Emergency (ambulance, fire, police) and public utility (electricity, gas and water) vehicles attending an emergency have priority on all roads.

- Speed limits are 50kph (31mph) in towns (unless a lower limit is posted), 70kph (43mph) on faster urban roads, 90kph (56mph) on secondary extraurban (i.e. rural) roads, 110kph (68mph) on principal extraurban roads and 130kph (81mph) on *autostrade*. Cars towing caravans (trailers) are limited to 80kph (50mph) on extraurban roads and 100kph (62mph) on *autostrade*. Speeding fines are around Lit. 200,000 regardless of how much your speed was above the speed limit. Note that you can lose your driving licence if you're caught speeding three times!

- Alcohol is a major factor in many of Italy's road accidents. The permitted blood alcohol concentration in Italy is 80mg of alcohol per 100ml of blood, which is the same as in many other European countries (although some countries, such as France, have a lower limit of 50mg, which the EU has proposed for all EU countries). Random breath tests (*il palloncino/etilometri*) can be carried out by the police at any time and motorists who are involved in accidents or who infringe motoring regulations are routinely breathalysed.

- All motorists must carry a red breakdown triangle, which must be placed 30m/100ft behind a broken down vehicle, and it's advisable to carry a spare set of bulbs/fuses, a fire extinguisher and a first-aid kit.

- Most main roads are designated priority (*dare precedenza*) roads, indicated by a sign. The most common priority sign is a yellow diamond on a white background, in use throughout most of Europe. The end of priority is shown by the same sign with a black diagonal line through it. On secondary roads *without* priority signs and in built-up areas, you must give way to vehicles coming from your RIGHT. **Failure to observe this rule is the cause of many accidents.** The priority rule was fine when there was little traffic, but nowadays most countries (Italy included) realise the necessity of having 'stop' or 'give way' (*cedere passaggio*) signs at junctions. Most Italian motorists no longer treat priority as a God-given right, although some still pull out without looking. The priority to the right rule usually also applies in car parks, but never when exiting *from* car parks or dirt tracks. If you're ever in doubt about who has the right of way, it's wise to give way (particularly to large trucks!).

- The wearing of seat belts is *compulsory* in Italy and includes passengers in rear seats, when seat belts are fitted. Children must use an approved safety seat or a safety belt suitable for their age. You can be fined Lit. 60,000 on-the-spot for not wearing a seat belt. Note that if you have an accident and aren't wearing a seat belt, your insurance company can refuse to pay a claim for personal injury. Nevertheless, many Italians use them only on *autostrade* (the safest of all roads), if at all.

- On roundabouts (traffic circles or rotaries), vehicles entering them usually have priority and not those already on it. However, this rule is changing to conform with other EU countries where vehicles on roundabouts have priority and traffic entering it is faced with a give way or stop sign. You're likely to encounter both types in Italy, so take care. Traffic flows anti-clockwise round roundabouts and not clockwise as in Britain and other countries driving on the left.

- For left-hand turns off a main road with traffic lights, there's often a specially marked filter lane or circle to the *right*, where you wait to cross the main road at right angles (indicated by a stop sign or traffic lights).

- A yellow or green filter light, usually flashing and with a direction arrow, may be shown in addition to the main signal. This means that you may drive in the direction shown by the arrow, but must give priority to pedestrians or other traffic. If you get into the wrong lane by mistake, you will no doubt be informed by the irate honking of motorists behind you! Flashing yellow lights are a warning to proceed with caution and are often used at crossroads during periods when traffic is light (e.g. after midnight). You must give priority to traffic coming from your right.

- Don't drive in bus, taxi or cycle lanes (unless you're an Italian) as you can be fined for doing so, although it's permitted when necessary to avoid a stationary vehicle or an obstruction. Be sure to keep clear of tram lines and outside the restricted area, delineated by a line. Note that trams always have priority over other vehicles.

- The use of horns is forbidden in cities and areas indicated by a 'silence zone' (*zona di silenzio*) sign. However, it's tolerated by wedding parties, New Year revellers, football fans (e.g. when Juventus have won the European Cup) and cars trapped by large vehicles or double/treble parked cars.

- The sequence of Italian traffic lights (*semaforo*) is red, green, yellow (amber) and back to red. Yellow means stop at the stop line; you may proceed only if the yellow light appears after you have crossed the stop line or when stopping may cause an accident. You can be fined around Lit. 120,000 for running a red light (or get a ticket to the next life!), which nevertheless is a national sport in Italy.

- Always come to a complete stop when required at intersections and ensure that you stop behind the white line (intersections are a favourite spot for police patrols waiting for motorists to put a wheel a few centimetres over the line).

- White or yellow lines mark the separation of traffic lanes. A solid single line or two solid lines means no overtaking (*sorpassare*) in either direction. A solid line to the right of the centre line, i.e. on your side of the road, means that overtaking is prohibited in your direction. You may overtake only when there's a single broken line in the middle of the road or double lines with a broken line on your side of the road. No overtaking may also be shown by the international road sign of two cars side by side (one red and one black). Always check your rear view and wing mirrors carefully before overtaking, as Italian motorists often appear from nowhere and zoom past at a 'zillion' miles an hour, particularly on country roads. If you drive a right-hand drive (RHD) car, take extra care when overtaking – the most dangerous manoeuvre in motoring. It's wise to have a special 'overtaking mirror' fitted to a RHD car.

- Moped (*ciclomotore* or *motorini*) and scooters are extremely popular in Italy (which could claim to having invented them) and are excellent for getting around cities, but a menace if you're a motorist. Be particularly wary of moped riders and cyclists. It isn't always easy to see them, particularly when they're hidden by the blind spots of a car or are riding at night without lights. Many young moped riders seem to have a death wish and tragically hundreds lose their lives annually in Italy (14 years of age is too young to let them loose on the roads). They are constantly pulling out into traffic or turning without looking or signalling. **Follow the example set by Italian motorists, who when overtaking mopeds and cyclists, ALWAYS give them a wide . . . . WIDE berth.** If you knock them off their bikes you may have a difficult time convincing the police that it wasn't your fault; far better to avoid them (and the police).

- An 'I' nationality plate must be affixed to the rear of a Italian-registered car when motoring abroad and drivers of foreign registered cars in Italy must have the appropriate nationality plate affixed to the rear of their vehicles. You can be fined on the spot for not displaying it, although it isn't often enforced judging by the number of cars without them.

- Be careful where you park, particularly in cities where your car can be towed away or clamped (with a 'boot' on a wheel) in a flash. *Never* park across entrances, at bus stops or taxi ranks, in front of fire and ambulance stations and schools (which may be indicated by yellow kerbstones) or near pedestrian crossings. 'No parking' may be shown by a sign. Always read all parking signs carefully and look for kerb markings (ask someone if you aren't sure whether parking is permitted). Any city parking that appears to be free is almost certainly illegal! In some areas local 'minders' (protection racketeers) may offer to look after your car for a small fee to ensure that it doesn't get damaged.

- Take particular care when crossing the road, even when using a pedestrian crossing, as drivers aren't required to stop, only to slow down (being hit by a 'slow' truck or bus can still kill you!). Cross quickly when and where there's plenty of space for drivers to see you and slow accordingly.

- All motorists in Italy must be familiar with the Italian 'highway code' which is published in a guide (*guida pratica alla soluzione dei nuovi quiz ministeriali*) for each category of licence.

- Italy adheres to the international standards for road signs, although there are also many signs with written instructions, some of which are listed below:

Italian	**English**
Accendere le luci/i fari (in galleria)	use headlights (in tunnel)
Attenzione	caution
Caduta massi	falling rocks
Casello a *** Metri	toll in *** metres
Curve	bends ahead
Dare precendenza	give way
Deviazione	diversion (detour)
Divieto di accesso	no entry
Divieto di sorpasso	no overtaking
Divieto di sosta	no stopping
Divieto di transitio	no right of way
Entrata	entrance
Incrocio	crossroads
Lavori in corso	road works ahead
Passagio a livello	level crossing
Pedaggio	toll
Pedoni	pedestrians
Pericolo	danger
Rallentare	slow
Senso unico	one-way street
Senso vietato (vietato lingresso veicoli)	no entry (for vehicles)
Sosta autorizzata	parking permitted
Sosta vietata	no parking
Strada ghiacciata	icy road
Svolta	bend
Tenere la destra	keep to the right

Transito interrotto	no through road
Uscita (camion)	exit (for trucks)
Veicoli al passo	dead slow

Car Rental

Car rental (*autonoleggio*) companies such as Alamo, Avis, Budget, Dollar, Europcar, Hertz and National InterRent have offices in most large towns and at major airports in Italy. If you're a visitor, it's advisable to reserve a rental car before arriving in Italy, which is generally cheaper. Fly-drive deals are available through most airlines and travel agents. Car rental in Italy is *very* expensive, particularly for short periods, and includes value added tax (IVA) at 20 per cent. There's also a 10 per cent government tax for pick up from a major airport. Hertz charge Lit. 120,000 (including optional insurances and taxes) for a one day rental for their cheapest models, e.g. a Fiat Punto or similar. This is for limited mileage of 100km/62mi per day only, after which there's a charge per kilometre. The weekly rate for a Fiat Punto is Lit. 600,000 with limited mileage and Lit. 900,000 with unlimited mileage. Special rates are available for weekends, usually from noon on Friday to 9am on Monday. Local rental companies (e.g. Holiday Auto – ☎ 0990-300400) are usually cheaper than the multinationals, although cars must be returned to the pick-up point.

Rates reduce considerably over long periods, e.g. a week or a month. They usually include Collision Damage Waiver (CDW) and Personal Accident Insurance (PAI), although you may need additional insurance (e.g. theft). When paying with a credit or charge card, your card company may cover damage to a vehicle through its own insurance. Always ensure that you know what's included in (and excluded from) the price and what your liabilities are. Note that a diesel car is much cheaper to run in Italy than a petrol-engined car. If required, check in advance that you're permitted to take a car out of Italy, which may be prohibited. To hire a car in Italy you must usually be aged at least 21, although it can be up to 25 or even as high as 30 for some vehicles. Drivers must have held a full licence for a minimum of one year and most companies have an upper age limit of 60 or 65. If payment isn't with a credit card there's usually a cash deposit and possibly the whole rental period must be paid in advance.

Rental cars can be ordered with a portable telephone and luggage rack, and child seats can be fitted for an extra charge. You can also hire a 4-wheel drive vehicle, station wagon, minibus, prestige luxury car, armoured limousine or a convertible, possibly with a choice of manual or automatic gearbox. There are also moped and motorcycle rental companies in the major cities. Minibuses accessible to wheelchairs can also be hired, e.g. from Hertz. Older cars can be rented from many garages at lower rates than those charged by the multinational companies, although they aren't always in good condition and can even be unsafe. Vans and pick-ups are available from some major rental companies by the hour, half-day or day, or from smaller local companies (which, once again, are cheaper).

Note that cars can be rented from multinational companies at a saving of up to 50 per cent on local rates by booking through their American offices, e.g. Alamo (☎ 1-800-327-9633), Avis (☎ 1-800-331-1212), Budget (☎ 1-800-527-0700), Dollar (☎ 1-800-800-4000), Hertz (☎ 1-800-654-30011) and National InterRent (☎ 1-800-227-3876), and paying by credit card. Toll-free (800) numbers of other

US-based rental companies can be obtained from international directory enquiries, although you pay international rates when phoning from abroad. Car hire companies have no way of knowing where the calls were made and therefore are unable to prevent people from booking from outside the USA.

2.

FURTHER
CONSIDERATIONS

This chapter contains important considerations for most people planning to buy a home in Italy, particularly those planning to live there permanently or semi-permanently. It includes information about the climate, geography, health, insurance, shopping, pets, television and radio, learning Italian, crime, public holidays and time difference.

CLIMATE

Italy generally has a temperate climate influenced by the Mediterranean and Adriatic Seas and the protective Alps encircling the north. The islands of Sicily and Sardinia and southern Italy enjoy a mild Mediterranean climate, as does the Italian Riviera. Italy enjoys warm dry summers and relatively mild winters in most regions, although there's a marked contrast between the far north and the south of the country. Rome is generally recognised as the dividing point between the colder north and the hotter southern regions. The best seasons throughout the country are spring and autumn, when it's neither too hot nor too cold in most regions.

Summers are generally very hot everywhere, when thunderstorms are common in inland areas, with average temperatures in July and August around 24°C (75°F). Summers are short and not too hot in Alpine and the northern lake areas, while the Po Valley has warm and sunny summers, but can be humid. Summers are dry and hot to sweltering the further south you go (too hot for most people), although sea breezes alleviate the heat in coastal areas. In Rome and further south the *Sirocco* wind from Africa can produce stifling hot weather in August with temperatures well above 30°C.

Winters are relatively mild in most areas with some rainy spells. They are, however, very cold (but usually sunny) in the Alpine regions, where snowfalls are frequent. The first snowfall in the Alps is usually in November, although light snow sometimes falls in mid-September and heavy snow can fall in October. The Alps shield northern Lombardy and the lakes area (including Milan) from the extremes of the northern European winter. Fog is common throughout northern Italy from the autumn through to February and winters can be severe in the Po Valley, the plains of Lombardy and Emilia-Romagna. Venice can be quite cold in winter (it often snows there) and it's often flooded when the sea level rises and inundates the city. Florence is cold in winter, while winters are moderate in Rome where it rarely snows. The Italian Riviera and Liguria experience mild winters and enjoy a mild Mediterranean climate as they are protected by both the Alps and the Appennini. Sicily and southern Italy have the mildest winters with daytime temperatures between 10°C and 20°C (50°F and 68°F).

Rainfall is moderate to low in most regions and is rare anywhere in summer. The northern half of the country and the Adriatic coast are wetter than the rest of Italy. There's a lot of rain in the central regions of Tuscany and Umbria in winter, although they suffer neither extreme heat nor cold most of the year. There's a shortage of water in many areas during summer, when the supply is often turned off during the day and households are limited to a number of cubic metres per year.

Italy is prone to earthquakes and volcanic eruptions (see **Geography** below). There has been a government campaign in recent years to inform people and allay their fears about earthquakes, although it has probably had the opposite effect! Officially some 3,000 towns out of a total of 8,000 are in constant threat from earthquakes. These communities contain some ten million homes, at least two-thirds of which aren't earthquake proof (even those that are supposedly 'earthquake proof' often aren't). The regions most at risk are Calabria, Friuli-Venezia-Giuila, Marche and Sicily. The area extending from Tuscany to Basilicata (with the exception of Puglia) have a medium to high risk, while all other regions are low or low to medium risk.

Average daily maximum/minimum temperatures (in Centigrade) for selected towns are show below:

Location	Spring (April)	Summer (July)	Autumn (October)	Winter (January)
Brindisi	18/11	29/21	22/15	12/6
Cagliari	19/11	30/21	23/15	14/7
Milan	18/10	29/20	17/11	5/0
Naples	18/9	29/18	22/12	12/4
Palermo	20/11	30/21	25/16	16/8
Rome	19/10	30/20	22/13	11/5
Venice	17/10	27/19	19/11	6/1

A quick way to make a *rough* conversion from Centigrade to Fahrenheit is to multiply by two and add 30. Weather forecasts (*previsioni del tempo*) are broadcast on TV and radio stations and published in daily newspapers.

GEOGRAPHY

Italy covers an area of 301,245km² (116,319mi²) and comprises a long peninsula shaped like a boot, which is instantly recognisable and tends to give the impression that the country is much larger than it actually is (it covers around the same area as the US state of Arizona or the British Isles). The country is 1,200km (750mi) in length and between 150 and 250km (93 to 155mi) in width. Italy has borders with France, Switzerland, Austria and Slovenia, and encompasses two independent states within its borders: the Vatican City (109 acres) in Rome, established in 1929, and the Republic of San Marino within the Marche region.

It's a land of stark contrasts including towering mountains and vast plains, huge lakes and wide valleys. It has a wide variety of landscape and vegetation, characterised by its two mountain ranges, the Alps and the Apennines (almost 80 per cent of the country is covered by hills and mountains). The Alps (*Alpi*) form the border in the north stretching from the Gulf of Genoa (*Golfo di Genova*) in the west to the Adriatic Sea (north of Trieste) in the east. The highest mountain peak is Monte Bianco (Mont Blanc), on the border with France (4,807m/15,770ft), and the highest peak in the Italian Alps is Monte Rosa (4,634m/15,203ft) on the Swiss border. The Alps are divided into three main groups, western, central and eastern, and are at their most spectacular in the Dolomites (*Dolomiti*) in the east.

The Appenines form the backbone of Italy extending for 1,220km/758mi from Liguria near Genoa to the tip of Calabria and into Sicily. The highest peak in the Appenines is the Corno Grande (2,914m/9,560ft) in the Gran Sasso d'Italia range in

Abruzzo. The Apuan Alps (*Alpi Apuane*) in the north-west of Tuscany form part of the sub-Appenines and are composed almost entirely of marble and have been mined since the Roman times. In the south, the Gargano and Sila massifs cross the spur and foot of the boot respectively.

The Alpine foothills are characterised by the vast Po Valley and the lakes of Como, Garda and Maggiore. Northern Italy has large areas of forest and farmland, while the south is mostly scrubland. Lowlands or plains comprise less than a quarter of Italy's total land mass. The largest plain is the Po Valley (bounded by the Alps, the Appenines and the Adriatic Sea), a heavily populated and industrialised area. The Po is Italy's longest river, flowing from west to east across the plain of Lombardy in the north into the Adriatic. Its tributaries include the Adige, Piave, Reno and Tagliamento rivers. Other major rivers include the Tiber (Rome) and the Arno (Tuscany). A coastal plain runs along the Tyrrhenian Sea from southern Tuscany through Lazio into Puglia (Tavoliere di Puglia), while another smaller plain is Pianura Campana near Mount Vesuvuis. Italy has a number of great national parks including Abruzzo in the Appenines and the Alpine Gran Paradiso between Valle d'Aosta and Piedmont.

The country is surrounded by sea on all sides except in the extreme north. The Ligurian and Tyrrenian seas bound the west of the peninsula; the Ionian Sea lies off the coasts of Puglia, Basilicata and Calabria in the south; and the Adriatic Sea in the east separates Italy from the former Yugoslavia (now the independent states of Slovenia, Croatia and Bosnia). Italy has a vast and varied coastline of some 7,500km (4,660mi), highlights of which include the Amalfi Coast (south of Naples), the crescent of Liguria (the Italian Riviera) and the Gargano Massif (the spur jutting into the Adriatic). Coastal areas vary considerably from the generally flat Adriatic coast to the dramatic cliffs of Liguria and Calabria.

The country encompasses a number of islands including Sicily (situated across the Strait of Messina), the largest and most densely populated island in the Mediterranean. The islands of Pantelleria, Linosa, Lampedusa lie between Sicily and Tunisia, and many small islands surround Sicily offering excellent facilities for scuba-diving and underwater fishing and spectacular scenery. These include the Lipari group of islands (encompassing Lipari itself plus Vulcano, Panarea and Stromboli), Ustica, Favignana, Levanzo, Marittimo, Pantelleria and Lampedusa. Italy's (and the Mediterranean's) second-largest island is Sardinia (*Sardegna*), situated in the Tyrrhenian Sea to the west of the mainland and south of the island of Corsica (France). It's the country's most sparsely populated region with a coastline of some 1,300km (800mi), and is one of Italy's most unspoilt regions.

Among Italy's most famous and attractive islands are Capri, Ischia and Procida in the Gulf of Naples. The seven islands of the Tuscan archipelego (off the Maremma coast) are among the most appealing of all the Mediterranean islands and include Elba, Capraia, Pianosa, Montecristo, Gorgona, Giglio and Giannutri. The beautiful island of Elba (where Napoleon was exiled from May 1814 to February 1815) covers an area of 224km^2 (86mi^2), two-thirds of which is woodland, and has some excellent sandy beaches. Other islands include the virtually unknown (five) Pontine islands some 32km (20mi) off the coast of Lazio.

Italy has a number of active volcanoes including Mount Etna on Sicily (3,274m/10,741ft), Stromboli (on the Isle of Eolie off the west coast of southern Italy) and Vesuvius (near Naples). Etna (which last erupted in 1992) and Stromboli are among the world's most active volcanoes, while Vesuvius hasn't erupted since 1944. Italy is also prone to earthquakes and a European fault line runs through the centre of the country from north to south down to Sicily. The highest risk areas are in southern Italy where some 70 per cent of the terrain is susceptible to earthquakes. The country's last big earthquake hit Messina and Reggio di Calabria in 1908 killing some 85,000 people. More recently there have been earthquakes in Friuli (1976), Irpinia, south-east of Naples (1980) and Umbria (1997).

Italy is divided into 20 regions (and 96 provinces), shown on the map in **Appendix E**. A map of Italy showing the major cities and geographical features is on page 6.

HEALTH

One of the most important aspects of living in Italy (or anywhere else for that matter) is maintaining good health. The quality of health care and health care facilities in Italy varies from poor to excellent, depending on the region and whether you have private health insurance. Italian doctors and other medical staff are well trained and the best Italian doctors are among the finest in the world (many pioneering operations are performed in Italy) and the best hospitals are the equal of any country. On the other hand, the worst public hospitals are among the poorest in Europe. There's a stark contrast between public and private health facilities in Italy, which has a disintegrating public health service that's over-stretched and under-funded, particularly in Rome and southern regions (where corruption is rife).

There are English-speaking and foreign doctors in resort areas and major cities. Hospital facilities are limited in some areas and nursing care and post-hospital assistance in Italy are well below what most northern Europeans and North Americans take for granted. Not surprisingly, health care costs per head in Italy are among the lowest in the EU and the country spends a relatively small percentage of its GDP on health. The country has comparatively few dentists per head of population and treatment can be astronomically expensive (patients also need to be wary of unnecessary treatment). Private health insurance is highly recommended, although free medical treatment is usually available for the uninsured (unlike in some other countries).

Italy's national health service (*Servizio Sanitario Nazionale/SSN*) provides free or low cost health care for those who contribute to Italian social security (*Tassa Sulla Salute/TSS*) and their families, plus university students and retirees (including those from other EU countries). From 1998, Italian employers have paid their employees' state health contributions. The public health service provides free hospital accommodation and treatment, medical tests and specialist consultations, and up to 90 per cent of the cost of prescription drugs and medicines. However, it provides no funding for visits to family doctors (GPs) and dentists, and pays only 75 per cent of out-patient and after-care treatment. Many medical expenses can be totally or partially deducted for tax purposes, including spectacles, contact lenses and hearing aids. Newcomers who pay Italian social security must register with their local *Azienda Sanitaria Locale/ASL* (previously *Unità Sanitaria Locale /USL)* and obtain a national health number as soon as possible after their arrival (you will receive a health card or *tessera sanitaria).* USLs can provide a list of local doctors, public health centres and hospitals. You will need to register with a doctor *(medico convenzionato).*

If you don't qualify for health care under the public health service, it's essential to have private health insurance (in fact, you won't usually get a residence permit without it). This is often advisable in any case if you can afford it, due to the inadequacy of public health services in many areas and long waiting lists for specialist appointments and non-urgent operations. Visitors to Italy should have holiday health insurance (see page 60) if they aren't covered by a reciprocal arrangement.

Pharmacies *(farmacia),* denoted by a large green cross, are generally open from 8.30am to 1pm and from 4pm to 8pm. There are also duty pharmacies outside normal business hours and 24-hour pharmacies in major cities. Pharmacists *(farmacista)* provide general health advice and recommend treatments or a visit to a doctor. Many medicines are sold over-the-counter in Italy that would require a prescription in many other countries and many pharmacies provide homeopathic *(omeopatia)* medicines. Italians often have a holistic approach to medicine, firmly believing that nature is the best healer and there are many health and herbal *(erboristerie)* stores in Italy.

It's possible to have medication sent from abroad, when no import duty or value added tax is usually payable. If you're visiting a holiday home in Italy for a limited period, you should take sufficient medication to cover your stay. In an emergency a local doctor will write a prescription that can be filled at a local pharmacy or a hospital may refill a prescription from its own pharmacy. It's also advisable to take some of your favourite non-prescription drugs (e.g. aspirins, cold and flu remedies, lotions, etc.) with you, as they may be difficult or impossible to obtain in Italy or may be much more expensive. If applicable, take a spare pair of spectacles, contact lenses, dentures or a hearing aid with you.

The Italians are generally healthy and have one of the highest life expectancies in Europe (around 82 for women and 78 for men). The incidence of heart disease in Italy is among the lowest in the world, a fact officially contributed in part to their healthy Mediterranean diet (which includes lots of fresh fruit and vegetables, garlic, olive oil and red wine), as is the incidence of cancers. However, the country has a high incidence of smoking-related health problems (the percentage of smokers in Italy is among the highest in the EU) and liver *(fegato)* problems as a result of too much alcohol are fairly common.

Common health problems among expatriates include sunburn and sunstroke, stomach and bowel problems (due to the change of diet and more often, water, but they can also be caused by poor hygiene), and various problems caused by excess alcohol (including a high incidence of alcoholism). Other health problems are caused by the high level of airborne pollen in spring in some areas (which particularly affects asthma and hay fever sufferers) and noise and traffic pollution, particularly in Italy's major cities. If you aren't used to Italy's hot sun, you should limit your exposure and avoid it altogether during the hottest part of the day, wear protective clothing (including a hat) and use a sun block. Too much sun and too little protection will dry your skin and cause premature ageing, to say nothing of the risks of skin cancer. Care should also be taken to replace the natural oils lost from too many hours in the sun and the elderly should take particular care not to exert themselves during hot weather.

Italy's mild climate (at least during the summer) is therapeutic, particularly for sufferers of rheumatism and arthritis and those who are prone to bronchitis, colds and pneumonia. Italy's slower pace of life is also beneficial for those who are prone to stress (it's difficult to remain up-tight while napping in the sun), although it takes many foreigners some time to adjust. The climate and lifestyle in any country has a marked affect on mental health and people who live in hot climes are generally happier and more relaxed than those who live in cold, wet climates (such as northern Europe). When you've had a surfeit of Italy's good life, a variety of health 'cures' are available at spas (*terme*) and health farms, which are also of benefit to those who suffer from arthritis and similar health problems (treatment is partly paid for by the national health service or private health insurance).

Health (and health insurance) is an important issue for anyone retiring to Italy. Many people are ill-prepared for old age and the possibility of health problems. There's a shortage of welfare and home-nursing services for the elderly in Italy, either state or private, and foreigners who are no longer able to care for themselves are often forced to return to their home countries. There are few state residential nursing homes in Italy or hospices for the terminally ill, although there are a number of private, purpose-built, retirement developments. Italy's provision for handicapped travellers is also poor, and wheelchair access to buildings and public transport is well below average for Western Europe.

If you're planning to take up residence in Italy, even for part of the year only, it's wise to have a health check (medical or screening, eyes, teeth, etc.) before your arrival, particularly if you have a record of poor health or are elderly. If you're already taking regular medication, you should bear in mind that the brand names of drugs and medicines vary from country to country, and should ask your doctor for the generic name. If you wish to match medication prescribed abroad, you will need a prescription with the medication's trade name, the manufacturer's name, the chemical name and the dosage. Most drugs have an equivalent in other countries, although particular brands may be difficult or impossible to obtain in Italy.

There are no special health risks in Italy and no immunisations are required unless you arrive from an area infected with yellow fever. Note that babies are issued with a vaccination record (*libretto delle vaccinazioni*) and children must have certain vaccinations in order to attend school. You can safely drink the water (unless there's a sign to the contrary, e.g. *acqua non potabile*), although it sometimes tastes awful. Many people prefer bottled water when not drinking red wine (which isn't only tastier, but is even beneficial to your health – **providing it's consumed in moderation!**) and various other alcoholic beverages. *Salute!*

INSURANCE

An important aspect of owning a home in Italy is insurance, not only for your home and its contents, but also for your family when visiting Italy. If you live in Italy permanently you will require additional insurance. It's unnecessary to spend half your income insuring yourself against every eventuality from the common cold to being sued for your last lira, but it's important to insure against any event that could precipitate a major financial disaster, such as a serious accident or your house being demolished by a storm. The cost of being uninsured or under-insured can be astronomical. Note that you may already have insurance in your home country that can be extended or which covers you for a limited period in Italy.

As with anything connected with finance, it's important to shop around when buying insurance. Simply collecting a few brochures from insurance agents or companies (listed in yellow pages under *Assicurazioni*) or making a few telephone calls could save you a lot of money. Note, however, that not all insurance companies are equally reliable or have the same financial stability, and it may be better to insure with a large international company with a good reputation than with a small Italian company, even if this means paying a higher premium. Read all insurance policies carefully and make sure that you understand the terms and the cover provided before signing them. Some insurance companies will do almost anything to avoid paying out on claims and will use any available legal loophole, therefore it pays to deal only with reputable companies (not that this provides a foolproof guarantee). Policies often contain traps and legal loopholes in the small print and it's sometimes advisable to obtain legal advice before signing a contract.

In all matters regarding insurance, you're responsible for ensuring that you and your family are legally insured in Italy. Regrettably you cannot insure yourself against being uninsured or sue your insurance agent for giving you bad advice! Bear in mind that if you wish to make a claim on an insurance policy, you may be required to report an incident to the police within 24 hours (this may also be a legal requirement). The law in Italy may differ considerably from that in your home country or your previous country of residence, and you should *never* assume that it's the same. If you're unsure of your rights, you're advised to obtain legal advice for anything other than a minor claim. Note that insurance policies are automatically renewed unless you cancel them in writing.

This section contains information about health insurance, household insurance, and holiday and travel insurance. See also **Car Insurance** on page 38.

Health Insurance

If you're visiting, living or working in Italy, it's extremely risky not to have health insurance for your family, as if you're uninsured or under-insured you could be faced with some very high medical bills. When deciding on the type and extent of health insurance, make sure that it covers *all* your family's present and future health requirements in Italy before you receive a large bill. A health insurance policy should cover you for *all* essential health care whatever the reason, including accidents (e.g. sports accidents) and injuries, whether they occur in your home, at your place of work or while travelling. Don't take anything for granted, but check in advance.

Long stay visitors should have travel or long stay health insurance or an international health policy (see **Health Insurance for Visitors** on page 57). If your stay in Italy is limited, you may be covered by a reciprocal agreement between your home country and Italy (see page 58). When travelling in Italy, you should carry proof of your health insurance with you.

Health Insurance for Residents

If you're planning to take up residence in Italy and will be contributing to Italian social security (*Servizio Sanitario Nazionale/SSN*), you and your family will be entitled to subsidised or free medical treatment. Most residents also subscribe to a complementary health insurance fund, called a *mutuo*, which pays the portion of medical bills that isn't paid by social security. Residents who don't contribute to social security should have private health insurance, which is mandatory for non-EU residents when applying for a visa or residence permit (*certificato di residenza*). Retirees who aren't automatically covered under the Italian national health service can join but are required to pay 7.5 per cent of their income (in which case private health insurance is usually a better option). Note that some foreign insurance companies don't provide sufficient cover to satisfy Italian regulations, therefore you should check the minimum cover necessary with a Italian consulate in your country of residence.

If you contribute to Italian social security, you and your family are entitled to free or subsidised medical treatment. Benefits include general and specialist care, hospitalisation, laboratory services, discounted drugs and medicines, maternity care, appliances and transportation. Many Italians belong to a mutual (*mutuo*) insurance scheme through their employers which 'tops up' the state scheme. Most Italians are covered by Italy's public health service, including retired EU residents (with a residence card) receiving a state pension. If you aren't entitled to public health benefits through payment of Italian social security or by receiving a state pension from another EU country, you must usually have private health insurance and must present proof of your insurance when applying for a residence permit. If you're an EU national of retirement age, who isn't in receipt of a pension, you may be entitled to public health benefits if you can show that you cannot afford private health insurance.

Anyone who has paid regular social security contributions in another European Union (EU) country for two full years prior to coming to Italy (e.g. to look for a job) is entitled to public health cover for a limited period from the date of the last contribution made in their home country. Social security form E106 must be obtained from the social security authorities in your home country and given to your local social security office in Italy. Similarly, pensioners and those in receipt of invalidity benefits must obtain form E121 from their home country's social security administration.

You will be registered as a member of social security and will be given a social security card, a list of local medical practitioners and hospitals, and general information about services and charges. If you're receiving an invalidity pension or other social security benefits on the grounds of ill-health, you should establish exactly how living in Italy will affect those benefits. In some countries there are reciprocal agreements regarding invalidity rights, but you must confirm that they apply in your case. Citizens of EU and European Economic Area (EEA) countries (Iceland, Liechtenstein and Norway) are able to make payments in their home country entitling them to use public health services in Italy and other EU and EEA countries.

The Italian health service places the emphasis on cure rather than prevention and treats sickness rather than promotes good health. There's little preventive medicine in Italy such as regular health checks. The public health service has limited resources for out-patient treatment, nursing and post-operative care, geriatric assistance, terminal illnesses and psychiatric treatment. Perfunctory treatment due to staff shortages, long waiting lists as a result of a lack of hospital facilities, and a general dehumanisation of patients are frequent complaints made against Italy's health system. Many problems are related to crippling bureaucracy, bad management and general disorganisation.

Private Insurance: If you aren't covered by the Italian health service you should take out private health insurance. Most private health insurance policies don't pay family doctors' fees or pay for medication that isn't provided in a hospital or there's an 'excess', e.g. the equivalent of around Lit. 150,000 for each 'illness', which may exceed the cost of treatment. Most will, however, pay for 100 per cent of specialists' fees and hospital treatment in the best Italian hospitals. Private policies vary considerably in price but generally cost from Lit. 2.5 to 4 million a year for a family of four, although they are higher for the elderly. You should avoid a company that reserves the right to cancel a policy when you reach a certain age, e.g. 65 or 70, or which increases premiums sharply as you get older, as to take out a new policy at the age of 65 or more for a reasonable premium is difficult. Those aged over 70 or 75 have a difficult time obtaining cover. Italian policies often have a period (e.g. five years) during which the insurance company cannot exclude you from cover (*rinuncia alla diritto di recessione*), even if you have a serious illness costing the insurance company a lot of money. Many companies, retirement groups and other organisations offer beneficial group rates.

Generally, the higher the premium, the more choice you have regarding doctors, specialists and hospitals. Most policies include disability pay if you're unable to work for a period after an illness or accident. The largest insurers in Italy include Instituto Nazionale delle Assicurazioni (INA), once state owned but now privatised, Sanicard, Filo Diretto, Europa Assistance and Pronto Assistance. Bear in mind that (as in many countries) Italian insurance companies are loathe to pay claims. One of the reasons they don't insist on a medical examination is so that they can refuse to pay a claim because you omitted to tell them you had a heavy cold three years previously. Britons and other Europeans can usually take out an international policy in their home country that covers them in Italy. American can take out a travellers' policy that covers them for their first year in Italy, although they should note that American and international hospitals in Italy may accept only Blue Cross or Blue Shield. If you already have private health insurance in another country, you may be able to extend it to cover you in Italy.

Changing Employers or Insurance Companies: When changing employers or leaving Italy, you should ensure that you have continuous health insurance. If you and your family are covered by a company health scheme, your insurance will probably cease after your last official day of employment. **If you're planning to change your health insurance company, you should ensure that important**

benefits aren't lost, e.g. existing medical conditions won't usually be covered by a new insurer. When changing health insurance companies, it's advisable to inform your old company if you have any outstanding bills for which they are liable.

Health Insurance for Visitors

Visitors spending short periods in Italy (e.g. up to a month) should have a travel health insurance policy (see page 60), particularly if they aren't covered by an international health policy. If you plan to spend up to six months in Italy you should either take out a travel policy, a special long stay policy or an international health policy. Premiums vary considerably and it's important to shop around. Most international health policies include repatriation or evacuation (although it may be optional), which may also include shipment (by air) of the body of a person who dies abroad to his home country for burial. An international policy also allows you to choose to have non-urgent medical treatment in the country of your choice.

Most international insurance companies offer health policies for different areas, e.g. Europe, world-wide excluding North America, and world-wide including North America. Most companies offer different levels of cover, for example basic, standard, comprehensive and prestige. There's always a limit on the total annual medical costs, which should be at least Lit. 750 million (although many companies provide cover of up to Lit. 3,000 million) and some companies also limit the charges for specific treatment or care such as specialists' fees, operations and hospital accommodation. A medical examination isn't usually required for international health policies, although pre-existing health problems are excluded for a period, e.g. two years.

Claims are usually settled in all major currencies and large claims are usually settled directly by insurance companies (although your choice of hospitals may be limited). Always check whether an insurance company will settle large medical bills directly, as if you're required to pay bills and claim reimbursement from an insurance company, it can take several months before you receive your money (some companies are slow to pay). It isn't usually necessary to translate bills into English or another language, although you should check a company's policy. Most international health insurance companies provide emergency telephone assistance.

The cost of international health insurance varies considerably depending on your age and the extent of cover. Note that with most international insurance policies, you must enrol before you reach a certain age, e.g. between 60 and 80, to be guaranteed continuous cover in your old age. Premiums can sometimes be paid monthly, quarterly or annually, although some companies insist on payment annually in advance. When comparing policies, carefully check the extent of cover and exactly what's included and excluded from a policy (often indicated only in the *very* small print), in addition to premiums and excess charges. In some countries, premium increases are limited by law, although this may apply only to residents in the country where a company is registered and not to overseas policy holders. Although there may be significant differences in premiums, generally you get what you pay for and can tailor premiums to your requirements. The most important questions to ask yourself are: does the policy provide the cover required and is it good value for money? If you're in good health and are able to pay for your own out-patient treatment, such as visits to your family doctor and prescriptions, then the best value is usually a policy covering specialist and hospital treatment only.

Reciprocal Health Agreements: If you're entitled to social security health benefits in another EU country or in a country with a reciprocal health agreement with Italy, you will receive free or reduced cost medical treatment in Italy. EU residents must apply for a certificate of entitlement to treatment (form E111) from their local social security office (usually around three weeks before they plan to travel to Italy). An E111 is open-ended and valid for life. However, you must continue to make social security contributions in the country where it was issued and if you become a resident in another country (e.g. another EU country) it becomes invalid. It covers emergency hospital treatment but doesn't include prescribed medicines, special examinations, X-rays, laboratory tests, physiotherapy and dental treatment. If you use the E111 in Italy, you must apply for reimbursement to Italian social security (instructions are provided with the form), which can take months. **Note, however, that you can still get a large bill from an Italian hospital, as your local health authority assumes only a percentage of the cost.**

Participating countries include all EU member states and most other European countries, **excluding** Albania, Switzerland and Turkey. The USA doesn't have a reciprocal health agreement with Italy and therefore American students and other Americans who aren't covered by Italian social security *must* have private health insurance in Italy. British visitors or Britons planning to live in Italy can obtain information about reciprocal health treatment in Italy from the Department of Social Security, Overseas Branch, Newcastle-upon-Tyne, NE98 1YX, UK.

Household Insurance

Household insurance in Italy generally includes building and contents insurance, all of which are usually contained in a multi-risk household insurance policy.

Building (*edificio*): There's no requirement to have cover for your home or personal belongings in Italy and most Italians don't bother to insure their home or its contents. However, if you have a mortgage (*ipoteca*) on a property, your lender will require you to have insurance. However, it highly advisable to take out insurance covering damage to the building due to fire, water, explosion, storm, freezing, snow, theft, malicious damage, acts of terrorism, broken windows and natural catastrophes. There are maximum limits for each risk. Note that in certain cases, claims for damaged property aren't considered unless the government declares the situation a natural catastrophe or Act of God. It's particularly important to have insurance for storm damage in Italy, which can be severe in some areas. Read the small print and check that you're covered for natural disasters such as floods. Note, however, that if you live in an area that's hit by a succession of natural disasters (such as floods), your insurance may be cancelled.

In the event of total loss, building insurance is based on the cost of rebuilding your home. **Make sure that you insure your property for the true cost of rebuilding.** If you have a property restored or modernised, you will need a professional valuation on completion for insurance purposes. You cannot insure against earthquakes on an Italian policy, although a foreign insurance company may offer cover at an exorbitant price. If there's an earthquake the Italian government assumes responsibility, which is limited to the value stated in the land registry (which may be well below a property's actual value), although the insured value of your home is also taken into consideration.

Contents (*contenuto*): Contents are usually insured for the same risks as a building (see above) and are insured for their replacement value. Some companies offer combined household policies while others require separate fire, theft and liability policies. A basic insurance policy may cover only fire and damage (*incendio ed altri danni ai beni*) with an extra premium for theft (*furto*). Although bottled gas is very safe, if you use it you must inform your insurance company as there's an extra premium to pay. Household polices are restrictive with regard to security including locks, window shutters or grilles (all windows less than 3m/10ft from the ground must be barred), armoured doors, unprotected openings, etc. All security requirements must be adhered to otherwise any claims are reduced or won't be paid. You cannot usually insure valuables (e.g. jewellery) unless they've been valued by an Italian expert and they normally need to be stored in a safe, which must be approved by your insurance company. When claiming for contents, if possible you should produce the original bills (always keep bills for expensive items) and should bear in mind that replacing imported items may be much more expensive in Italy.

Apartments: If you own an apartment or a property that shares common elements with other properties (see page 153), building insurance is included in your service charges, although you should check exactly what's covered. You must, however, still be insured for third party risks in the event that you cause damage to neighbouring apartments, e.g. through flood or fire.

Holiday Homes: Premiums are generally higher for holiday homes due to their high vulnerability (particularly to burglaries) and are usually based on the number of days a year a property is inhabited and the interval between periods of occupancy. Cover for theft, storm, flood and malicious damage may be suspended when a property is left empty for more than three weeks at a time (or if there's no visible forced entry). It's possible to negotiate cover for periods of absence for a hefty surcharge, although valuable items are usually excluded. If you're absent from your property for long periods, e.g. more than 60 days a year, you may also be required to pay an excess on a claim arising from an occurrence that takes place during your absence (and theft may be excluded). You should read all small print in policies. **Note that, where applicable, it's important to ensure that a policy specifies a holiday home and not a principal home.**

In areas with a high risk of theft (e.g. most major cities and resort areas), you may be required to fit extra locks and other security measures. Some companies may not insure holiday homes in high risk areas. It's unwise to leave valuable or irreplaceable items in a holiday home or a home that will be vacant for long periods. **Note that some insurance companies will do their utmost to find a loophole which makes you negligent and relieves them of their liability.** Always carefully check that the details listed in a policy are correct, otherwise your policy could be void.

Rented Property: Your landlord will usually insist that you have third party liability insurance, as detailed in the rental contract. A lease requires you to insure against 'tenant's risks', including damage you may make to the rental property and to other properties if you live in an apartment, e.g. due to flood, fire or explosion. You can choose your own insurance company.

Premiums: Premiums are usually calculated on the size of the property, either the habitable area in square metres or the number of rooms, rather than its value. Usually the sum insured (house and contents) is unlimited, providing the property doesn't exceed a certain size and is under a certain age. Premiums depend on the area, although you should expect the premium for a policy that includes theft to be around double what you would expect to pay in another western European country. The cost of multi-risk property insurance in a *low-risk* area is around Lit. 150,000 a year for a property with one or two bedrooms, Lit. 300,000 for three or four bedrooms and around Lit. 600,000 a year for five or six bedrooms. Premiums can be much higher in high risk areas. If you have an index linked policy, cover is increased each year in line with inflation.

It's possible (and legal) to take out building and contents insurance in another country for a property in Italy, although the policy may still be written under Italian law (so always check). The advantage is that you will have a policy you can understand and you will be able to handle claims in your own language (you may also be more likely to be paid or be paid earlier). This may seem like a good option for a holiday home in Italy, although it may be more expensive than insuring with a Italian company and can lead to conflicts if the building is insured with a Italian company and the contents with a foreign company.

Claims: If you wish to make a claim, you must usually inform your insurance company in writing (by registered letter) within two to five days of the incident or 24 hours in the case of theft. Thefts should also be reported to the local police within 24 hours, as the police statement, of which you receive a copy for your insurance company, usually constitutes irrefutable evidence of your claim. Check whether you're covered for damage or thefts that occur while you're away from the property and are therefore unable to inform your insurance company immediately. Note that Italian insurance companies are notoriously slow to pay claims and in some cases are reluctant to pay up at all!

Holiday & Travel Insurance

Holiday and travel insurance is recommended for all who don't wish to risk having their holiday or travel ruined by financial problems or to arrive home broke. As you probably know, anything can and often does go wrong with a holiday, sometimes before you even get started (particularly when you *don't* have insurance). The following information applies equally to both residents and non-residents, whether they are travelling to or from Italy or within Italy. Nobody should visit Italy without travel (and health) insurance.

Travel insurance is available from many sources including travel agents, insurance companies and brokers, banks, automobile clubs and transport companies (airline, rail and bus). Package holiday companies and tour operators also offer insurance policies, some of which are compulsory, too expensive **and don't provide adequate cover.** You can also buy 24-hour accident and flight insurance at major airports, although it's expensive and doesn't offer the best cover. Before taking out travel insurance, you should carefully consider the range and level of cover you require and compare policies. Short-term holiday and travel insurance policies may include cover for holiday cancellation or interruption; missed flights; departure delay at both the start *and* end of a holiday (a common occurrence); delayed, lost or damaged baggage; personal effects and money; medical expenses and accidents (including evacuation home); flight insurance; personal liability and legal expenses; and default or bankruptcy insurance, e.g. a tour operator or airline going bust. You may also need cover for transport strikes in Italy!

Health Cover: Medical expenses are an important aspect of travel insurance and you shouldn't rely on insurance provided by reciprocal health arrangements (see page 58), charge and credit card companies, household policies or private medical insurance (unless it's an international policy), none of which usually provide adequate cover, although you should take advantage of what they offer. The minimum medical insurance recommended by experts is Lit. 750 million in Italy and the rest of Europe and Lit. 3,000 million for the rest of the world (many policies have limits of between Lit. 4,500 to 15,000 million). If applicable, check whether pregnancy related claims are covered and whether there are any restrictions for those over a certain age, e.g. 65 or 70 (travel insurance is becoming increasingly more expensive for those aged over 65, although they don't usually need to worry about pregnancy – particularly the men!).

Always check any exclusion clauses in contracts by obtaining a copy of the full policy document, as not all relevant information will be included in an insurance leaflet. High risk sports and pursuits should be specifically covered and *listed* in a policy (there's usually an additional premium). Special winter sports policies are available and more expensive than normal holiday insurance ('dangerous' sports are excluded from most standard policies). Third-party liability cover should be Lit. 6,000 million in North America and Lit. 3,000 million in the rest of the world. **Note, however, that this doesn't cover you when you're using a car or other mechanically propelled vehicle.**

Visitors: Travel insurance for visitors to Italy should include personal liability and repatriation expenses. If your travel insurance expires while you're visiting Italy, you can buy further insurance from an insurance agent, although this won't include repatriation expenses. Flight insurance and comprehensive travel insurance is available from insurance desks at most airports, including travel accident, personal accident, world-wide medical expenses and in-transit baggage.

Cost: The cost of travel insurance varies considerably, depending on where you buy it, how long you intend to stay in Italy and your age. Generally the longer the period covered, the cheaper the daily cost, although the maximum period covered is usually limited, e.g. six months. With some policies, an excess (deductible) must be paid for each claim; with others the excess applies only to certain items such as luggage, money and medical expenses. As a rough guide, travel insurance for Italy (and most other European countries) costs from around Lit. 60,000 for one week, Lit. 90,000 for two weeks and Lit. 150,000 for a month for a family of four (two adults and two children under 16). Premiums may be higher for those aged over 65 or 70.

Annual Policies: For people who travel abroad frequently, whether on business or pleasure, an annual travel policy usually provides the best value, but carefully check exactly what it includes. Many insurance companies (e.g. Europ Assistance) offer annual travel policies for the equivalent of around Lit. 300,000 to 450,000 a year for an individual (the equivalent of around two to three months insurance with a standard travel insurance policy), which are excellent value for frequent travellers. Some insurance companies also offer an 'emergency travel policy' for holiday homeowners who need to travel abroad at short notice to inspect a property, e.g. after a severe storm. The cost of an annual policy may depend on the area covered, e.g. Europe, world-wide (excluding North America) and world-wide (including North America), although it doesn't usually cover travel within your country of residence. There's also a limit on the number of trips a year and the duration of each trip, e.g. 90

or 120 days. An annual policy is usually a good choice for owners of a holiday home in Italy who travel there frequently for relatively short periods. **However, carefully check exactly what's covered (or omitted), as an annual policy may not provide adequate cover.**

Claims: If you need to make a claim, you should provide as much documentary evidence as possible to support it. Travel insurance companies gladly take your money, but they aren't always so keen to pay claims and you may need to persevere before they pay up. Always be persistent and make a claim *irrespective* of any small print, as this may be unreasonable and therefore invalid in law. Insurance companies usually require you to report a loss (or any incident for which you intend to make a claim) to the local police or carriers within 24 hours and obtain a written report. Failure to do so may mean that a claim won't be considered.

SHOPPING

Italy is one of the world's great shopping countries and Italian shops are designed to seduce you with their artful displays of beautiful and exotic merchandise. Shopping (which is almost as popular as tax evasion!) is both an art form and a pleasure in Italy, particularly food shopping, when most people prefer to shop in traditional small family stores rather than anonymous supermarkets. The major cities, such as Rome, Milan and Florence, are a shoppers' paradise, where even the shop windows are a delight, although they aren't generally the best places to find bargains. It's difficult to say which is Italy's finest shopping city; some say Milan or Rome, while others plump for Florence or Venice – all have their own unique attractions.

Italy draws an army of foreign shoppers keen to pay for top quality Italian labels such as Armani, Ferretti, Gucci, Ungaro, Valentino and Versace. Italian products are synonymous with craftsmanship, quality and style (not to mention their high prices), whether it's high fashion, furniture, cars or jewellery. In general prices are high, but then so is the quality. Large department (*grandi magazzini*) and chain stores such as COIN, Co-op, Esselunga, Metro, Oviesse, La Rinascente, Standa and UPIM, are the best outlets for basics. Every region of Italy has its particular specialities. Among the best buys are clothing, shoes, luggage, contemporary art, prints, engravings, leather goods, jewellery (particularly gold), perfumes, food (ham, cheese, olive oil, pasta,

etc.), wine, spirits, liquors, ceramics, pottery, mosaics, marble, basketwork, straw goods, brass, fabrics, linens, glassware, porcelain, china, furniture, soft furnishings, household goods, inlaid wood, carvings, antiques, lace, embroidery, paper goods and electrical appliances.

Italians aren't into convenience shopping and shopping at all hours, and there are strict opening hours in Italy. These are generally from 8.30 or 9am to between 12.30 and 1.30pm and from 3.30 or 4pm to 7.30 or 8pm, from Monday to Saturday, although there are variations depending on the region and season. Most small stores and businesses close for around three hours for lunch (*pausa* or *siesta*), although department stores and supermarkets tend to remain open (*orario continuato/nonstop*) all day, and some tobacconists, pharmacies and petrol stations open 24-hours a day. Most shops close on certain days or half-days of the week (often Monday mornings), which varies depending on the kind of shop and the region. Many small shops close for a few weeks in summer (August is the most popular month) for holidays. A new law passed in 1998 allows limited evening and Sunday opening.

Food can be expensive in Italy and some Italian products are more expensive in Italy than they are abroad! Less food is bought in supermarkets (*supermercati*) and hypermarkets (*ipermercati*) in Italy than in many other western European countries and therefore it's generally more expensive (Italian supermarkets are also often smaller than those in other European countries). The major supermarket chains include Coop, Esselunga, Euromercato, GS, Pam, SMA, Standa, Unes and Upim, and there are also discount supermarkets such as i Discount, Lidl and Sosty (good for unbranded staple foods). Large supermarkets and hypermarkets tend to open from around 9am until 9pm. Produce (fruit and vegetables) tends to be seasonal and there isn't as much imported produce in Italy as, for example, in the UK and USA.

Imported foods are available in the major cities and can also be purchased by mail (but are expensive). There are many foreign food shops, delicatessens and gourmet shops in the major cities. Food markets (*mercati*) are excellent and the best places to buy fresh produce, meat and fish. Most villages have a weekly travelling market and larger towns have a daily (usually including Sundays) municipal or community market (*mercati communali coperti*). Other markets include foreign food markets, dedicated fish markets, flea markets and antique markets (which are held year round throughout Italy).

As in most countries, it's important to shop around and compare prices in Italy, which can vary considerably, not only between small shops and hypermarkets, but also between different supermarkets and hypermarkets in the same town. Note, however, that price differences usually reflect different quality, therefore make sure that you're comparing similar products. Prices in small village shops are much higher than in large towns, which in turn are higher than supermarkets.

In general, Italian shops are limited to just two sales (*saldi*) a year, which are usually held from early January until mid-February and from August to September, each for a maximum duration of two months. Goods purchased in sales cannot be returned. It's also possible to buy goods direct from factory outlets in Italy, with discounts of 50 per cent or more, although factory shops aren't nearly as common as in some countries (e.g. the USA). There are also wholesale stores (that sell retail) and discount stores.

You may be able to obtain a reduction when buying a large quantity of goods or expensive items, particularly if you offer to pay cash (which may result in a 5 to 10 per cent discount). Shops with fixed prices may display a 'fixed price' (*prezzi fissi*) sign. On the other hand, bargaining is common and even expected in street markets, although usually not when buying food (unless you're buying it by the tonne!). When haggling, never offer anything you aren't willing to pay, as if your offer is accepted you're expected to buy. Don't be deterred from haggling if your efforts are dismissed out of hand – just try the next stall-holder. You should beware of counterfeit goods, as many top Italian fashion brands are the target of counterfeiters. If a bargain seems too good to be true, then it probably is.

One particular idiosyncrasy (idiocy?) you should be aware of in Italy is that in many shops you order goods from one person, pay for them at a separate cash register (*cassa*), and then return with your receipt (*scontrino* or *ricevuta fiscale*) to collect your goods (Italian bureaucracy at its finest – why do something in one operation when you can take three?). Incidentally, it's illegal for a shopkeeper not to give you a receipt and also for you not to ask for one (it's supposed to prevent tax fraud – ho! ho!). You can be fined by the 'finance police' (*guarda di finanza*) for leaving a store without a receipt.

There are a number of books for dedicated shoppers in Italy including Frommer's *Born to Shop Italy* by Suzy Gersham & George McDonald (Macmillan), *Made in Italy* by Annie Brody & Patricia Schultz (Workman), and *Bargain Hunting in Italy, Lo Scoprioccasioni* (the bargain hunter's bible in Italian, but easy to understand) and *Designer Bargains in Italy*. The latter three are written by Teodora Van Meurs and available from Editore Shopping, Via Pestalozza 8, 20131 Milan (☎ 02-7063 8088, e-mail: info@scoprioccasioni.it). Catalogue shopping is available via Skymail (☎ 02-5530 3366), which also offers magazine subscriptions.

In Rome and other cities, or anywhere there are lots of tourists, you *must* be wary of pickpockets and bag-snatchers. *Never* tempt fate with an exposed wallet or purse, or by flashing your money around.

Furniture & Furnishings

Furniture (*mobili*) is generally more expensive in Italy than in many other European countries, although a wide range of modern and traditional furniture is available. Modern furniture is popular and is sold in furniture stores in industrial zones and large hypermarkets throughout Italy, although there are few nationwide, cut-price discount stores. Department stores also sell a wide range of (mostly up-market) furniture. UnoPiu and DuePiu have huge factory outlets north of Rome selling wooden furniture, garden and summer home furniture (such as rattan and bamboo items), DIY furniture and household goods. They produce beautiful catalogues and you can order by telephone (☎ 0761-7581 for a catalogue). Tucano and Oltrefrontiera have a wide selection of furniture and home furnishing, many imported from around the world. Inexpensive chain stores include Coin, Habitat, Home Shop, Rinascente, Standa and Upim. A number of international designer companies have elegant boutiques in Italy including Biggie Best, English Home and Designers Guild.

Most stores make deliveries or loan or rent self-drive vans at reasonable rates. Pine furniture is inexpensive and popular. Beware of buying complicated home-assembled furniture with indecipherable Italian instructions and too few screws. If you want reasonably priced, good quality, modern furniture, you need look no farther than Ikea, a Swedish company manufacturing furniture for home assembly which has stores in a number of cities. There are also many good carpet stores in Italy, although like most home furnishings they can be expensive.

Exclusive modern and traditional furniture is available everywhere, although not everyone can afford the exclusive prices, including bizarre designer pieces for those with money to burn. Many regions of Italy have a reputation for quality handmade furniture. Italian furniture and furnishing stores often offer design services (which may be free) and stock a wide range of beautiful fabrics and materials in patterns and colours ideally suited to Italian homes and the climate and conditions.

If you're spending a lot of money, don't be reluctant to ask for a reduction as most stores will give you a discount. The best time to buy furniture and furnishings is during sales (particularly in winter), when prices of many items are slashed. Most furniture stores also offer special deals on furniture packages for a complete room or home. It's possible for residents to pay for furniture (and large household appliances) interest-free over one year or with interest over a longer period, e.g. five years. It may be worthwhile comparing the cost of furniture in a neighbouring country with that in Italy, although it usually doesn't pay to buy new furniture abroad to furnish a Italian home (particularly as you must usually add shipping costs).

If you're looking for antique furniture at affordable prices, you may find a few bargains at antique fairs (*fiera d'antiquariato*) and flea markets, although genuine antiques are expensive and difficult to find. If you do come across anything worthwhile you must usually drive a hard bargain, as the asking prices are often ridiculous, particularly in tourist areas during the summer. Markets are, however, good for fabric (e.g. for curtains), bed linen and wallpaper. There's a reasonable market for second-hand furniture in Italy and many sellers and dealers advertise in the expatriate and local press (such as *Wanted in Rome*). Charity shops are also an Aladdin's cave of household goods and furniture (they also hold periodic sales).

The kind of furniture you buy for your Italian home will depend on a number of factors including the style and size of your home, whether it's a permanent or holiday home, your budget, the local climate, and not least, your personal taste. If you intend to furnish a holiday home with antiques or expensive modern furniture, bear in mind that you will need adequate security and insurance. If you own a holiday home in Italy, it's usually worthwhile shipping surplus items of furniture you have in your home abroad (unless you live in Australia!). If you intend to move permanently to Italy in a number of years and already have a house full of good furniture abroad, there's little point in buying expensive furniture in Italy.

There are do-it-yourself hypermarkets in some areas, selling everything for the home including DIY supplies, furniture, bathrooms, kitchens, decorating and lighting, plus services such as tool rental and wood cutting. There are also salvage and second-hand companies selling old doors, window frames, fireplaces, tiles and other materials that are invaluable when restoring an old home or wishing to add a 'lived-in' feel to a modern home. Note, however, that many modern DIY supplies and materials aren't as easy to find in Italy as in many other European countries and are more expensive, therefore you may prefer to import them.

Household Goods

Household goods in Italy are generally of good quality with a large choice. Prices compare favourably with other European countries and bargains can be found at supermarkets and hypermarkets. Not surprisingly for a nation that spends much of its time in the kitchen (the rest is spent eating!), Italian kitchenware, crockery, cutlery and glasses can all be purchased cheaply and the quality is usually excellent. It's advisable to buy white goods (such as refrigerators and washing machines) in Italy, as imported appliances may not function properly due to differences in the electrical supply (and they may also be difficult to get repaired). Note also that the standard size of kitchen appliances and cupboard units in Italy *isn't* the same as in some other countries, and it may be difficult to fit an imported dishwasher or washing machine into a Italian kitchen. Check the size *and* the latest Italian safety regulations before shipping these items to Italy or buying them abroad, as they may need expensive modifications.

If you already own small household appliances, it's worthwhile bringing them to Italy, as usually all that's required is a change of plug. If you bring appliances with you, don't forget to bring a supply of spares and refills such as bulbs for a refrigerator or sewing machine, and spare bags for a vacuum cleaner (unless you have a Dyson!). If you're coming from a country with a 110/115V electricity supply, such as the USA, you'll need a lot of expensive transformers and it's usually better to buy new appliances in Italy. Small appliances such as vacuum cleaners, grills, toasters and electric irons are inexpensive in Italy and are of good quality. Don't bring a television without checking its compatibility first, as TVs from many countries won't work in Italy (see page 69).

If you need kitchen measuring equipment and cannot cope with decimal measures, you will need to bring your own measuring scales, jugs, cups and thermometers. Foreign pillow sizes (e.g. American and British) aren't the same as in Italy and duvets are much more expensive than in some other countries, so are worth taking.

Shopping Abroad

Shopping abroad (e.g. in Austria, France, Slovenia or Switzerland) makes a pleasant change from all those 'boring' Italian shops full of tempting and expensive luxuries (although the information in this section applies equally to foreign residents shopping in Italy as it does to Italian residents shopping abroad). It can also save you money and makes a pleasant day out for the family. Don't forget your passports or identity cards, car papers, children, dog's vaccination papers and foreign currency. Most shops in border towns eagerly accept Italian lire, but will usually give you a lower exchange rate than a bank. Whatever you're looking for, compare prices and quality before buying. Bear in mind that if you buy goods that are faulty or need repair, you may need to return them to the place of purchase.

From 1993 there have been no cross-border shopping restrictions within the European Union for goods purchased duty and tax paid, providing all goods are for personal consumption or use and not for resale. Although there are no restrictions, there are 'indicative levels' for certain items, above which goods may be classified as commercial quantities. For example, persons entering Italy aged 17 or over may import the following amounts of alcohol and tobacco without question:

- 10 litres of spirits (over 22° proof);

- 20 litres of sherry or fortified wine (under 22° proof);

- 90 litres of wine (or 120 x 0.75 litre bottles/10 cases) of which a maximum of 60 litres may be sparkling wine;

- 110 litres of beer;

- 800 cigarettes and 400 cigarillos and 200 cigars and 1kg of smoking tobacco.

There's no limit on perfume or toilet water. If you exceed the above amounts you may need to convince the customs authorities that you aren't planning to sell the goods. There are fines for anyone who sells duty-paid alcohol and tobacco, which is classed as smuggling.

Never attempt to import illegal goods into Italy and don't agree to bring a parcel into Italy or deliver a parcel in another country without knowing exactly what it contains. A popular confidence trick is to ask someone to post a parcel in Italy (usually to a poste restante address) or to leave a parcel at a railway station or restaurant. **THE PARCEL USUALLY CONTAINS DRUGS!**

Duty-Free Allowances

Under European Union (EU) rules, duty-free (*esente da dazio*) shopping within the EU is due to be abolished on 1st July 1999 (although it may get a reprieve). Duty-free allowances are the same whether or not passengers are travelling within the EU or from a country outside the EU. For each journey to another EU member state, travellers aged 17 or over are entitled to import the following goods purchased duty-free:

- one litre of spirits (over 22° proof) *or* two litres of fortified wine (under 22° proof) *or* two litres of wine;
- two litres of still table wine;
- 200 cigarettes *or* 100 cigarillos *or* 50 cigars* *or* 250g of tobacco;
- 60ml of perfume;
- 250ml of toilet water;
- other goods including gifts and souvenirs to the value of Lit. 67,000.

* Residents of non-EU states are entitled to import 150 cigars.

Duty-free allowances apply to both outward and return journeys, even if both are made on the same day, and the combined total (i.e. double the above limits) can be imported into your 'home' country.

VAT Refunds: If you live outside the EU you can obtain a VAT refund (20 per cent on most goods) on purchases providing the value (excluding books, food, services and some other items) amounts to Lit. 360,000 or more in one store (stores providing this service usually display a 'Tax-Free' sticker in their windows). Large department stores may have a special counter where non-EU shoppers can arrange for the shipment of duty-free goods. An export sales invoice (or 'tax-free shopping cheque') is provided by retailers, listing all purchases. When you leave Italy your purchases must be validated by customs (*dogana*) staff at the airport, port or railway station (so don't pack them in your checked baggage!). Refunds may be made on the spot at special 'tax-free' counters, otherwise they can be made by mail within 90 days of the date of purchase. You can choose to have a refund paid to a credit card or bank account or to receive a cheque.

PETS

If you plan to take a pet (*animale domestico*) to Italy, it's important to check the latest regulations. Ensure you have the correct papers, not only for Italy but for any countries you will pass through to reach Italy. Particular consideration must be given before exporting a pet from a country with strict quarantine regulations, such as the UK. If you need to return prematurely, even after a few hours or days in Italy, your pet must go into quarantine, e.g. for six months in the UK, which apart from the expense is distressing for both pets and owners (although this is likely to change in the near future if, as expected, the UK abolishes quarantine).

There's no quarantine period for pets in Italy, but they need a health certificate issued by an approved veterinary surgeon. Dogs and cats need a rabies vaccination not less than 20 days or more than 11 months prior to the date of issue of the health certificate. Those aged under 12 weeks are exempt, but must have a health certificate and a certificate stating that no cases of rabies have occurred for at least six months in the local area. British owners must complete an *Application for a Ministry Export Certificate for dogs, cats and rabies susceptible animals* (form EXA1), available from the Ministry of Agriculture, Fisheries & Food (MAFF), Animal Health (International Trade) Division B, Hook Rise South, Tolworth, Surbiton, Surrey KT6 7NF, UK (☎ 0181-330 4411). A health inspection must be performed by a licensed veterinary officer before you're issued with an export health certificate (bilingual, Italian-English) that's valid for 30 days. Animals may be examined at the Italian port of entry by a veterinary officer.

If you're transporting a pet to Italy by ship or ferry, you should notify the ferry company. Some companies insist that pets are left in vehicles (if applicable), while others allow pets to be kept in cabins. If your pet is of nervous disposition or unused to travelling, it's best to tranquillise it on a long sea crossing. Pets can also be transported by air.

At the age of three months, a dog must be registered at the local 'dog bureau' (*anagrafe canina*) and some municipalities issue dog tags. Italian regulations require dogs to be tattooed on their body (not just their ear) as a means of registration, although a new microchip identification system is being introduced and will eventually replace tattooing. Tattooing must be done by a veterinary surgeon (*veterinari*) or the Unita Santaria Locale (who do it for free). Dogs and cats don't need to wear identification discs in Italy and there's no system of licensing (a dog tax was abolished because country people claimed their dogs were working animals and refused to pay it). All dogs must be kept on a leash and muzzled when in a public area in towns (although many people ignore the law) or on public transport, but not in the country. You must usually pay full fare for a dog that isn't carried (e.g. in a container) on public transport.

Health insurance for pets is available from a number of insurance companies and it's advisable to have third party insurance in case your pet bites someone or causes an accident. In areas where there are poisonous snakes, some owners keep anti-venom in their refrigerator (which must be changed annually). Although not exactly a nation of animal lovers (in Italy, animals and birds are something to shoot at or eat), pets are rarely restricted or banned from long-term rental or holiday accommodation (but check when renting an apartment).

The unpleasant aspect of Italy's dog population is abundantly evident on the streets of Italian towns and cities, where dogs routinely leave their 'calling cards'. You must *always* watch where you walk in Italy. Most dog owners don't take their pets on long country walks, but just to a local park or car park or simply let them loose in the streets to do their business. Owners of dogs that soil footpaths can be fined, although there's no pooper-scooper law requiring them to clean up after their pets (some cities have attempted to introduce them without success). Although it's of little consolation, it's purportedly good luck to tread in something unpleasant!

The Ente Nazionale per la Protezione degli Animali (national association for the protection of animals) is the main organisation for animal welfare in Italy and it operates shelters for stray and abused animals, and inexpensive pet hospitals in many cities.

TELEVISION & RADIO

Television

Until 1976, all Italian television (TV) stations were state-owned and under the control of the government. However, there has been something of a revolution in the last few decades, although there are still three public TV stations. Cable TV is available in the main Italian cities and towns, although it's much less common in Italy than in many other western European countries. Satellite TV is also popular in Italy, particularly among expatriates. Italy is a nation of TV addicts and almost every Italian household has at least one TV. Like most people, the Italians complain endlessly about their TV, particularly its lack of quality, surfeit of advertising, dependence on trashy foreign programmes, moronic game shows and endless repeats, although it's generally no worse than most other European countries. However, although Italy prides itself on its culture, this isn't evident from its TV programmes. The most popular programmes are films, sport, theatre, variety, serials and game shows. TV and radio programmes are listed in daily newspapers and weekly magazines, most of which provide free weekly programme guides with reviews and comments. Weekly TV magazines include *tv Sette*, *TV Guide* and *Sorrisi e Canzoni TV*.

Standards: The standards for TV reception in Italy aren't the same as in some other countries. Italy uses the standard European PAL B/G system and therefore TVs and video recorders (VCRs) operating on the British PAL I, French (SECAM) or the North American (NTSC) systems won't work there. Machines operating on the British PAL I system can be converted, although you're usually better off buying a new TV or VCR. It's possible to buy a multi-standard European TV (and VCR) containing automatic circuitry that switches between different systems such as PAL and SECAM. Some multi-standard TVs also include the North American NTSC standard and have an NTSC-in jack plug connection allowing you to play American videos. Some people opt for two TVs, one to receive Italian and cable/satellite programmes and another (e.g. SECAM or NTSC) to play their favourite videos. Some modern VCRs can play PAL, NTSC and SECAM video tapes. If you decide to buy a TV in Italy, you will find it advantageous to buy one with teletext, which apart from allowing you to display programme schedules, also provides a wealth of useful and interesting information.

Stations: Italy has six terrestrial stations broadcasting throughout the country. These include three government-owned stations (*Radiotelevisione Italiana*), RAI-UNO, RAI-DUE and RAI-TRE (RAI one, two and three), and three privately-owned channels, Canale 5, Italia 1 and Rete 4 (controlled by Silvio Berlusconi, the media magnate and former prime minister, through his Fininvest company). RAI generally provides higher quality programmes than the commercial stations and isn't as politically biased as previously. The RAI and private channels each have around half the Italian TV audience. Other channels available via cable and satellite include Antenna 3, Antenne 2 (France), Italia 7/Telecity, Italia 8, Odeon, Rete A-Mtv, Telelombardia, Telenova/Cinque Stelle, Telepiù 3 and Videomusic/Tmc 2. You can also receive TeleMonteCarlo (Tmc) in some 70 per cent of Italy and if you live in northern Italy you can receive terrestrial broadcasts from Austria, France and Switzerland. There are also local TV stations (*Tv locali*) throughout Italy.

As in many countries, programmes consist largely of mindless game shows, soaps, dubbed reruns of foreign sitcoms, chat shows, TV shopping, soccer and mild pornography, with not much serious news reporting or discussion. Almost all foreign programmes are dubbed. Sexist TV is rife and topless ladies commonplace (a popular show on British satellite TV channel Bravo is *Italian Stripping Housewives*), although between 7am and 10.30pm, programmes containing explicit sexual content and violence aren't broadcast.

TV Licence: A TV tax (*canone*) is payable in Italy of Lit. 170,000 a year for a colour TV, although it can also be paid quarterly or half-yearly (at a post office) by 31st January. A single licence covers any number of TVs in a household. When you buy a TV in Italy your name is automatically registered with the authorities, although many people avoid it by buying a second-hand TV or making an 'arrangement' with the vendor. The tax must be paid to customs if you personally import a TV. The authorities have powerful detector vans to discover those watching TV and check whether they have paid the tax. Fines for non-payment are high.

Italian Pay TV: Italian pay TV is broadcast via satellite rather than cable (as in some countries) and includes Telepiù 1 and 2, Tele+1 to 3, TMC (TeleMontecarlo), TMC2 (mostly video clips), CNN, BBC World, MTV, Discovery Channel, Cartoon Network and DMX (radio music channels). Telepiù 1 shows films which may have a double audio track (*doppio audio*) allowing you to switch from Italian to the original (usually English) soundtrack. Telepiù 2 shows mainly sports, including all matches live from *Serie A*, Italy's premier football league (you can sign up for all 34 of a team's matches, depending on where you live, or just their 17 away games). To receive Italian pay TV you must buy a decoder for around Lit. 160,000, available from a TV store, and pay a monthly or annual subscription to receive programmes. The subscription depends on what you want to watch (there are discounts if you subscribe to all channels). Around one million people subscribe to pay TV.

Satellite TV: Around 25 geostationary satellites are positioned over Europe, carrying over 200 TV stations broadcasting in a variety of languages. All the European satellite TV stations can be received throughout Italy, although the size of the dish required varies depending on the location.

Astra: TV addicts (easily recognised by their antennae and square eyes) are offered a huge choice of English and foreign-language stations via Astra satellites.

Although it wasn't the first in Europe (which was Eutelsat), the European satellite revolution really took off with the launch of the Astra 1A satellite in 1988 (operated by the Luxembourg-based *Société Européenne des Satellites* or SES), positioned 36,000km (22,300mi) above the earth. Since 1988 a number of additional Astra satellites have been launched, increasing the number of available channels to 64 (or over 200 via digital). An added bonus is the availability of foreign radio stations via satellite, including all the main British Broadcasting Corporation (BBC) stations (see **Cable & Satellite Radio** on page 73).

Among the many English-language stations available on Astra are Sky One, Movimax, Sky Premier, Sky Cinema, Film Four, Sky News, Sky Sports (three channels), UK Gold, Channel 5, Granada Plus, TNT, Eurosport, CNN, CNBC Europe, UK Style, UK Horizons, The Disney Channel and the Discovery Channel. Other stations broadcast in Dutch, German, Japanese, Swedish and various Indian languages. The signal from many stations is encrypted or scrambled (*codificato*), with the decoder usually built into the receiver, and viewers must pay a monthly subscription fee to receive programmes. You can buy pirate decoders for some channels. The best served by clear (unscrambled or *in chiaro*) stations are German-speakers (most German stations on Astra are clear).

Eutelsat: Eutelsat (owned by a consortium of national telephone operators) was the first company to introduce satellite TV to Europe (in 1983) and it now runs a fleet of communications satellites carrying TV stations to over 50 million homes. Until 1995 they had broadcast primarily advertising-based, clear-access cable channels. Following the launch in March 1995 of their Hot Bird satellite, Eutelsat hoped to become a major competitor to Astra, although its stations are mostly non-English. The English-language stations on Eutelsat include Eurosport, Euronews, BBC World, European Business News, CNBC Europe and Worldnet. Other channels broadcast in Arabic, French, German, Hungarian, Italian (including RAI one, two and three), Polish, Portuguese, Spanish and Turkish.

Sky Television: You must buy a Videocrypt decoder, an integral part of the receiver in most models, and pay a monthly subscription to receive all Sky stations except Sky News (which isn't scrambled). Various packages are available costing from between GB£10 and GB£30 per month (for the premium package offering all movie channels plus Sky Sports). To receive scrambled channels such as Movimax and Sky Sports you need an address in Britain. Subscribers are sent a coded 'smart' card (similar to a credit card), which must be inserted in the decoder to switch it on (cards are frequently updated to thwart counterfeiters). Sky won't send smart cards to overseas viewers as they have the copyright for a British-based audience only and overseas homeowners need to obtain a card through a friend or relative in Britain. However, a number of companies and retailers in Europe (some of which advertise in the expatriate press in Italy) supply genuine Sky cards and pirate cards may also be available.

Digital Television: Digital TV was launched on 1st October 1998 by Sky Television in the UK. The benefits include a superior picture, better (CD) quality sound, widescreen cinema format and access to many more stations. To watch digital TV you require a Digibox and a (digital) Minidish, which in 1998 could be purchased at a subsidised price by existing Sky customers. Customers must sign up for a 12-month subscription and agree to have the connection via a phone line (to allow for future interactive services). In addition to the usual analogue channels (see above), digital TV offers BBC 1, BBC 2 and Channel 4 (but not ITV or ITV2), plus many new digital channels (a total of 200 with up to 500 possible later). ONdigital launched a rival digital service on 15th November 1998, which although it's cheaper, provides a total of 30 channels only (15 free and 15 subscription) including BBC, ITV, ITV2, Channel 4 and Channel 5. Cable & Wireless also plan to launch a digital service in 1999. Widescreen digital TVs cost around GB£1,000, but will inevitably become cheaper as more models become available and the demand increases. At the time of writing, digital satellite TV wasn't available in Italy.

BBC Worldwide Television: The BBC's commercial subsidiary, BBC Worldwide Television, broadcasts two 24-hour channels: BBC Prime (general entertainment) and BBC World (24-hour news and information). BBC World is free-to-air and is transmitted via the Eutelsat Hot Bird satellite, while BBC Prime is encrypted and transmitted via the Intelsat satellite. BBC Prime requires a D2-MAC decoder and a smartcard costing around £25 and an annual £75 subscription fee plus VAT. Smartcards are available from TV Extra, PO Box 304, 59124 Motala, Sweden (☎ 46-141-56060). For more information and a programming guide contact BBC Worldwide Television, Woodlands, 80 Wood Lane, London W12 0TT, UK (☎ UK 0181-576 2555). The BBC publishes a monthly magazine, *BBC On Air*, giving comprehensive information about BBC Worldwide Television programmes. A programme guide is also listed on the Internet (www.bbc.co.uk/schedules) and both BBC World and BBC Prime have their own websites (www.bbcworld.com and www.bbcprime.com). When accessing them, you need to enter the name of the country (e.g. Italy) so that the schedules appear in local time.

Equipment: A satellite receiver should have a built-in Videocrypt decoder (and others such as Eurocrypt, Syster or SECAM if required) and be capable of receiving satellite stereo radio. An 85cm dish is adequate north of Rome, although a larger dish or a signal booster may be required in southern areas of Italy. A basic fixed satellite system (which will receive programmes from one satellite only) costs around Lit. 750,000 and a motorised dish (which will automatically adjust its orientation so that you can receive programmes from other satellites) will set you back three or four times as much. If you wish to receive satellite TV on two or more TVs, you can buy a satellite system with two or more receptors. To receive stations from two (or more) satellites simultaneously, you need a motorised dish or a dish with a double feed antenna (dual LNBs). There are many satellite sales and installation companies in Italy. Shop around and compare prices. Alternatively you can import your own satellite dish and receiver and install it yourself. Before buying a system, ensure that it can receive programmes from all existing and planned satellites.

Location: To receive programmes from any satellite, there must be no obstacles between the satellite and your dish, i.e. no trees, buildings or mountains must obstruct the signal, therefore check before renting or buying a home. Before buying or erecting a satellite dish, check whether you need permission from your landlord or the local authorities. In general, dishes of up to 1m in diameter don't require planning permission providing that they aren't positioned on the front wall or roof and don't protrude above the top of the roof, and that there's only one per house. Dishes can usually be mounted in a variety of unobtrusive positions and can be painted or patterned to blend in with the background. New blocks of flats or apartments are generally fitted with at least one communal satellite dish.

Videos: There are video stores where films can be rented (*noleggio*) in Italy's major cities and most video rental stores have some films in English. Look in the yellow pages under *Audiovisivi*. There are also international video mail-order companies that sell or rent videos.

Programme Guides: Many satellite stations provide teletext information and most broadcast in stereo. Sky satellite programme listings are provided in a number of British publications such as *What Satellite, Satellite Times* and *Satellite TV* (the best), which are available on subscription. The annual *World Radio and TV Handbook* (Billboard) contains over 600 pages of information and the frequencies of all radio and TV stations world-wide.

Radio

Radio was deregulated in Italy in 1976, at the same time as television. Since then there has been an explosion in the number of stations available and there are now some 2,500, from large national stations to small local stations with just a handful of listeners. The three main channels are Radio 1, 2 and 3 operated by the state controlled company RAI. Radio 1 and 2 feature light (dance) music and general entertainment, while Radio 3 broadcasts serious discussion programmes and classical music. There are also Radio 1 and 2 popular music stations which are also part of RAI. Radio is very popular in Italy with an estimated audience of some 35 million people, over a third of whom listen exclusively to popular music stations. During the summer, RAI broadcasts daily news in English and Vatican Radio also broadcasts the news in English at various time during the day. There are also expatriate English-language radio stations in the major cities.

BBC: The BBC World Service is broadcast on short wave on several frequencies (e.g. 12095, 9410, 7325, 6195, 3955, 648 and 198 khz) simultaneously and you can usually receive a good signal on one of them. The signal strength varies depending on where you live in Italy, the time of day and year, the power and positioning of your receiver, and atmospheric conditions. All BBC radio stations, including the World Service, are also available on the Astra satellite (see below). The BBC publish a monthly magazine, *BBC On Air*, containing comprehensive information about BBC World Service radio and TV programmes. For a free copy and frequency information write to BBC On Air, Room 205 NW, Bush House, Strand, London WC2B 4PH, UK (an annual subscription costs GB£24).

Cable & Satellite Radio: If you have cable or satellite TV, you can also receive many radio stations via your cable or satellite link. For example, BBC Radio 1, 2, 3, 4 and 5, BBC World Service, Sky Radio, Virgin 1215 and many foreign-language stations are broadcast via the Astra satellites (see page 70). Satellite radio stations are listed in British satellite TV magazines such as the *Satellite Times*. If you're interested in receiving radio stations from further afield you should obtain a copy of the *World Radio TV Handbook* (Billboard).

LEARNING ITALIAN

Although Italian is the national language of Italy, sizeable minorities speak German (Alto Adige), French (Valle d'Aosta), Slovene and Ladino. There are also numerous (some 600!) regional dialects, many of which are difficult or impossible to understand (e.g. Neopolitan and Sicilian), even for fluent Italian speakers. Sardinian is virtually a separate language and has more in common with Catalán (the language of Catalonia in Spain) than Italian. Standard Italian (*italiano standard*) is, however, taught in all state schools and almost everyone can understand it (although older people may know only their own regional dialect). French is widely understood and English is spoken in the major cities and tourist centres. The ability to speak English confers prestige in Italy and anyone with a smattering (most waiters) are keen to show it off. Note, however, that English isn't spoken as widely in Italy as in many other European countries and you shouldn't expect to find English speakers in rural areas. English is more widely spoken in the north than the south of the country.

Unlike the French, Italians appreciate any attempt to speak their language, however tortured. Italian is a relatively easy language to learn (if that can ever be said of any language!) as it's phonetic and pronounced exactly as it's written, with each syllable pronounced (although Italians often express themselves with their hands!). It has many similarities to French and Spanish and you will have a head start if you can speak either of these languages.

If you don't speak Italian fluently, you may wish to enrol in a language course. If you want to make the most of the Italian way of life and your time in Italy, it's essential to learn Italian as soon as possible. For people living in Italy permanently, learning Italian isn't an option, but a necessity, both professionally and socially. Although it isn't always easy, even the most non-linguistic person can acquire a working knowledge of Italian. All that's required is a little hard work, some help and perseverance (particularly if you have only English-speaking colleagues and friends). **Note that your business and social enjoyment and success in Italy will be directly related to the degree to which you master Italian.**

Most people can teach themselves a great deal through the use of books, tapes, videos and even CD-ROM computer-based courses. However, even the best students require some help. Teaching Italian is big business in Italy, with classes offered by language schools, Italian and foreign colleges and universities (which sponsor programmes for foreigners), private and international schools, foreign and international organisations (such as the British Institute in Rome), local associations and clubs, and private teachers. Tuition ranges from language courses for complete beginners, through specialised business or cultural courses, to university-level courses leading to recognised diplomas. Most Italian universities provide language courses and many organisations offer residential holiday courses all year round, particularly for children and young adults (it's best to stay with a local Italian family).

There are many language schools (*scuole di lingue*) in all Italian cities and large towns. Most schools run various classes depending on your language ability, how many hours you wish to study a week, how much money you want to spend and how quickly you wish to learn. For those for whom money is no object, there are total immersion courses where you study for up to nine hours a day, five days a week. The cost for a one-week (45 hours) total immersion course is usually between Lit. 4.5

million and 6 million depending on the school. Rates vary so shop around. Language classes generally fall into the following categories:

extensive	4-10	hours per week
intensive	15-20	"
total immersion	20-40+	"

Don't expect to become fluent in a short time unless you have a particular flair for languages or already have a good command of Italian. Unless you desperately need to learn Italian quickly, it's best to arrange your lessons over a long period. However, don't commit yourself to a long course of study, particularly an expensive one, before ensuring that it's the right course. Most schools offer free tests to help you find your appropriate level and a free introductory lesson.

You may prefer to have private lessons, which are a quicker, although more expensive way of learning a language. The main advantage of private lessons is that you learn at your own speed and aren't held back by slow learners or left floundering in the wake of the class genius. You can advertise for a teacher in your local newspapers, on shopping centre/supermarket bulletin boards, on university notice boards, and through your or your spouse's employer. Don't forget to ask your friends, neighbours and colleagues if they can recommend a private teacher. Private lessons cost from around Lit. 100,000 an hour at a school or Lit. 30,000 to 60,000 for a private tutor.

Language schools are listed in the yellow pages under *Scuole Varie – Scuole di Lingue* or you can contact the Association of Language Schools of Italian as a Foreign Language (ASILS), Corso Vittorio Emanuele, 39, 00186 Rome (☎ 06-679 8896, Internet: www.bwline.com/itschools/). A useful book for anyone wishing to visit Italy to study the Italian language and culture is *Study Holidays*, containing practical information on accommodation, travel, and sources of bursaries, grants and scholarships. It's published by the Central Bureau, Seymour Mews House, Seymour Mews, London W1H 9PE, UK (☎ 0171-486 5101).

CRIME

The crime rate in Italy varies considerably from region to region and is around average for Europe. Violent crime is rare in most areas, although muggings do occur in resort areas and cities. Despite its often violent reputation, there's actually *less* violent street crime such as muggings and robbery with violence in most parts of Italy than in many other European countries, and it's generally a very safe place for children. Sexual harassment and even assault can be a problem for women in some areas, although most men draw the line at cat-calls and whistles. Foreigners should take care when travelling in the south of Italy, where highway robbery and kidnappings of foreigners occasionally take place.

Housebreaking and burglary are rife in Italy, where 'holiday' or second homes are a popular target. Many residents keep dogs as a protection or warning against burglars and have triple-locked and steel-reinforced doors. However, crime in rural areas remains relatively low and it's still common for people in villages and small towns not to lock their homes or cars. Car theft and theft from cars is widespread in cities, where foreign-registered cars are a popular target, particularly expensive models, which are often stolen to order and spirited abroad. It's advisable to use as many high-security locks as you can carry to protect a bicycle, moped or scooter.

Beware of bag snatchers (*scippatori*) in towns and cities, who operate on foot, scooters, motorcycles or even from cars. Always carry bags defensively slung across your body (make sure it has a strong strap that cannot easily be cut (otherwise you should carry it firmly in your hand). Fanny-packs (that are stowed above your bottom) are vulnerable and should be avoided, as should small back-packs which can be easily cut. Confidence tricksters and hustlers are also rife in Italy, where it's advisable to avoid all strangers trying to attract your attention. Many stage accidents, such as spilling something on your clothes (or pointing out something which has been done by an accomplice), in order to rob you. Be alert to any incident that could be designed to attract your attention. Don't accept an offer from someone to take your photograph with your camera (they are likely to run off with it); if you must ask someone to take a photo, ask a tourist.

Pickpockets and bag-snatchers are a plague in the major cities, where the street urchins (often Albanians or Gypsies) are highly organised and trained pickpockets (if you get jostled check for your wallet). They try to surround you and often use newspapers or large pieces of cardboard to distract you and hide their roaming hands. Keep them at arm's length, if necessary by force, and keep a firm grip on your valuables. If you're targeted shout 'Va Via!' (go away) in a loud voice (a loud whistle can also be useful to scare off prospective attackers or pickpockets).

Always remain vigilant in tourist haunts, queues, on public transport (particularly on night trains) and anywhere that there are crowds. Never tempt fate with an exposed wallet or purse or by flashing your money around and hang on tight to your shoulder bag. Don't carry a lot of cash or expose expensive jewellery, watches or sunglasses when out walking. One of the most effective methods of protecting your passport, money, travellers' cheques and credit cards, is with an old-fashioned money belt (worn under your clothing) or a pouch on a string around your neck. Always keep some emergency money and a credit card in separate places in case of theft and a copy of important documents such as your passport.

The Mafia holds a death grip on the south of Italy, where business people are often forced to pay protection money (*pizzo*) to the mobsters to ensure their businesses are safe. Despite many high profile arrests in recent years, rumours of the Mafia's demise or loss of influence is premature and they reportedly have their fingers in every facet of government right up to the Prime Minister's office in Rome!

However, although organised crime and gang warfare is rife in some areas, it has no discernible impact on the lives of most foreigners in Italy (particularly in the north of the country).

Don't let the foregoing catalogue of crime and mayhem put you off Italy. You can usually safely walk almost anywhere at any time of day or night and there's no need for anxiety or paranoia about crime. However, you should be 'street-wise' and take certain elementary precautions. These include avoiding high-risk areas at night (such as parks and car parks) and those frequented by drug addicts, prostitutes and pickpockets. You can safely travel on most *metròs* at any time, although some stations are best avoided late at night. When you're in an unfamiliar city, ask a policeman, taxi driver or other local person whether there are any unsafe neighbourhoods – and avoid them!

See also **Car Crime** on page 39, **Home Security** on page 179 and **Household Insurance** on page 58.

PUBLIC HOLIDAYS

The government has established ten statutory national public holidays (*feste nazionali*) a year plus one official local holiday. The following days are official national public holidays:

Date	Holiday
1st January	New Year's Day (*Il Capodanno* or *San Silvestro*)
6th January	Epiphany (*La Befana or Epifania*)
March or April	Easter Monday (*Pasquetta, Lunedi di Pasqua or Sant' Angelo*)
25th April	Liberation Day (*Anniversario della Liberazione*)
1st May	Labour Day (*Giornata del Lavoro or Primo Maggio*)
15th August	Assumption of the Blessed Virgin Mary (*Assunzione/Ferragosto*)
1st November	All Saints (*Ognissanti or Tutti I Santi*)
8th December	Immaculate Conception (*Concezione Immacolata*)
25th December	Christmas Day (*Natale*)
26th December	St. Stephen's or Boxing Day (*Santo Stefano*)

When a holiday falls on a Saturday or Sunday, another day isn't usually granted as a holiday unless the number of public holidays in a particular year falls below a minimum number. Holidays are occasionally moved to form long weekends and when a holiday falls on a Thursday or Tuesday, it's customary to create a long weekend or make a 'bridge' (*fare ponte*) by taking the following or preceding day off as well. When a holiday falls on a Friday or Monday many businesses close for the entire holiday weekend (assuming they would normally work on a Saturday or Sunday). All public offices, banks and businesses are closed on public holidays, when only essential work is performed. Note that foreign embassies and consulates in Italy usually observe Italian public holidays plus their own country's national holidays.

In addition to the national public holidays listed above, each province or town has its own saints' days and festivals (*festas*), fairs (*fieras*) and pilgrimages (*pellegrinaggios*). For example 29th June (*San Pietro*) in Rome, 7th December (*San Ambrogio*) in Milan and 24th June (*San Giovanni*) in Florence, Genoa and Turin.

Although regional holidays aren't always official public holidays, most local businesses are closed for the day or part of the day. Public holidays are marked on most calendars, some of which also show saints' days (calendars are distributed free by local businesses such as banks in December/January). Note that many businesses and shops also close for summer holidays, which may be for two to four weeks, usually in August.

TIME DIFFERENCE

Like most of the continent of Europe, Italy is on Central European Time (CET). This is Greenwich Mean Time (GMT) plus one hour from the last Sunday in September until the last Sunday in March, and GMT plus two hours during daylight saving from the last Sunday in March to the last Sunday in September. Time changes are announced in local newspapers and on radio and TV. The time is given on the telephone 'speaking clock' service number (see your local phone book) and shown on a TV with a 'time' button. When making international telephone calls or travelling long-distance by air, check the local time difference, which is shown in phone books.

Times in Italy, for example in timetables, are usually written using the 24-hour clock, when 10am is written as 1000 and 10pm as 2200. Midday (*mezzogiorno*) is 1200 and midnight (*mezzanotte*) is 2400. When writing times, Italians put a comma between hours and minutes, e.g. 9,00 is 9am and 21,00 is 9pm. The international time difference in winter (October to March) between Rome at noon (1200) and some major international cities is shown below:

ROME	LONDON	JO'BURG	SYDNEY	AUCKLAND	NEW YORK
1200	1100	1300	2100	2300	0600

3.

FINANCE

One of the most important aspects of buying a home in Italy and living there (even for relatively brief periods) is finance, which includes everything from transferring and changing money to mortgages and taxes. If you're planning to invest in a property or business in Italy financed with imported funds, it's important to consider both the present and possible future exchange rates. On the other hand, if you live and work in Italy and are paid in lire (or euros), this may affect your financial commitments abroad. **Bear in mind that if your income is received in a currency other than lire it can be exposed to risks beyond your control when you live in Italy, particularly regarding inflation and exchange rate fluctuations.**

If you own a home in Italy you can employ an Italian accountant or tax adviser to look after your financial affairs there, and declare and pay your local taxes. You can also have your financial representative receive your bank statements, ensure that your bank is paying your standing orders (e.g. for utilities) and that you have sufficient funds to pay them. If you let a home in Italy through an Italian company, they may perform the above tasks as part of their services.

Although the Italians prefer to pay cash (which cannot be traced by the taxman!) rather than use credit or charge cards, it's wise to have at least one credit card when visiting or living in Italy. Even if you don't like credit cards and shun any form of credit, they do have their uses, for example no-deposit car rentals, no pre-paying hotel bills (plus guaranteed bookings), obtaining cash 24-hours a day, simple telephone and mail-order payments, greater safety and security than cash, and above all, convenience. Note, however, that not all Italian businesses accept credit cards, particularly small businesses, and you should check in advance.

Wealth Warning: If you plan to live in Italy you must ensure that your income is (and will remain) sufficient to live on, bearing in mind currency devaluations and exchange rate fluctuations (if your income isn't paid in lire or euros), rises in the cost of living (see page 108), and unforeseen expenses such as medical bills or anything else that may reduce your income (such as stock market crashes and recessions!). Foreigners, particularly retirees, often under-estimate the cost of living in Italy and some are forced to return to their home countries after a few years. Note also that Italy is one of the highest taxed countries in the European Union (EU) when both direct and indirect taxes (including social security) are taken into consideration.

This section includes information on importing and exporting money; banking; mortgages; taxes (property, income, capital gains, inheritance, gift and VAT); wills; and the cost of living.

FISCAL CODE

All residents of Italy need a fiscal code (*codice fiscale*), that Italians receive at birth, which is required to apply for a job, open a bank account, register a car, buy or rent a home, or even pay utility bills. You can obtain a fiscal code from your local tax office (*intendenza di finanza*) for which you will need your passport and a copy of the pages containing your particulars. Codes for individuals are comprised of letters and figures (figures only for companies). The code is made up of the first, third and fourth consonants of your surname (or fewer if there aren't enough), the year and month (A-L) of your birth, and your day of birth (1-31 for men, 41-71 for women). Each *comune* has its own number for fiscal code purposes, although for foreigners the country of birth is shown. Husbands and wives have separate codes, as a wife in Italy retains and uses her maiden name after she's married.

You should inform your local tax office when you move home, although you will retain the same fiscal number. Your fiscal number must be used on all official correspondence with the tax authorities and on tax declarations. It's useful to keep a note of your number with you at all times as you never know when you may be required to provide it.

ITALIAN CURRENCY

As you're probably aware, the Italian unit of currency is the lira (plural *lire*), which is also the currency of the Republic of San Marino and the Vatican City. It has been devalued many times in recent decades and has traditionally been one of the weakest currencies in Western Europe. This is, however, good news if you receive your income in a strong currency that has appreciated against the lira in recent years. On 1st January 1999 the euro was introduced in Italy (plus Austria, Belgium, Finland, France, Germany, Ireland, Luxembourg, the Netherlands, Portugal and Spain) and will eventually become the country's currency. The currencies of all 11 euro countries are locked into a fixed exchange rate (set by the European Central Bank) with the euro and consequently with each other. On 1st January 1999, the exchange rate between the euro and the lira was set at 1936.27 lire. The lira will continue to circulate until 1st January 2002, when it will be withdrawn and replaced by the euro (euro coins and notes will be introduced earlier in some countries and will circulate alongside the national currency, but they won't become legal currency until 2002). Although you will no longer be a millionaire with the demise of the lire, you will at least be able to manage the numbers!

Not surprisingly, given Italy's woeful fiscal management, the rules to allow Italy entry to the euro were blatantly fudged (Italy had a public debt well above the level specified in the Maastricht Treaty) and it's the weakest link in the euro group of 11 countries. However, it's hoped that the discipline imposed by the euro and the possibility of being thrown out if it doesn't stick to the rules, will finally knock the Italian financial system into shape and drag it screaming and kicking into the 21st century (some people believe it hasn't even made it into the 20th century yet!). There has been very little opposition in Italy to replacing the lira with the euro and most Italians look forward to having what's expected to be a very strong currency.

Italian coins (*monete*) are minted in values of 5, 10, 20, 50, 100, 200, 500 and 1,000 lire. The 5, 10 and 20 lire coins are hardly ever seen in circulation, although they are still legal tender and haven't been recalled by the Banca d'Italia (they are useful for old-fashioned lifts that require a coin to use them). Coins can be confusing with a number of different coins minted for the same value. Banknotes (*banconote*) are printed in values of 1,000, 2,000, 5,000, 10,000, 20,000, 50,000, 100,000 lire and the new 500,000. The abbreviation for *lire italiane* is Lit. (as used by banks and in this book) or £, not to be confused with the sign for sterling (so don't have a heart attack when you're charged £2,000 for a cup of coffee!). Note that when writing figures in Italy, a period (.) is used to separate units of millions and thousands and a comma is used to denote fractions.

It's advisable to obtain some Italian coins and banknotes before arriving in Italy and to familiarise yourself with them. You should have some lire in cash, e.g. Lit.

150,000 to 300,000 in small notes, when you arrive. This will save you having to queue to change money on arrival at an Italian airport (where exchange rates are poor). It's best to avoid Lit. 100,000 and 500,000 notes, which sometimes aren't accepted, particularly for small purchases or on public transport! However, you should avoid carrying a lot of cash. Beware of short-changing, which is common in some areas (always check your change, particularly when tendering a large note).

IMPORTING & EXPORTING MONEY

There are no exchange controls in Italy and no restrictions on the import or export of funds. An Italian resident is permitted to open a bank account in any country and to export an unlimited amount of money from Italy. You may import or export up to Lit. 20 million in any combination of foreign currency, Italian currency and travellers' cheques without formality. Amounts over Lit. 20 million (e.g. to buy a home) must be declared in order to prevent money laundering and provide statistical data for the Bank of Italy (*Banca d'Italia*).

When transferring or sending money to (or from) Italy you should be aware of the alternatives and shop around for the best deal. One way to do this is via a bank draft (*assegno circolare*), which should be sent by registered mail. Note, however, that in the unlikely event that it's lost or stolen, it's impossible to stop payment and you must wait six months before a new draft can be issued. Bank drafts aren't treated as cash in Italy and must be cleared, as with personal cheques. One of the safest and quickest methods of transferring money is to make a direct transfer or a telex or electronic transfer (e.g. via the SWIFT system in Europe) between banks. A 'normal' transfer should take three to seven days, but in reality it usually takes much longer and an international bank transfer between non-affiliated banks can take weeks! A SWIFT telex transfer *should* be completed in a few hours, with funds being available within 24 hours. The cost of transfers vary considerably, not only commission and exchange rates, but also transfer charges (such as the telex charge for a SWIFT transfer). Note that it's usually quicker and cheaper to transfer funds between branches of the same bank than between non-affiliated banks.

Always check charges and exchange rates in advance and agree them with your bank (you may be able to negotiate a lower charge or a better exchange rate). Shop around a number of banks and compare fees. Some foreign banks levy a flat-fee for electronic transfers, irrespective of the amount. British banks charge between £10 and £45 for 'express' electronic transfers taking from one to five days or longer. When you have money transferred to a bank in Italy, make sure that you give the account holder's name, the account number, the branch number and the bank code. If money is 'lost' while being transferred to or from an Italian bank account, it can take weeks to locate it. If you plan to send a large amount of money to Italy or abroad for a business transaction such as buying property, you should ensure that you receive the commercial rate of exchange rather than the tourist rate.

Italian banks (along with Portuguese and Spanish) are among the slowest in Europe to process bank transfers and you should expect them to take at least twice as long as a bank says it will. It isn't unusual for transfers to and from Italy to get 'stuck' in the pipeline, which allows the Italian bank to use your money for a period interest free. For example, transfers between British and Italian banks sometimes take from three to six weeks and the money can 'disappear' for months or even completely! Except for the fastest (and most expensive) methods, transfers between international banks are a joke in the age of electronic banking, when powerful financiers can switch funds almost instantaneously.

You can also send money by international money order from a post office or with a telegraphic transfer, e.g. via Western Union, the quickest and safest method, but also the most expensive. Western Union transfers can be picked up from a post office in Italy (and 100 other countries) just 15 minutes after being paid into a post office abroad. Money can be sent via American Express offices by Amex cardholders. Postcheques can be cashed at any post office in Italy and most credit and charge cards can be used to obtain cash advances. It's also possible to pay some bills by personal cheques and Eurocheques, although these take a long time to clear (a number of weeks) and fees are high. **Note that most Italian banks don't accept cheques drawn on foreign banks.**

Most banks in major cities have foreign exchange windows and there are banks or exchange bureaux (*ufficio di cambio*) with extended opening hours at airports, major railway stations and in all major cities. Here you can buy or sell foreign currencies, buy and cash travellers' cheques and eurocheques (up to Lit. 300,000 per cheque and a maximum of Lit. 900,000/three cheques in one transaction), and obtain a cash advance on credit and charge cards. Note, however, that eurocheques aren't used a lot in Italy and some Italian banks refuse to cash them. At airports and in tourist areas in major cities, there are automatic change machines accepting up to 15 currencies including US$, sterling, Deutschmarks, and French and Swiss francs. **Note, however, that airports (and change machines) usually offer the worst exchange rates and charge the highest fees (e.g. handling charges).**

There are many private exchange bureaux in the major cities and resorts with longer business hours than banks, particularly at weekends. Most offer competitive exchange rates and low or no commission (but always check). They are easier to deal with than banks and if you're changing a lot of money you can usually negotiate a better exchange rate. Never use unofficial money changers, who are likely to short change you or leave you with worthless foreign notes rather than lire. Banks tend to offer the best exchange rates and the post office the lowest charges. The post office charges a flat rate of Lit. 1,000 per cash transaction (regardless of the amount), while banks charge Lit. 2,500 or more. The exchange rate (*tasso di cambio*) against the lire for most European and major international currencies is listed in banks and daily newspapers. Exchange rates are better when obtaining cash with a credit or debit card as you're given the wholesale rate, although there's a 1.5 per cent charge on cash advances and ATM transactions in foreign currencies. Note that in Italy you need a PIN composed of numbers rather than letters, as many Italian ATMs have only numerical keypads (some ATMs may reject foreign cards – if this happens try again and if necessary try another ATM).

Travellers' Cheques: If you're visiting Italy, it's safer to carry travellers' cheques (*assegni turistici*) than cash. There are no bank charges if you buy lire travellers' cheques, although you may be better to buy cheques in a major currency such as $US or sterling when visiting Italy, which can be used anywhere in Europe. Travellers' cheques aren't as easy to cash in Italy as in some other countries, e.g. the USA, and they are difficult or impossible to change in rural areas. They aren't usually accepted as cash by businesses, except perhaps in hotels, restaurants and shops in Rome and other major cities, which usually offer a poor exchange rate. You can buy travellers' cheques from any Italian bank, usually for a fee of 1 per cent of the face value. Fees and rates vary considerably when cashing travellers' cheques in Italy. Some banks charge Lit. 1,000 per cheque with a Lit. 3,000 minimum, while the post office charges Lit. 2,000 for amounts up to Lit. 100,000 and Lit. 5,000 above Lit. 100,000. Buying large denomination cheques saves on per-cheque exchange charges. Note that American Express and Thomas Cook offices don't charge for cashing their own cheques. Banks usually offer a better exchange rate for travellers' cheques than for banknotes.

Always keep a separate record of cheque numbers and note where and when they were cashed. American Express provides a free, three-hour replacement service for lost or stolen travellers' cheques at any of their offices world-wide, providing you know the serial numbers of the lost cheques. Without the serial numbers, replacement can take three days or longer. Most companies provide toll-free numbers for reporting lost or stolen travellers' cheques in Italy.

One thing to bear in mind when travelling anywhere is not to rely on one source of funds only.

BANKS

There are around 1,000 banks (*bancos*) in Italy, including some 50 branches of foreign banks (mostly in Rome and Milan), around 250 of which are large (*grandi*). The remaining 750 or so are primarily local banks with few branches. The number of banks in Italy is continually reducing as banks merge or are taken over. There are three types of bank in Italy: ordinary credit banks, co-operative banks (*banchi popolari cooperative*) and co-operative credit banks (*banche di credito cooperativo*). As in other countries, co-operative banks were established to provide loans (particularly home loans) to their customers. Co-operative credit banks are rural and artisan savings banks funded and owned by farmers and craftsmen. They comprise the largest number of banks in Italy, but because their average size is very small they account for just a small percentage of total deposits.

The Banca Nazionale del Lavoro, Banca d'Italia, Cassa di Riparmio, Banca Commerciale Italiana, Banca di Roma, Banco di Napoli and Banco di Sicilia all have nationwide branch networks. The top ten banks hold some 35 per cent of total bank assets. Creditwest, a joint venture between Credito Italiano and the British National Westminster Bank, has around 30 branches in Rome, Milan and Naples. The post office serves as a savings bank for many Italians and foreigners with a fiscal code.

Bank opening hours vary depending on the bank and town, and are generally from 8.30am until 1pm or 1.30pm and for one to one and a half hours in the afternoon, e.g. from 2.30 or 3pm until 4 or 4.30pm. Some city banks also open from 9am to noon on Saturdays. Note that banks usually open only in the morning on the day before a public holiday. Offices at major airports and railway stations have longer opening hours for changing money and cashing travellers' cheques, and there are also exchange bureaux in major cities and resorts with extended opening hours.

The Bank of Usury or The Loan Shark Banking Corp. would be a more appropriate name for most Italian banks, which levy some of the highest charges in the world. The interest rates charged by many Italian banks equate to usury, particularly for business and consumer loans, and would actually be illegal in some countries. The interest rate on credit cards are also exorbitant. However, lenders are now required to publish the highest rates they charge and the market average, so that borrowers can make comparisons. Shop around and compare rates before signing any contracts or taking out a loan. Note that with the introduction of the euro with low base rates, borrowing in euros should become much cheaper. Despite the extortionate charges and interest rates, it has traditionally been difficult to obtain loans from Italian banks. Due to the high fees (and taxes) levied by banks, many Italians prefer to keep their money in cash at home (away from the prying eyes of the tax man!).

Italy has one of the least efficient and most ponderous banking services in Europe, where even the simplest operation is inordinately complicated and time-consuming (Russians will feel at home). Banks have little or no concept of customer service and staff are akin to state bureaucrats and have about the same interest in their customers (nil). Although banking has become highly automated in recent years, Italian banks lag far behind those in many other European countries (notably Britain, Germany, the Netherlands and Switzerland) in terms of efficiency and the range and quality of services provided. Decisions regarding loans and other transactions often aren't made by managers at local level and must be referred to a regional or national head office. Italian banks will need to become *much* more competitive and efficient to compete with other EU banks with the introduction of the euro. On the other hand, Italians banks are quite safe and most deposits are covered by a Bank Deposit Insurance Fund (*Fondo Interbancario di Garanzia dei Depositi*).

Opening an Account

You can open a bank account in Italy whether you're a resident or a non-resident. It's best to open an Italian bank account in person, rather than by correspondence from abroad. Ask your friends, neighbours or colleagues for their recommendations and just go along to the bank of your choice and introduce yourself. You must be aged at least 18 and provide proof of identity, e.g. a passport, and your address in Italy (a utility bill will usually suffice). Before choosing a bank, it's advisable to compare the fees charged for international money transfers and other services, which can be very high.

If you wish to open an account with an Italian bank while abroad, you must obtain an application form from a branch of an Italian bank (either in Italy or your home country). You need to select a branch from the list provided, which should be close to your home or place of business in Italy. If you open an account by correspondence, you must provide a reference from your bank, including a certificate of signature or a signature witnessed by a solicitor or lawyer. You also need a photocopy of the relevant pages of your passport and a lire draft to open the account.

Non-Residents: If you're a non-resident, you're entitled to open a non-resident account (*conto estero*) only. Only foreign currency or imported lire can be paid into a non-resident account, which pays higher interest than resident accounts. There's no withholding tax on interest earned on deposits in non-resident accounts, as there is for resident lire accounts (when withholding tax is deducted at source). If you're a non-resident it's possible to survive without an Italian account by using eurocheques, travellers' cheques and credit cards, although this isn't wise and is an expensive option. If you have a second home in Italy, you can have all documentation (e.g.

cheque books, statements, etc.) sent to an address abroad and some Italian banks also provide written communications in English.

Residents: You're considered to be a resident of Italy (*residenti valutari*) if you have your main centre of interest there, i.e. you live or work there more or less permanently. To open a resident's account you must usually have a residence permit (*certificato di residenza*) or evidence that you have a job in Italy.

It isn't advisable to close your bank accounts abroad when you're living permanently in Italy, unless you're absolutely certain that you won't need them in the future. Even when you're resident in Italy, it's cheaper to keep some money in local currency in an account in a country that you visit regularly, rather than pay commission to convert lire. Many foreigners living in Italy maintain at least two accounts; a foreign account (possibly offshore) for international transactions and a local account with an Italian bank for day to day business.

All banks provide credit and debit cards (called Bancomat cards) to obtain cash throughout Italy and also abroad, usually via the CIRRUS and NYCE networks. However, it's unwise to rely solely on ATMs (also referred to as Bancomats in Italy) to obtain cash as they often run out of money or are out of operation. Note also that daily withdrawals with a Bancomat card are generally a maximum of Lit. 500,000.

Cheque Accounts

The normal bank account for day-to-day transactions in Italy is a cheque or current account (*conto corrente/interno*). Non-EU residents need Italian residency and a fiscal number (*codice fiscale*) to open a current account. Couples can open a joint account (*conto corrente cointestato*) and some banks have special accounts and deals for children, pensioners, students and women. Always shop around and compare fees and benefits before opening an account. When opening a cheque account, you should request a Bancomat debit card, which can be used to pay for goods and pay bills throughout Italy. You will receive a cheque book (*libretto di assegni*) and your Bancomat card, which you must usually collect in person from your branch, around two to three weeks after opening an account.

Interest is paid on cheque accounts biannually or annually, although it may be as little as 0.5 per cent. Many banks offer accounts where the balance above a sum of your choice (e.g. Lit. 5 million) is automatically invested in mutual funds. There's a fee for a cheque book (stamp duty) and a fee for each cheque you write, which is around Lit. 1,000 or more when charges, duty and insurance is included. Current account charges vary and may be negotiable depending on factors such as the number of cheques you write and the average balance maintained. Charges are higher on non-resident than resident accounts. A damning reflection of the state of banking in Italy is that only some 25 per cent of Italians have a cheque account, while in other western countries most people have at least one and often two or more.

Cheques (*assegni*) may be crossed (*sbarrato*) or open (*non-sbarrato*), which are the most common. Cheques require endorsement on the back before they can be paid into an account. Note that open cheques are freely negotiable and even crossed cheques can be endorsed to a third party (up to Lit. 20 million), although you can write not transferable (*non trasferibile*) on the back of a cheque to prevent it from being endorsed. Cheque cards (*carte di garanzia*), that guarantee a cheque up to a specified amount, are available in Italy, but few people accept personal cheques even with a guarantee card (you're unlikely to be able to use your cheque book outside your local area anyway). Cheques are, however, accepted by utility companies and other business with which you regularly do business. To obtain cash over the counter you need to complete a form or write a cheque made out to yourself (*me medesimo*, usually written as *m.m.*, or *me stesso*), which can usually be done only at your own branch. Cheques must be written in blue or black ink and when writing the amount in words no capitals are used and all words are connected. Most banks now have tellers who can cash cheques, thus eliminating the previous two-step operation where you presented the cheque/form at one counter and were given a receipt to take to a cash desk (*cassa*) to obtain your money.

It's illegal to bounce cheques (*assegno a vuoto*) in Italy, for which you can be banned from holding a bank account and can also be prosecuted. You should also take care not to become overdrawn, which can be very expensive (overdrafts may be possible for a hefty interest rate). There's no such thing as post-dated cheques in Italy, which are against the law, and all cheques can be presented for payment on the day they are written irrespective of their date. The time taken to clear cheques (after which the funds are credited to your account and start earning interest) varies from two days for a cheque drawn on the same bank to a week or longer for a cheque drawn on a different bank. Note that you can stop payment of a cheque only when it has been lost or stolen (not simply because you have changed your mind), when a report must be made to the local police.

Bank statements (*estratto conto*) are issued monthly or quarterly (you can usually choose) and contain your account details such as your bank, branch and account number at the top. This information is required when payments are to be made directly to or from your account, e.g. by standing order (*ordine di pagamento*) or direct debit (*domiciliazione*). Regular bills (such as utility bills) are best paid by direct debit, for which there's a charge of around Lit. 1,500. If you're a non-resident, it's advisable to keep an emergency amount on deposit for unexpected (or unexpectedly high) bills. Bills can also be paid in cash at banks by completing a payment slip (*richiesta di bonifico*).

Offshore Banking

If you have a sum of money to invest or wish to protect your inheritance from the tax man, it may be worthwhile investigating the accounts and services (such as pensions and trusts) provided by offshore banking centres in tax havens such as the Channel Islands (Guernsey and Jersey), Gibraltar and the Isle of Man (around 50 locations world-wide are officially classified as tax havens). Offshore banking has had· a good deal of media attention in recent years, during which it has also been under investigation by the EU. The big attractions are that money can be deposited in a wide range of currencies, customers are usually guaranteed complete anonymity, there are no double taxation agreements, no withholding tax is payable and interest is paid tax-free. Many offshore banks also offer telephone banking (usually 24 hours a day, seven days a week).

A large number of American, British and other European banks and financial institutions provide offshore banking facilities in one or more locations. Most institutions offer high-interest deposit accounts for long-term savings and investment portfolios, in which funds can be deposited in any major currency. Many people living abroad keep a local account for everyday business and maintain an offshore account for international transactions and investment purposes. However, most financial experts advise investors not to rush into the expatriate life and invest their life savings in an offshore tax haven until they know what their long-term plans are.

Accounts have minimum deposits levels which usually range from the equivalent of around GB£500 to GB£10,000, with some as high as GB£100,000. In addition to large minimum balances, accounts may also have strict terms and conditions, such as restrictions on withdrawals or high early withdrawal penalties. You can deposit funds on call (instant access) or for a fixed period, e.g. from 90 days to one year (usually for larger sums). Interest is usually paid monthly or annually; monthly interest payments are slightly lower than annual payments, but they have the advantage of providing a regular income. There are usually no charges providing that a specified minimum balance is maintained. Many accounts offer a cash or credit card (e.g. Mastercard or Visa) which can be used to obtain cash from cash machines (ATMs) throughout the world.

When selecting a financial institution and offshore banking centre, your first priority should be for the safety of your money. In some offshore banking centres, all bank deposits are guaranteed under a deposit protection scheme, whereby a maximum sum is guaranteed should the financial institution go to the wall (the Isle of Man, Guernsey and Jersey all have such schemes). Unless you're planning to bank with a major international bank (which is only likely to fold the day after the end of the world!), you should check the credit rating of a financial institution before depositing any money, particularly if it doesn't provide deposit insurance. All banks have a credit rating (the highest is 'AAA') and a bank with a high rating will happily tell you what it is (but get it in writing). You can also check the rating of an international bank or financial organisation with Moody's Investor Service. You should be wary of institutions offering higher than average interest rates; if it looks too good to be true it probably will be – like the Bank of International Commerce and Credit (BICC) that went bust in 1992.

MORTGAGES

Mortgages (home loans) are available from all major Italian banks (both for residents and non-residents) and many foreign banks. Mortgages (*ipoteche*) from Italian banks can take a long time to be approved (although it's now much faster than it was) and you may be able to obtain better terms and a larger loan from a foreign lender. Italian mortgages are repaid using the capital and interest method (repayment), and endowment and pension-linked mortgages aren't offered. Italian loans can be arranged with a fixed or variable interest rate (*tasso*). When comparing rates, the fixed rate (*tasso fisso*) is usually higher than the variable rate (*tasso variabile*) to reflect the increased risk to the lender. The advantage of a fixed rate is that you know exactly how much you must pay over the whole term. You can usually convert a variable rate mortgage to a fixed rate at any time.

Interest rates in Italy have traditionally been very high and Italian lenders' margins and fees are among the highest in Europe (mortgages may also contain restrictive clauses). Many Italians have mortgages with a high fixed interest rate that they would like to renegotiate or pay off early, but they are prevented or discouraged from doing so by punitive penalties. You may be able to renegotiate your current mortgage for one with a lower interest rate, although many Italian mortgages contain clauses that don't allow homeowners to do this.

The government interest rate was reduced to 4 per cent in October 1998 – a 25-year low. Mortgage rates in 1998 were are as low as 5 per cent and were expected to fall even further in 1999 with the introduction of the euro (the base rate throughout the euro zone was set at 3 per cent in December 1999). The first banks to offer home loans under 5 per cent were the British banks, Abbey National and Woolwich. These two banks lead the way on mortgages in Italy, while Banco Popolare di Milano (BPM) and Rolo (the bank with the toffee centre) were among the first Italian banks to offer the same sort of rates. Loans are also now available from telephone mortgage lenders such as Banca Manager, who offer a fast response and lower fees than most traditional banks. When looking for a mortgage, shop around for the best deal. Note that it's also possible to assume the mortgage of a vendor.

Those seeking a first mortgage are usually offered the best deals. Many lenders offer low start mortgages, which are fixed (*tasso/rata d'ingresso*) for two or three years, after which they may change to a variable rate. Some banks offer lower interest rates to attract buyers in certain areas. You can have a clause in your mortgage whereby you aren't required to accept an increase of over 10 per cent in your payments or more than the standard of living index (i.e. inflation). Any additional amount owed is added to your loan or the loan period is extended. Most banks don't have a maximum limit for mortgages, although some limit the minimum loan to between Lit. 100 and 200 million. Mortgages repayments are generally limited to a maximum around 30 per cent of your net income.

It's inadvisable to over-stretch your finances when taking out a mortgage as there will inevitably be added costs that you haven't bargained for. Some foreign lenders apply stricter rules than Italian lenders regarding income, employment and the type of property on which they will lend, although some are willing to lend more than an Italian lender. If you default on your mortgage repayments, your property can be repossessed and sold at auction, although most lenders are willing to negotiate and arrange lower repayments when borrowers get into financial difficulties.

Up to the mid-'90s, Italian banks rarely lent more than 50 per cent of the value of a property, although this has now risen to 80 per cent. Mortgages of 95 or 100 per cent aren't available in Italy, although it may be possible to obtain a larger (e.g. 90 per cent) mortgage for a property requiring restoration (*mutuo per ristrutturazione*). Loans are usually repaid over a shorter period (*durata*) in Italy (e.g. 10 or 15 years) than in many other countries (including the UK and USA), where a 20 to 30-year repayment period is common. However, some Italian banks now offer mortgages for up to 30 years. The maximum loan for a second home is generally around 50 or 60 per cent. If you're buying a new property off-plan where payments are made in stages, a bank will provide a 'staggered' loan, where the loan amount is advanced in instalments as required by the

contract. During the period before completion, interest is payable on a monthly basis on the amount advanced by the bank (plus insurance). When the final payment has been made and the loan is fully drawn, the mortgage enters its amortisation period (*periodo di ammortamento/durata del mutuo*).

Note that when buying a property in Italy, the deposit paid when signing the preliminary contract (*compromesso di vendita*) is automatically protected under Italian law should you fail to obtain a mortgage. It's possible to obtain a mortgage guarantee from most lenders, valid for two to four months, during which period you're guaranteed a mortgage for a specified sum, subject to an acceptable property valuation. To obtain a mortgage from an Italian bank, you must provide proof of your monthly income and all out-goings, such as existing mortgage payments, rent and other loans or commitments. Proof of income usually includes three month's pay slips for employees, confirmation of income from your employer and tax returns. If you're self-employed you require an audited copy of your balance sheets and trading accounts for the past three years, plus your last tax return. If you want an Italian mortgage to buy a property for commercial purposes, you must provide a detailed business plan (in Italian).

There are various fees (*spese istruttoria*) associated with mortgages. All lenders charge an arrangement fee for establishing a loan, usually around 1 per cent of the loan amount. There's a registration tax of 2 per cent of the mortgage value plus interest and a fixed payment of Lit. 200,000. A fee is also payable to the notary (*notaio*) for registering the charge against the property (see **Fees** on page 147). Most lenders impose an administration fee of around 1 per cent of the loan with minimum and maximum fees. It isn't usual to have a survey in Italy, where an Italian lender may value a property or simply accept the fiscal value, although foreign lenders usually insist on a 'valuation' before they will grant a loan. It's customary in Italy for a property to be held as security for a loan taken out on it, i.e. the lender takes a first charge on the property.

Mortgages for Second Homes

It's more difficult for non-residents to obtain a mortgage for a second home in Italy and usually only 50 or 60 per cent of its value can be borrowed. Interest rates for non-residents are also usually higher than for residents. Most people find it difficult to obtain a mortgage outside of Italy for an Italian home without collateral. However, if you have spare equity in an existing property (either in Italy or abroad), then it may be more cost effective to remortgage (or take out a second mortgage) on that property, than take out a new mortgage for a second home. It involves less paperwork and therefore lower legal fees, and a plan can be tailored to meet your individual requirements. Depending on the equity in your existing property and the cost of your Italian property, this may enable you to pay cash for a second home.

It's also possible to obtain a foreign currency mortgage, other than lire, e.g. sterling, French or Swiss francs, $US, Deutschmarks, Dutch guilders or even euros. However, you should be wary of taking out a foreign currency mortgage, as interest rate gains can be wiped out overnight by currency swings and devaluations. It's generally recognised that you should take out a loan in the currency in which you're paid or in the currency of the country where a home is situated, i.e. lire or euros. In this case if the foreign currency is devalued, you will have the consolation of knowing that the value of your Italian property will ('theoretically') have increased by the same percentage, when converted back into the foreign currency. When choosing between a lire loan and a foreign currency loan, be sure to take into account all charges, fees, interest rates and possible currency fluctuations. However you finance the purchase of a second home in Italy, you should obtain professional advice from your bank manager and accountant.

Note that if you have a foreign currency mortgage, you must usually pay commission charges each time you make a transfer to pay your mortgage or remit money to Italy. However, some lenders will transfer mortgage payments to Italy each month free of charge or for a nominal amount. If you let a second home, you may be able to offset the interest on your mortgage against rental income, but pro rata only. For example if you let an Italian property for three months of the year, you may be able to offset a quarter of your annual mortgage interest against your rental income.

TAXES

Italy is one of the highest taxed countries in the EU and is also estimated to have the highest number of tax dodgers (tax evasion is a national sport). There seems·to be a tax stamp (*bollo*) for everything in Italy (the Beatles must have had Italy in mind when they wrote their song *The Tax Man*). To make matters worse, Italian tax law is inordinately complicated (amazingly they have actually been simplified in recent years) and the taxes, regulations and procedures are constantly changing (just when you think you understand them they change everything and hit you with new taxes). In 1997, there was a major overhaul of the Italian tax system when a number of existing taxes were abolished and new taxes were introduced. It's important to check all tax information with an accountant or tax office (but get it in writing) in order to establish that it's correct, including the information contained in this book.

VALUE ADDED TAX (VAT)

Value added tax (VAT or the 'Voracious Administration Tax'), called *Imposta sul Valore Aggiunto (IVA)* in Italy, is a general tax on goods and services. Most prices of goods and services in Italy are quoted inclusive of tax, although sometimes they are given exclusive of tax, e.g. for office supplies and business equipment. Italy has the following rates of VAT:

Rate	Percentage	Applicable To
Reduced	4%	Consumer goods; basic foodstuffs; newspapers, magazines and books; property (excluding luxury homes); meals in company restaurants, schools and canteens; home care assistants for the sick; and equipment for the disabled.
Intermediate	10%	Foods (including game and courtyard birds, rabbits, fish, shellfish, molluscs, prosciutto cotto, breakfast cereals, soups, condiments, sugar, spices, pork and beef, olive husk oil, long-life milk, cream, yogurt, tea, eggs, honey, chocolate and biscuits); theatre

		scripts; hotel bills; cinema tickets; ornamental plants; tickets for urban public transport (except air, train and boat travel); and satellite and cable TV.
Standard	20%	'Luxury' food and drink including wine, beer, mineral water and coffee; crayfish, oysters, lobster, caviar and similar products; clothing, fabric and textiles; raw materials and semi-finished building products; marble materials and products; recorded music and films; petrol and other fuels; telephones and telephone bills; electrical appliances; cars, motorcycles and boats; cigarettes; leather and fur; gold jewellery; plants and flowers used to make perfume and medicine; and perfume, cosmetics and soaps.

There are a number of exempt goods and services in Italy including exported goods; services supplied outside the country; ships and aircraft; interest; insurance; shares and bonds; postal and medical services; businesses; and books and newspapers. Non-profit organisations are also exempt from VAT.

If you're in business or self-employed you usually need an VAT number (*partita IVA*) and must charge VAT on all your services and goods. You must maintain accounts in officially stamped books (*registri*) that are used to calculate the tax payable. Where applicable, you must apply for a VAT number from your *comune* within 30 days of starting business or a number can be assigned by an accountant (*commercialista*). The VAT number of companies is also used as their fiscal code (*codice fiscale*).

Businesses with a turnover of over Lit. 360 million (services) or over Lit. 1 billion (industry or commerce) must pay their VAT monthly, while others can choose to pay quarterly. VAT paid on a monthly basis must be paid by the 18th of each month. If you pay quarterly, VAT is payable by the 5th day of the second month after the end of the fiscal quarter, e.g. the first quarter's IVA is due on 5th May, the second quarter's on 5th August, the third by 5th November and the fourth by 5th March (one month later than usual). You must pay interest of 0.5 per cent on the amount payable in the last quarter. An annual IVA declaration must be completed by 5th March each year. Even if you have no income you should file an annual return in order to prevent suspicion of fraud and to keep your IVA number active (if you don't file it could be cancelled). Although there are huge fines and even prison sentences for avoiding VAT, many Italians will do their utmost to avoid paying it.

INCOME TAX

Income tax (*Imposta sul Reddito delle Persone Fisiche/IRPEF*) in Italy has traditionally been among the highest in the European Union and although the rates have been reduced in recent years, they are still above average for the European Union. Belgians, Dutch and Scandinavians will find Italian income tax lower, while most other western Europeans will pay around the same or higher taxes. Paying Italian income tax can be advantageous for some people, as there are more allowances than in some other countries. If you're able to choose the country where you're taxed, you should obtain advice from an international tax expert. Italy doesn't have a pay-as-you-earn (PAYE) system of income tax, whereby employees' tax is withheld at source by employers, and individuals are responsible for paying their own income tax. Anyone who's liable for Italian income tax must register at their local tax office (*intendenza di finanza*). The tax year in Italy is the same as the calendar year and income is taxed in the year in which the payment or advantage is actually received. Each person is taxed individually and although a married couple may file a joint tax return, they are taxed separately.

Moving to Italy (or another country) often offers opportunities for legal 'favourable tax planning'. To make the most of your situation, it's advisable to obtain professional income tax advice before moving to Italy, as there are usually a number of things you can do in advance to reduce your tax liability, both in Italy and abroad. Be sure to consult a tax adviser who's familiar with both the Italian tax system and that of your present country of residence. For example, you may be able to avoid paying tax on a business abroad if you establish both residency and domicile in Italy before you sell. On the other hand, if you sell a foreign home after establishing your principal residence in Italy, it becomes a second home and you may then be liable to capital gains tax abroad (this is a complicated subject and you will need expert advice). You should inform the tax authorities in your former country of residence that you're going to live permanently in Italy. Information about income tax in Italy is available from your local tax office.

Tax evasion (*l'evasione fiscale*) is rife in Italy, where avoiding taxes is more popular than soccer (Italians may not be world champions at soccer, but they certainly are when it comes to tax evasion). The worst offenders are businesses and the self-employed, and it's common knowledge that tax inspectors accept bribes to 'turn a blind eye' to tax evasion. The tax authorities may estimate your taxable income based on your perceived wealth. It's necessary to list (on a one-page *riccometro* form) your personal belongings and situation such as homes, cars, boats, motorbikes, whether you employ household help, whether your spouse works, dependent family members, and family means, among other things. This information is used to determine your actual financial situation and whether you're entitled to certain social services. Therefore if you're a millionaire and declare the income of a shop assistant, it would be wise not to live in a *palazzo* and drive a Ferrari! New (larger) fines were introduced for tax evasion in 1998.

Liability

Your liability for Italian income tax depends on where you're domiciled. Your domicile is normally the country you regard as your permanent home and where you live most of the year. A foreigner working in Italy for an Italian company who has taken up residency in Italy and has no income tax liability abroad, is considered to have his tax domicile (*domicilio fiscale*) in Italy. A person can be resident in more than one country at any given time, but can be domiciled only in one country. The domicile of a married woman isn't necessarily the same as her husband's, but is determined using the same criteria as anyone capable of having an independent domicile. Your country of domicile is particularly important regarding inheritance tax (see page 105). You're considered to be an Italian resident and liable to Italian tax if any of the following apply:

- your permanent home (i.e. family or principal residence) is in Italy;
- you spend over 183 days in Italy during any calendar year;
- you carry out paid professional activities or employment in Italy, except when secondary to business activities conducted in another country;
- your centre of vital economic interest, e.g. investments or business, is in Italy;

If you're registered as a resident (*residenza anagrafica*) in your *comune*, you're automatically tax resident in Italy.

If you intend to live permanently in Italy, you should notify the tax authorities in your present country (you will be asked to complete a form, e.g. a form P85 in Britain). You may be entitled to a tax refund if you depart during the tax year, which usually necessitates the completion of a tax return. The authorities may require evidence that you're leaving the country, e.g. evidence of a job in Italy or of having purchased or rented a property there. If you move to Italy to take up a job or start a business, you must register with the local tax authorities soon after your arrival.

Double-Taxation Treaties: Italian residents are taxed on their world-wide income, subject to certain treaty exceptions (non-residents are taxed only on income arising in Italy). Citizens of most countries are exempt from paying taxes in their home country when they spend a minimum period abroad, e.g. one year. Italy has double-taxation treaties with over 60 countries including all members of the European Union, Australia, Canada, China, the Czech Republic, Cyprus, Hungary, India, Israel, Japan, Malaysia, Malta, New Zealand, Norway, Pakistan, the Philippines, Poland, Rumania, Russia, Singapore, the Slovak Republic, Sri Lanka, Switzerland, Turkey, the USA and Yugoslavia.

Treaties are designed to ensure that income that has already been taxed in one treaty country isn't taxed again in another treaty country. The treaty establishes a tax credit or exemption on certain kinds of income, either in the country of residence or the country where the income was earned. Where applicable, a double-taxation treaty prevails over domestic law. If a country has a double-taxation treaty with Italy, it will contain rules that determine in which country an individual is resident. Note that the 183 day rule (mentioned above) also applies to other EU countries and many countries (e.g. Britain) limit visits by non-residents to 182 days in any one year or an average of 90 days per tax year over a four-year period. Many people living abroad switch their investments to offshore holdings to circumvent double-taxation agreements.

If you're in doubt about your tax liability in your home country, contact your nearest embassy or consulate in Italy. The USA is the only country that taxes its non-resident citizens on income earned abroad (American citizens can obtain a copy of a brochure, *Tax Guide for Americans Abroad*, from American consulates).

Allowances & Deductions

Before you're liable for income tax, you can deduct social security payments and certain allowances and deductions from your taxable income. Income tax is calculated upon both earned income and unearned income. If you have an average income and receive interest on bank deposits only, tax on unearned income won't apply as tax is deducted from bank interest before you receive it. Although the tax rates in Italy are relatively high, your net income tax can be considerably reduced by allowances and deductions.

Taxable income includes base pay; overseas and cost of living allowances; contributions to profit sharing plans; bonuses (annual, performance, etc.); storage and relocation allowances; language lessons provided for a spouse; personal company car; payments in kind (such as free accommodation or meals); stock options; home leave or vacations (paid by your employer); children's education; and property and investment income (dividends and interest). Some income, such as certain social security benefits, isn't subject to income tax.

Taxable income in Italy is officially divided into the following six categories, each of which is defined by law: employment; self-employment; business; real estate (land and buildings); capital (principally dividends and interest); and other 'miscellaneous' income. Tax is applied on aggregate income, which for residents includes all income earned and for non-residents income earned in Italy only. Income from employment includes bonuses, stock options, interest-free loans, overseas adjustments, cost of living allowances, housing allowance, education allowance, tax reimbursements and car allowance. Benefits in kind are valued for tax purposes at their fair market value. The following items aren't included in taxable employment income:

- Mandatory social security contributions;

- Contributions up to Lit. 2.5 million paid to Italian qualified pension funds;

- Contributions up to Lit. 7 million paid to entities or funds for the sole purpose of medical assistance in accordance with collective labour contracts or company agreements and regulations;

- Reimbursement for travel and accommodation for business trips up to a maximum of Lit. 90,000 within Italy and Lit. 150,000 abroad;

- Share purchase plans granted under certain conditions.

Deductible expenses: No expenses are specifically deductible from taxable income, although mandatory social security contributions paid by an employee and alimony paid to a spouse (from whom the taxpayer is legally separated or divorced) may be deducted from gross income. A tax credit of up to 19 per cent of the following expenses is also granted:

- Interest on a mortgage on a principal residence (*prima casa*) or land in Italy, providing that the loan is taken out in a European Union country, up to a maximum of Lit. 1.33 million.

- Medical expenses in excess of Lit. 250,000 (including surgical expenses, specialist treatment, prostheses, spectacles, contact lenses and hearing aids) for both the taxpayer and his dependants.

- Funeral expenses up to a maximum of Lit. 190,000.

- Tuition expenses at universities up to the equivalent cost of attendance at a state establishment.

- Premiums for life insurance and health insurance up to a total of Lit. 475, 000.

Personal Allowances: A dependent spouse (i.e. someone earning less than Lit. 5.5 million) can claim an allowance of from Lit. 817,522 to 1,057,552, depending on a couple's taxable income (as shown in the table below). There's an allowance of Lit. 336,000 for each dependent child (irrespective of his/her age) or other dependent family members. A couple must share this allowances between them, e.g. a couple with one child each receive an deduction of Lit. 168,000. A one-parent family can claim a deduction equal to a spouse's deduction and deductions for children as for two-parent families. These allowances can be claimed by residents irrespective of their category of income. Deductions for a dependent spouse (1998) are shown below:

Taxable Income (in millions)	Deduction (Lit.)
Up to Lit. 30	1,057,552
Lit. 30 to 60	961,552
Lit. 60 to 100	889,552
Over Lit. 100	817,552

From 1998 the deductions for independent workers and pensioners have been increased to compensate for the increase in IRPEF on gross income, as shown below:

Taxable Income (in millions)	Deduction (Lit.)
Up to Lit. 9.1	1,680,000
Lit. 9.1 to 9.3	1,600,000
Lit. 9.3 to 15.3	1,500,000
Lit. 15.3 to 15.6	1,250,000
Lit. 15.6 to 15.9	1,150,000
Lit. 15.9 to 30	1,050,000
Lit. 30 to 40	950,000
Lit. 40 to 50	850,000
Lit. 50 to 60	750,000
Lit. 60 to 60.3	650,000
Lit. 60.3 to 70	550,000
Lit. 70 to 80	450,000
Lit. 80 to 90	350,000
Lit. 90 to 90.4	250,000
Lit. 90.4 to 100	150,000
Over Lit. 100	100,000

Pensioners who receive more than one pension (with the total not exceeding Lit. 18 million) are eligible for a further deduction of Lit. 70,000 if they don't have any income from property and related areas. From 1998, anyone receiving more than one pension has been required to subtract withholding tax calculated on the total amount received. From 1999 those who receive more than one pension and don't have other sources of income are no longer required to file an income tax return and don't need to pre-pay their taxes. However, those with other income in addition to pensions must pay income tax, but only on the non-pension income.

Tax Rates & Calculation

Italian income tax is progressive and levied at rates of between 19 and 45 per cent (1998), as shown in the table below:

Taxable Income	Tax Rate	Cumulative Tax*
Up to Lit. 15m	19%	Lit. 2,850,000
Lit. 15m to 30m	27%	Lit. 6,900,000
Lit. 30m to 60m	34%	Lit. 17,100,000
Lit. 60m to 135m	40%	Lit. 47,100,000
Over Lit. 135m	46%	

* In the above table the first column shows taxable income; the second column shows the tax rate payable on the income band shown in the first column; and the third column the cumulative tax payable on the maximum income in that band, e.g. Lit. 6,900,000 is the tax payable on an income of Lit. 30 million. If your taxable income is Lit. 50 million you would pay Lit. 6,900,000 on the first Lit. 30 million and 6,800,000 on the balance (Lit. 20 million x 34%), making a total tax bill of Lit. 13,700,000. **The above rates include a 0.5 per cent regional surtax.** This is fixed at this rate for 1998-1999, after which the regions can increase it up to a maximum of 1 per cent.

Tax Calculation

The following tax calculation is for a married employee with a dependent spouse and two children, interest on a home loan of Lit. 6 million and a net cadastral income of the owner's home of Lit. 1 million.

Item		Sum (lire)
Gross Income		100,000,000
Social Security Contributions (9%)		9,000,000
Net Income		91,000,000
Net Cadastral Income of the Owner's Home		1,000,000
Taxable Income		92,000,000
Income Tax (IRPEF)		29,900,000
Less Personal Allowances:		
Dependent Spouse	889,552	
2 Dependent Children	672,000	
Expenses Relating to Income	600,000	
Interest on Home Loan	1,140,000	(3,301,552)
Income Tax Payable		**26,598,448**

Regional Tax

A new regional tax (*Imposta Regionale sulle Attività Produttive/IRAP*) was introduced in January 1998 and replaced local income tax (ILOR) and various other taxes. IRAP is a tax on services and goods based on the value of production (without taking into account any expenses for personnel, interest, extra fees and accruals), and is payable by the self-employed, professionals, artists, companies and organisations. There are special requirements for autonomous workers whose earnings don't exceed Lit. 20 million a year. Check with your accountant.

The basic rate is 4.25 per cent. There's a 5 per cent rate for banks, insurance and financial services' companies, and a reduced agricultural rate of 3 per cent. There are tax breaks for companies operating in depressed areas. For 1998 and 1999, IRAP will be collected by the federal government, after which it will be paid regionally. IRAP is payable in the same way as income tax with estimated taxes payable in two tranches in May and November. The fine for non-payment is between 120 and 240 per cent of the amount due and if you underestimate your tax you will be fined twice the amount of the highest estimate due! There are also fines for late payment.

Taxation of Property Income

All property owners in Italy (whether residents or non-residents) must pay income tax based on a property's imputed income. Income from land and buildings is based on the cadastral value (*rendita catastale*), which is a nominal value attributed to land and buildings by the land registry (*catasto*). The value of land is calculated by multiplying the average ordinary income (fixed by the *catasto*) for the surface area, taking into consideration the kind of culture and the location of the land. The value of buildings is calculated by multiplying the surface area by a pre-determined amount (fixed by the cadastre) taking into consideration the location, age, class and category (see **Fees** on page 147) of the properties, as shown in the property deeds. There are minimum thresholds below which you don't pay IRPEF.

Rental Income: Income tax is payable in Italy on rental income from an Italian property, even if you live abroad and the money is paid there. All rental income must be declared to the Italian tax authorities whether you let a property for a few weeks to a friend or 52 weeks a year on a commercial basis. Rental income derived from real property is taxed as ordinary income, from 19 to 46 percent. You're eligible for deductions such as repairs and maintenance; security; cleaning costs; mortgage interest (Italian loans only); management and letting expenses (e.g. advertising); local taxes; and an allowance to cover depreciation and insurance. You should seek professional advice to ensure that you're claiming everything to which you're entitled. Many people find that there's little tax to pay after deducting their expenses.

Real estate is also subject to local municipal 'property tax' (see page 103).

Income Tax Returns & Tax Payment

The tax year in Italy is the same as the calendar year. All residents must file an income tax return (*dichiarazione dei redditi*) unless any of the following apply:

- you have no income;

- your income is exempt from tax, e.g. a war pension, certain state pensions such as the old age pension or an invalidity pension;

- you have already paid tax at source on income, e.g. dividends, bank interest, mortgage interest, etc.

- you're an employee and are taxed on a PAYE basis and have no other income.

Non-residents with income arising in Italy must also file a tax return. The tax system is based on self-assessment and the tax office won't send you a tax return or chase you to complete one. Tax returns must be purchased from a tobacconist or stationers or are available free from your local council (*municipio*).

Employees: The tax return for most taxpayers is the *modello 730*, which covers the following categories of people or income: dependent workers; pensioners; compensation paid to members of the clergy; wages paid to members of co-operatives; compensation paid to elected government officials (all levels); and anyone with a fixed-term contract (*tempo determinato*) that will be continued through the months of March to June. Those with additional income from land and real estate; dividends earned from corporations; and income derived from on-going work also use the 730. Income subject to separate taxes (without the option of being included under ordinary taxes) such as capital income, occasional autonomous work, inherited income received on an on-going basis; life insurance and accident policy premiums if policies are redeemed before five years; non-taxable TFR (severance indemnity) payments; and deductible taxes and fees which have been used as deductions (and reimbursed) in the previous year, can also be declared on form 730.

Self-Employed: If your self-employed (e.g. an artisan, merchant, artist) or a professional with a VAT number (*Partita IVA*), you must file a *Unico* form. This is a multifunctional, colour-coded (light blue, orange, green and dark blue) form that replaced the old form 740 in 1998. No additional documentation such as expense receipts or medical expenses need be attached. The various coloured sections denote the type of tax. The basic *Unico* form has four pages, but there are 14 other pages comprising a total of 44 sections. The completed form should be presented between 1st June and 31st July at a bank, post office or CAAF, from where it will be sent to the Department of Finance via computer. It shouldn't be sent to a service centre office.

Filing: *Modello 730* returns for the previous year must be filed between the 1st May and the 30th June. A married couple may file a joint tax return (both must sign) but are taxed separately, although payment is joint. However, one spouse's tax credit may be used to offset tax payable by the other spouse. A spouse with income below Lit. 5.5 million (1998) would be dependent for the purpose of the dependent relative tax credit. The disadvantage of filing a joint return is that although the assessment may be raised against only one of the couple, there's a common responsibility for payment. A couple can use form 730 if their combined income is earned from land and/or real estate and the total amount is less than Lit. 5.5 million. Otherwise they must use the *Unico* form (see **Self-Employment** above).

Personal income tax forms no longer needs to be filed at the local *comune* or sent to a service centre and hand-written forms are now accepted at banks and post offices. However, forms completed by professionals using computer systems must be lodged or sent directly to a service centre. Late filing within 30 days after the due date is subject to a penalty of 15 per cent of the tax due; after 30 days, penalties range from 120 to 245 per cent of the tax due! You should keep copies of all tax returns and receipts for six years.

Payment: Advance tax payments must be made equal to 98 per cent of the tax paid for the previous year or the amount due for the current year (whichever is less). Forty per cent of the advance tax payments (called an *acconto*) must be made by 31st May and the remaining 60 per cent by 30th November. If you have earned less you can claim a refund, although tax rebates can take years to be paid. Income tax can be paid in two to six monthly instalments, when interest of 6 per cent is payable. A portion of the total interest due must accompany each instalment. Those with a VAT number (*partita IVA*) must pay by the 15th of the month, others by the end of the month. If you choose to pay by instalments it must be noted on your income tax return. Taxpayers who pay overdue income tax between 1st and 20th June must pay a surcharge of 0.5 per cent. If a late payment is made between 21st June and 20th July, the surtax rate is 4.27 per cent and when payment is received after 20th July, a surtax of 40 per cent is payable plus 5 per cent annual interest (in addition to the 4.27 per cent surtax).

Accountants: Because of the complexity of the Italian tax system, it's advisable to use an accountant (*commercialista*, who's actually a combination of accountant and lawyer) to prepare your tax return, particularly if you're self-employed (obligatory unless you have a doctorate in Italian bureaucracy!). An accountant's fees are relatively low (although you should obtain a quotation) and he can also advise you on what you can and cannot claim regarding allowances and expenses.

PROPERTY TAX

Property tax (*Imposta Comunale sugli Immobili/ICI* or 'Ichy') is paid by anyone who owns property or land in Italy, whether resident or non-resident. It's levied at between 0.4 to 0.7 per cent of a property's fiscal value (*valore catastale*), the actual rate being decided by the local municipality depending on a property's size, location, age, class and category (see the table below), as shown in the property deeds (*rogito*). If a property is unfit for habitation, ICI is reduced by 50 per cent. The tax is paid in two instalments in June and December. The form for paying ICI is complicated and many people (particularly foreigners) employ an accountant (*commercialista*) or agent to do it for them. If tax isn't paid on time you can be fined in the form of a surcharge or additional tax (*sopratassa*) up to 100 to 200 per cent of the amount due. Payments must be up to date when a property is sold and you should check this when buying a property.

The cadastral category (*categoria*) of a property determines the property tax rate payable and also the minimum sum that must be declared as the purchase price in the deed of sale (*rogito*). Categories are decided by the land registry (*catasto*) and are as follows:

Category	Abitazione di Tipo (Housing Type)
A/1	*Signorile* (exclusive)
A/2	*Civile* (civilian)
A/3	*Economico* (economical)
A/4	*Populare* (working class)
A/5	*Unltrapopulare* (ultra working class)
A/6	*Rurale* (rural)
A/7	*Villini* (small detached)
A/8	*Ville* (detached)
A/9	*Castelli, palazzi di eminenti pregi*
	Artistici o storici (castle or building of eminent historic or artistic importance)
A/10	*Uffice e studi privati* (private offices and studios)
A/11	*Alloggi tipici dei luoghi* (typical housing of the region)

Property owners also pay income tax (*IRPEF*) on their property, which is based on its cadastral value (see **Taxation of Property Income** on page 101). Other property related taxes include communal services (*servizio riscossione tributi ruoli*) for owners of condominiums and other properties that share services or facilities (see page 153), garbage tax (*tassa communale dei rifiuti*) and water rates (see page 186).

When you buy a home in Italy you should go to the town hall (*municipio*) to register your ownership. After this date all bills for local services will be sent automatically and are payable at a post office or local bank (or by direct debit).

CAPITAL GAINS TAX

Capital gains tax (*Imposta Comunale sull'Incremento di Valore degli Immobili/INVIM*) has been abolished for new property owners. However, it's payable on gains accrued before 1ˢᵗ January 1993 when a property is sold before 1ˢᵗ January 2003. Where applicable, CGT is payable to the local community and varies from 3 per cent up to a maximum of 30 per cent on profits exceeding 200 per cent (as shown in the table below). CGT is reduced by 50 per cent when a property is sold to a principal residence (*prima casa*) buyer.

The capital gain is the difference between the purchase and sale price, less expenses for renovation, improvements, repairs, etc., and is based on the increase in the cadastral value (*rendita catastale*) of a property, not the increase in its actual market value. Note that calculating INVIM is complicated and it's advisable to employ an accountant (*commercialista*) to assess the sum payable. The tax is based on the price declared in the deed of sale (*rogito*). It isn't advisable to under-declare the value (too much), otherwise the authorities may arbitrarily assess a new sale price (although you can appeal against it). Where applicable, INVIM is deducted from the amount payable to the vendor by the notary (*notaio*) handling the sale. INVIM is payable at the following rates:

Profit	INVIM Payable
Up to 20%	3 to 5%
20 to 50%	5 to 10%
50 to 100%	10 to 15%
100 to 150%	15 to 20%
150 to 200%	20 to 25%
over 200%	25 to 30%

A new capital gains tax was introduced on 1ˢᵗ January 1999 and applies to gains made on stocks and shares. The tax is based on the average price quoted as at June '98 and is levied at two rates, 12.5 and 27 per cent, depending on the type of gain. From 1999, CGT has been based on the value of your assets at the beginning of the year. Capital gains that aren't realised from business activities are subject to CGT at 12.5 per cent. CGT is levied on the actual gain (selling price less purchase price re-valued to account for inflation). Capital losses are deductible from capital gains and may be carried forward for five years. Gains derived from qualified sales are subject to CGT at a rate of 27 per cent. A qualified sale is a sale of more than 2 per cent of the issued shares of a company quoted on the primary or secondary markets, or of more than 5 per cent of the shares of a non-listed company. Capital losses cannot be recovered for qualified sales.

INHERITANCE & GIFT TAX

As in most other western countries, dying doesn't free your assets from the clutches of Italian tax inspectors, and Italy imposes an Inheritance and gift tax (*Imposta sulle Successioni e Donazioni/ISD*).

Inheritance Tax: Inheritance tax, called estate tax or death duty in some countries, is levied on the estate of a deceased person. Both residents and non-residents are subject to inheritance tax if they own property in Italy. The country where you pay inheritance tax is decided by your domicile (see **Liability** on page 95). If a person is living permanently in Italy at the time of his death and has been doing so for some years, he's usually deemed to be domiciled there by the Italian tax authorities. If you're domiciled in Italy, then inheritance tax applies to your world-wide estate (excluding property), otherwise it applies only to assets located in Italy. It's important to make your domicile clear, so that there's no misunderstanding on your death. Note that Italian succession law is quire restrictive compared with the law in other countries and you cannot leave your entire estate to anyone you wish (or to a pet).

The taxable value is the value of the estate on the date of death, net of debts. Legacies made to the Italian state, local government, recognised non-profit organisations (*entri morali*), foundations and non-profit public hospitals are exempt from tax, and excluded from the total value of the estate. Inheritance tax is paid by individual beneficiaries, irrespective of where they are domiciled, and not by the estate. This sometimes results in property (such as real estate) needing to be sold before it can be inherited, although the payment of tax can sometimes be deferred or paid by instalments (when interest is payable). Italian banks may also provide a bridging loan for this purpose.

Inheritance tax varies depending on the relationship of beneficiaries to the deceased and is between 3 and 33 per cent. It's applied to the total assets (undivided inheritance or gift) *and* on the portion received by each heir or beneficiary. Estates valued below Lit. 250 million left to a spouse, parent or child are exempt from ISD, as are estates valued below Lit. 100 million left to brothers, sisters and direct relatives, as shown in the table below:

Taxable Amount (Lit. millions)	% Tax Payable on Estate or Gift*			
	Undivided	A	B	C
10 to 100	0	0	3	6
100 to 250	0	3	5	8
250 to 350	3	6	9	12
350 to 500	7	10	13	18
500 to 800	10	15	19	23
800 to 1,500	15	20	24	28
1,500 to 3,000	22	24	26	31
Over 3,000	27	25	27	33

* The First column ('Undivided') is applied to the total value of the taxable estate. Where there are several heirs or beneficiaries, the tax is assessed proportionately

between them. The other rates (columns A to C) represent additional tax payable by beneficiaries who are neither a spouse or parent nor a direct descendant (i.e. a child) of the deceased, as follows: A = brothers, sisters and direct relatives; B = other relatives to the 3rd and 4th degree; and C = other individuals.

Gift Tax: Gift tax is applied and calculated in the same way as inheritance tax, according to the relationship between the donor and the recipient, and the size of the gift. Any gifts made before the death of the donor must be included in the estate duty return. For non-residents, gift tax applies only to assets located in Italy.

It's important for both residents and non-residents with property in Italy to decide in advance how they wish to dispose of their Italian property. This should be decided before buying a house or other property in Italy. There are a number of ways of limiting or delaying the impact of Italian inheritance laws, particularly regarding property, which can be left in its entirety to a surviving spouse or be purchased through a company (either in Italy or abroad). A surviving spouse can also be given a life interest in an estate in priority to children or parents, although this may not apply to non-residents. Note that Italian law doesn't recognise the rights to inheritance of a non-married partner, although there are a number of solutions to this problem, e.g. a life insurance policy. Real estate transferred by inheritance or gift may also be subject to capital gains tax (see page 104), which may be credited against any inheritance or gift tax due.

Italy has treaties to prevent double taxation of estates with a number of countries including Denmark, France, Greece, Israel, Sweden, the UK and the USA. In the absence of a treaty, a tax credit may be available for any foreign taxes paid on assets located abroad.

Italian inheritance law is a complicated subject and professional advice should be sought from an experienced lawyer who understands both Italian inheritance law and the law of any other countries involved. Your will (see below) is also a vital component in reducing Italian inheritance and gift tax to the minimum or delaying its payment.

WILLS

It's an unfortunate fact of life that you're unable to take your hard-earned assets with you when you take your final bow (or come back and reclaim them in a later life!). All adults should make a will (*testamento*) regardless of how large or small their assets. The disposal of your estate depends on your country of domicile (see **Liability** on page 95). As a general rule, Italian law permits a foreigner who *isn't* domiciled in Italy to make a will in any language and under the law of any country, providing it's valid under the law of that country. A will must be in writing (but not necessarily in the hand of the testator) and in any language. Under Italian rules regarding conflict of law, the law that applies is the law of the country where the testator was a citizen at the time of his death.

Note, however, that 'immovable' property (or immovables) in Italy, i.e. land and buildings, *must* be disposed of (on death) in accordance with Italian law. All other property in Italy or elsewhere (defined as 'movables') may be disposed of in accordance with the law of your home country or domicile. Therefore, it's important to establish where you're domiciled under Italian law. One solution for a non-resident wishing to avoid Italian inheritance laws may be to buy a home through a company, in which case the shares of the company are 'movable' assets and are therefore governed by the succession laws of the owner's country of domicile.

Italian law gives the immediate family (i.e. spouse, children and parents) an absolute right to inherit a share of an estate (called *legittime*) and therefore it isn't possible to disinherit them as can be done in some other countries (e.g. Britain). However, a foreigner who wishes to dispose of his estate according to the laws of his home country can state this in an Italian will. There are three types of Italian will: a holographic will, a public will and a secret will.

Holographic will: The only requirements of a holographic will (*testamento olografo*) are that it must be written entirely in your own handwriting and signed and dated by you. This is a popular and common type of will in Italy because of it's simplicity (no witnesses are required) and that fact that it's free. However, legally it's the worst type of will you can have as it can easily 'disappear' or be forged.

Public will: A public will (*testamento pubblico*) is the safest type of will in Italy. It's prepared and recorded by a notary (*notaio*) and becomes part of his public records. It must be witnessed by two people (of any nationality), who must sign it in the presence of the notary, who also signs. Two copies are made; one for the testator and one for the notary. The notary may also write or oversee the writing of a public will.

Secret will: A secret will (*testamento segreto*) is written by the testator or a third person and handed to a notary in a sealed envelope. The testator declares the authenticity of the sealed will in the presence of the notary and two witnesses, none of whom actually see the will. Secret wills are rare in Italy.

For anyone with a modest Italian estate, for example a small property in Italy, a holographic will is sufficient. Note that where applicable, the rules relating to witnesses are strict and if they aren't followed precisely they may render a will null and void. In Italy, marriage doesn't automatically revoke a will, as in some other countries, e.g. Britain. Wills aren't made public in Italy and aren't available for inspection.

If you have a large estate in Italy, it's advisable to consult a lawyer (*avvocato*) when drawing up a will. It's possible to make two wills, one relating to Italian property and the other to any foreign property. Experts differ on whether you should have separate wills for Italian and foreign property, or a foreign will with a codicil (appendix) dealing with your Italian property (or vice versa). However, most lawyers believe that it's better to have an Italian will for your Italian property (and a will for any country where you own immovable property), which will speed up and reduce the cost of probate in Italy. If you have an Italian and a foreign will (or wills), make sure that they don't contradict one another. Note that a foreign will written in a foreign language must be translated into Italian (a certified translation is required) and proven in Italy in order to be valid there.

You'll also need someone to act as the executor of your estate, which can be particularly costly for modest estates. Under Italian law, the role of the executor is different from that in many other countries. Your bank, lawyer or other professional will usually act as the executor, although this should be avoided if at all possible as the fees can be astronomical. It's advisable to make your beneficiaries the executors, as they can then instruct a lawyer after your death should they require legal assistance. Note that probate (the proving of a will) can take a long time in Italy.

Keep a copy of your will(s) in a safe place and another copy with your lawyer or the executor of your estate. Don't leave them in a safe deposit box, which in the event of your death is sealed for a period under Italian law. You should keep information regarding bank accounts and insurance policies with your will(s), but don't forget to tell someone where they are!

Note that Italian inheritance law is a complicated subject and it's important to obtain professional legal advice when writing or altering your will(s).

COST OF LIVING

No doubt you would like to try to estimate how far your lire will stretch and how much money (if any) you will have left after paying your bills. Inflation in Italy in 1998 was less than 2 per cent and it has enjoyed a relatively stable and strong economy in recent years (which cannot be said of the government). Salaries are generally high and Italy has a high standard of living, although the combined burden of social security, income tax and indirect taxes make Italian taxes among the highest in the European Union (EU).

Anyone planning to live in Italy, particularly retirees, should take care not to underestimate the cost of living, which has increased considerably in the last decade. Italy is a relatively expensive country by American and British standards, and it's one of the most expensive countries in the EU, although there's a huge disparity between the cost and standard of living in the prosperous north and central regions of Italy, and the relatively poor south. The cost of living in Italy's major cities is much the same as in cities in Britain, France and Germany, although overall Italy has a slightly lower cost of living than northern European countries. Luxury and quality products are expensive, as are cars, but wine and spirits are inexpensive. However, you should be wary of cost of living comparisons with other countries, which are often wildly inaccurate and usually include irrelevant items which distort the results.

It's difficult to calculate an average cost of living in Italy as it depends on each individual's particular circumstances and life-style. The actual difference in your food bill will depend on what you eat and where you lived before arriving in Italy. Food is almost double the cost in the USA, but similar overall to most other western European countries, although you may need to modify your diet. From Lit. 600,000 to 750,000 will feed two adults for a month, excluding fillet steak, caviar and alcohol (other than a moderate amount of inexpensive beer or wine). Note, however, that it's possible to live frugally in Italy if you're willing to forego luxuries and live off the land. Shopping for selected 'luxury' and 'big-ticket' items (such as stereo equipment, electrical and electronic goods, computers, and photographic equipment) abroad can also yield significant savings.

A list of the approximate **MINIMUM** monthly major expenses for an average single person, couple or family with two children are shown in the table below (most people will no doubt agree that the figures are either too HIGH or too LOW). If you work in Italy, you need to deduct around 10 per cent of your gross salary for social security contributions and the appropriate percentage for income tax. The numbers (in brackets) refer to the notes following the table.

ITEM	MONTHLY COSTS (Lire)		
	Single	Couple	Couple with two children
Housing (1)	750,000	1,200,000	1,500,000
Food (2)	350,000	500,000	750,000
Utilities (3)	100,000	150,000	200,000
Leisure (4)	200,000	300,000	350,000
Transport (5)	200,000	200,000	250,000
Insurance (6)	100,000	200,000	225,000
Clothing	100,000	200,000	400,000
Total (Lit.)	**1,800,000**	**2,750,000**	**3,675,000**

1. Rent or mortgage payments for a modern or modernised apartment or house in an average suburb, excluding major cities and other high-cost areas. The properties envisaged are a studio or one-bedroom apartment for a single person, a two-bedroom property for a couple and a three-bedroom property for a couple with two children.

2. Doesn't include luxuries or liquid food (alcohol).

3. Includes electricity, gas, water, telephone, pay TV and heating costs.

4. Includes all entertainment, restaurant meals, sports and vacation expenses, plus newspapers and magazines.

5. Includes running costs for an average family car, plus third party insurance, annual taxes, petrol, servicing and repairs, **but excludes depreciation or credit purchase costs.**

6. Includes 'voluntary' insurance such as supplementary health insurance, disability, home contents, third party liability, legal, travel, automobile breakdown and life insurance.

4.

FINDING YOUR DREAM HOME

After having decided to buy a home in Italy, your first tasks will be to choose the region and what sort of home to buy. **If you're unsure where and what to buy, the best decision is usually to rent for a period.** The secret of successfully buying a home in Italy (or anywhere else) is research, research and yet more research, preferably before you even set foot there. You may be fortunate and buy the first property you see without doing any homework and live happily ever after. However, a successful purchase is much more likely if you thoroughly investigate the towns and communities in your chosen area; compare the range and prices of homes and their relative values; and study the procedure for buying property. It's a wise or lucky person who gets his choice absolutely right first time, but it's much more likely if you do your homework thoroughly.

Among the many things that attract homebuyers to Italy are the good value for money of rural property (providing you avoid the more fashionable areas) and the wonderful architecture and character of Italian homes. Architecturally, Italy is probably the most beautiful country in the world and many foreigners cherish the neglected 17th to 19th century buildings that abound throughout the country. Many Italians have a city apartment and a weekend house in the country, although they tend to choose modern homes rather than the old farmhouses and village houses favoured by many foreigners. There's a steady demand in Italy for retirement and second homes from both Italians and foreigners, although there are few holiday-home developments as are common in Italy and Spain.

Italians aren't very mobile and move house much less frequently than the Americans and British, which is reflected in the fairly stable property market. It generally isn't worth buying a home in Italy unless you plan to stay in the market for the medium to long term, say a minimum of five year and preferably 10 to 15 years. Italians don't generally buy domestic property as an investment, but as a home for life, and you shouldn't expect to make a quick profit when buying property in Italy. Property values generally increase at an average of around 5 per cent a year (or in line with inflation), meaning you must usually own a home for around three years simply to recover the high fees associated with buying. Property prices rise faster than average in some popular areas (such as Milan), although this is generally reflected in much higher purchase prices. The stable property market in most areas acts as a discouragement to speculators wishing to make a fast buck, particularly as many properties require a substantial investment in restoration or modernisation before they can be resold at a profit.

Italy boasts a huge range of properties to suit every pocket and taste. A slice of *la dolce vita* needn't cost the earth, with habitable cottages and terraced village homes available from around Lit. 60 million, modern apartments from around Lit. 90 million and large country homes from as little as Lit. 120 million. However, if you're seeking a home with a large plot of land and a swimming pool you will need to spend at least Lit. 180 million (depending on the area) and for those with the financial resources the sky's the limit, with luxury apartments in Rome and villas on the Italian Riviera costing billions of lire.

This chapter is designed to help you decide what sort of home to buy and, most importantly, its location. It will also help you avoid problems and contains information about regions, research, Italian homes, location, renting, cost, fees, buying new and old, community properties, timeshare (and other part-ownership schemes), real estate agents, inspections and surveys, garages and parking, conveyancing, purchase contracts, completion, renovation and restoration, moving house, moving in, security, utilities, heating and air-conditioning, property income and selling a home.

REGIONS

Italy is divided into 20 geographical regions, which are described below and shown on the map in **Appendix E**.

Abruzzo (Abruzzi): Abruzzo is situated in central Italy bordering Lazio to the west and with a long Adriatic coastline in the east. It contains the provinces of Chieti, L'Aquila (also the capital city), Pescara and Teramo, and used to take in Molise to the south, which became an independent region in 1963. The region has a population of 1.25 million and covers an area of 10,794km² (4,168mi²). Abruzzo is a mountainous region with the highest mountains in central Italy, that are part of the Appennines which form the backbone of the region on the western side. The highest peaks are in the Gran Sasso group (where Mussolini was kept prisoner), where the Corno Grande reaches a height of 2,912m (9,551ft). The region contains three national parks: Gran Sasso-Laga, Maiella-Morrone, and the National Park of Abruzzo, which is home to the rare endangered species of Marsican brown bears (which are unique to Italy), plus wolves, deer, chamois, and many other mammals and birds.

Abruzzo is sparsely populated (its density is 116 people per km²) due to its mountainous terrain and high emigration. However, its folk traditions endure through a myriad of rituals, festivals and pilgrimages, and the local dialect is still widely spoken. There has been an increase in prosperity in recent years thanks to state aid, new industry and the harnessing of water-power to create electricity from hydroelectric power plants. The area between Pescara and Chieti is the region's economic centre, with the highest per capita income in southern Italy and relatively low unemployment of around 10 per cent. Abruzzo has traditionally been dominated by a mountain economy and is noted for sheep farming – the migration of sheep towards the southern regions of Puglia and Lazio is a centuries old tradition. The region is also famous for its handicrafts.

L'Aquila (which means eagle), the region's capital, is a university city noted for its rich cultural life. It was founded in the 13ᵗʰ century with people drawn from 99 smaller centres, an event commemorated by a famous 99-spout fountain. In the 1400s, L'Aquila was the second most important city in the Spanish Kingdom of Naples and is one of the smallest (and the youngest) capital cities in Italy. The region contains a wealth of attractive historic towns including Atri, Lanciano, Penne and Vasto, while other interesting towns include Chieti, Lanciano, Pescara, Scanno (noted for its traditional copperware), Sulmona (known for its sugar-covered almonds or *confetti*) and Teramo. Pescara (whose name comes from the word *pesca* or fishing, once the main activity of the area) is a popular holiday resort and the only city in the region with a population of over 100,000. Other resorts include Francavilla al Mare, Guilianova, Montesilvano, Roseto degli Abruzzi, Silvi Marina and Vasto. Roccaraso and Pescasseroli in the Simbruini mountains are popular ski resorts among Romans, but its long, cold winters and tortuous roads doesn't make it popular with foreigners.

Traditional local architecture consists of roughly-built stone houses with small windows usually built in groups on hillsides while in towns severe stone *palazzi* are common. The price of old buildings in need of renovation is quite low compared with the rest of Italy, although the region isn't popular among foreigners. Abruzzo has good road communications with Rome due to the opening of the A24 autostrada in recent years. The nearest international airport is Rome and there's a regional airport at Pescara.

Basilicata (Lucania): Basilicata contains the provinces of Matera and Potenza (the regional capital). It's the least populated region of central and southern Italy and is one of the poorest and least developed regions of the *Mezzogiorno*, with one of its lowest per capita incomes and an unemployment rate of over 20 per cent. The population of Basilicata is around 600,000 and its area 9,991 km² (3,858mi²). It has a harsh terrain consisting of rugged mountains (rising to over 1,800m/6,000ft in the west) between Calabria and Apulia, and coastlines on both the Tyrrhenian and Ionian seas. The region's main economy is agriculture (mainly olives, livestock and sheep raising) and although only some 8 per cent of the land is suitable for cultivation, 40 per cent of the population is employed in agriculture, often on tiny parcels of land. Agricultural workers outnumber industrial workers, although there has been a flourish of industrial development in recent years, which has brought some welcome prosperity. The production of arts and crafts for the tourism industry is also an important industry. Basilicata has seen the widespread migration of its young to the north for many decades and consequently many villages (particularly those in mountainous and inhospitable areas) are dying, inhabited almost exclusively by the elderly. The region is also noted for its widespread corruption, inefficiency and organised crime.

The main city of Matera (45,000) is noted for the primeval beauty of its rupestre cave dwellings (*i Sassi*), which seem to grow from the surrounding tufa stone. These historic dwellings, where peasants used to sleep with their animals, are now a protected site. Basilicata isn't a popular tourist destination, although there are some splendid resorts on the two small strips of coast (such as Maratea on the Tyrrhenian coast). Other resorts include Bagnara Calabra, Copanello, Diamante, Paola, Pizzo, Praia a Mare, Scalea, Scilla and Soverato. Interesting historic towns include Venosa, with its Roman and medieval remains, and Melfi, once a Norman stronghold.

The region has poor rail and road communications with the rest of the country, although road links have improved in recent years. The nearest international airport is Naples and the nearest regional airport at Bari. The region is of little interest to foreign property buyers (but may be ideal for those wishing to 'get away from it all').

Calabria: Calabria (known as *Brutium* in Roman times) contains the provinces of Cantazaro, Cosenza and Reggio di Calabria. The regional capital is Cantazaro, founded by the Byzantines in the 9-10ᵗʰ centuries, while Reggio di Calabria (the region's largest city) has Greek origins. Other important towns include Cosenza, Crotone and Vibo Valentia. Calabria's population is around 2 million and its area 15,077km² (5,822mi²). It's the southernmost region of the peninsula (Sicily is further south, but is an island) and is dubbed the blue and green region. It's the most unspoilt region of Italy noted for its crystal clear seas, reflected in names such as the Costa Viola, that wash the deserted coastline. High mountains plunge into the sea creating an intricate and varied coastline with a medley of small bays, long sandy beaches and lush vegetation. Inland the mountains offer superb scenery and many attractive villages (with houses of grey stone and terracotta roofs) where traditional handicrafts are produced. Famous historic towns include Corigliano, Calabro, Castrovillari (a

Swabian stronghold) and Rossano, the Greek settlements of Locri and Gerace, and the picturesque seaside town of Tropea.

Calabria forms the 'toe' of the Italian 'boot' and boasts magnificent coastlines on both the Ionic and Tyrrenhian seas. Hemmed in by a coastal road and railway line, the mountainous interior remains inaccessible, with the Sila mountains to the north and vast forests and the Aspromonte in the south. The national parks of Calabria and Pollino were created to protect the natural resources of the forests. The southern region consists largely of flat land and large fertile plains (less than 9 per cent of the land), where olive and citrus groves contrast with ugly industrial developments such as those at Lamezia Terme. Calabria is an impoverished region that saw mass overseas migration in the early 20th century and to northern Italy and Europe in the '60s and '70s. The region has very high unemployment at around 27 per cent and the lowest per capita income in Italy. Crotone and Reggio di Calabria have a frightening criminal reputation and kidnapping is commonplace. Due to the poor economy, organised crime (the *mafia* or more correctly, *'ndrangheta*) is rife, although foreigners aren't prime targets.

The construction of a motorway link to the north and new railway lines has reduced the region's isolation, although it remains virtually unknown to most Italians and foreigners. There's a regional airport at Reggio di Calabria, although the nearest international airport is Palermo (Sicily). Tourism is an important industry with seaside properties priced at about L1 million per m² in Tropea and Scalea, although property isn't usually built to the same standards as in northern Italy and the region is of little interest to foreign property buyers.

Campania: Campania (named *Campania Felix* by the Romans) contains the provinces of Avellino, Benevento, Caserta, Naples (Napoli) and Salerno. Naples is the regional capital and, indeed, the capital of the whole of southern Italy. The population of Campania is around 5.6 million in an area of 35,208km² (13,595mi²). Agriculture is an important local industry, employing around a quarter of the workforce, while other important industries include livestock (e.g. buffalo for the production of mozzarella cheese), canning, textiles, and handicrafts such as leather, coral, inlaid wood and ceramics. The region has a high unemployment rate of around 25 per cent.

The area around Naples includes one of the most beautiful coastlines in Italy and the gulfs of Naples, Salerno and Policastro are home to a number of world famous resorts, including Positano, Ravello, Sorrento and Vietri sul Mare on the Amalfi Coast. The Bay of Naples and the Isle of Capri have been immortalised in song, although the island of Ischia is also a paradise (with its thermal baths such as the Therme di Poseidon) and beloved by northern visitors. Sorrento, famous for its lemon groves, is the largest and most popular Neapolitan resort. The region is steeped in history and contains a wealth of Roman sites and ruins, including Pompeii in the shadow of Mt. Vesuvius, whose eruption destroyed Pompeii and Herculaneum in the year AD79. These cities have been excavated and provide an excellent insight into how the ancient Romans lived. Other interesting cities include Padula (with its charterhouse), Sessa Aurunca, Santa Maria Cápua Vetere and Teano. The national parks of Cilento, Valle di Diano and Vesuvius were created in 1991 to protect areas of natural beauty from property speculators. The imposing Greek temples of Paestum in the south are among the best-preserved Greek architecture in the world and there's also a magnificent royal palace and park at Caserta.

Naples is famous for the vitality of its citizens, but also for corruption and the *mafia*, although in recent years the city's administrators have tried to improve its image in order to attract more tourists. The city's extreme poverty and the 'art of getting by' is the main reason for the high rate of petty crime, such as thefts and purse-snatching. The *Camorra* is the Neapolitan branch of the *mafia* and the city of Naples is considered by many to be a third-world city, infamous for its terrible traffic congestion (said to be the worst outside Cairo) and outrageous driving habits. With its splendid art treasures, such as those in the Museum of Capodimonte, and breathtaking natural setting, Naples is also a major tourist centre. The 19th century phrase 'see Naples and die' (coined in the days of the Grand Tour) referred to its unique appeal and charms, not forgetting its poverty, overcrowding and crime. A quarter of Campania's population lives around Naples, one-third of which is aged under 14. Among the city's traditions are its devotion to San Gennaro (the local patron saint) and to soccer (*calcio*).

Property on the islands in the archipelago of Capri, Ischia and Procida is very expensive, as are homes on the Amalfi coast, while inland prices fall dramatically. Property on Capri ranges from Lit. 5 to 12 million per m² for a prestigious apartment, while in Positano a similar property costs from Lit. 5 to 6.5 million per m². In stark contrast with the immaculately painted villas and *palazzi* in the wealthier resort areas, there are numerous half-abandoned villages in the interior and a plethora of poorly designed and shoddily built apartment blocks dotted along the coast. The region is noted for its high risk of earthquakes and landslides, particularly on the overbuilt coast.

Naples is an important rail and road junction with good communications to the north and south. Its airport has frequent flights to Rome and Milan and internationally, while the *autostrada* south from Salerno to Reggio Calabria is toll-free in recognition of the region's poverty. The tiny island of Procida, held by the English navy in 1799, is connected by ferry to the mainland, as are the neighbouring islands of Capri and Ischia.

Emilia Romagna: Emilia Romagna contains the provinces of Bologna (also the regional capital), Ferrara, Forli, Modena, Piacenza, Parma, Ravenna, Reggio Emilia and Rimini. It's one of the country's largest regions with an area of 22,075km² (8,524mi²) and a population of about four million, and takes its name from the ancient Roman road to Rome (the *Via Aemilia*) and the Romagna, name of the former Papal State. The region has an outstanding artistic heritage dating from Etruscan, Roman, Byzantine and Renaissance times. Emila Romagna encompasses the tiny

Republic of San Marino on top of Mount Titano, famous nowadays for duty-free shopping and its Formula one grand prix race. Situated between Lombardy and Tuscany, Emilia Romagna is a rich and fertile region with many important industries. The northern area consists of a flat and featureless wheat prairie, while in the south there are the foothills of the Appenines. The country's major river, the Po, forms a delta with the marshy area known as the Valli del Comacchio (famous for its eels) before emptying into the Adriatic. The intensely cultivated land is given over to large-scale farming and Emilia Romagna is the country's main producer of grain, sugar beet, soft fruit, tomatoes, grapes and rice.

The capital city of Bologna (500,000) is a beautiful and proud city with outstanding Renaissance architecture, covered porticos and towers. It's known as '*La Dotta*' (the erudite) as its university was founded in 1088 and is one of the oldest in the world. Bologna has a rich gastronomic heritage and boasts the best food in Italy including pasta (tortellini, lasagne and fettuccini), mortadella, *prosciutto di Parma* (fine cured ham), *Parmigiano,* Parmesan cheese and Lambrusco wines. It's a lively, congenial, cultivated and relatively tourist-free city, although it's also one of Italy's most expensive places to live. A thriving industrial area surrounds Bologna and only some 6 per cent of the region's population is unemployed.

Other interesting cities include Parma, which has a Romanesque cathedral and baptistry, and a charming opera house with strong connections with Verdi who lived at nearby Sant'Agata. Modena is home to the opera star Pavarotti and Ferrari motor cars, and is noted for its fine cuisine, exquisite Romanesque cathedral and the Este Gallery. Ferrara has a number of fine palaces associated with the Este family and Ravenna, with its many fascinating Romanesque buildings and mosaics, is the resting place of Italy's most famous poet, Dante, and the ancient capital of the Western Roman Empire during its decadence under Gothic and Byzantine domination. Small towns of interest include Carpi (known for works in scagliola), Cesena (home of the Malatesta dynasty), Comacchio, Correggio, Faenza (famous for ceramics) and Mirandola. The region contains a wealth of attractive historic town centres with arcaded streets, brick palazzi, cobbled plazas and splendid cathedrals.

The wide sandy beaches along the Adriatic coastline are home to number of thriving resorts including Cattolica, Cervia, Cesenatico, Milano Marittima, Rimini and Riccione, popular with young Italians and foreigners. Property on the coast costs from Lit. 2 million per m² in Cesenatico to Lit. 5.5 million per m² in Milano Marittima. The region doesn't contain many derelict properties at bargain prices as it has one of the highest standards of living in Italy, evidenced by the wealth of prestigious country properties with sky high prices. Emilia Romagna has excellent road, rail and air links with the rest of Italy. Bologna has an international airport and is a major rail junction with good rail and road links with the north and Rome.

Friuli-Venezia-Giuila: The region of Friuli-Venezia-Giuila contains the provinces of Gorizia, Pordenone, Trieste (also the capital city) and Udine, covering an area of 7,844km² (3,029mi²) with a population of around 1.25 million. It's situated in the north-east of the country bordering Austria and Slovenia, with the Gulf of Venice, the Adriatic Sea and the Veneto region to the south. Friuli was occupied by the Romans under Julius Caesar and is short for *Forum Iulii* or Julian Forum. The region was partitioned between Italy and Yugoslavia in the aftermath of WWII and its population is ethnically mixed, more middle European than Italian, and is accorded a special status taking into account its unique historical and ethnic background. The mountainous north contains peaks as high as 2,750m (9,000ft) and is famous for the heroic WWI battles fought in Carso, Gorizia and Udine. There are some plains in the south around the coasts of the Gulf of Trieste and the Adriatic, which are dotted with sandy beaches such as those at Grado and Lignano Sabbiadoro. The region is crammed with artistic treasures from the Roman, Byzantine and Romanesque-Gothic eras, and is one of the most cosmopolitan and culturally sophisticated in Italy. Among the many attractive cities of historic importance are Aquileia, with its Roman monuments and Byzantine mosaics, Grado ('golden island') with its elegant beaches and Cividale dei Friuli, founded by Julius Caesar.

Trieste is the largest seaport on the Adriatic and was once the port of the Austro-Hungarian empire. It's a splendid, ancient city, designed on a grid pattern, with superb neo-classical 18th century architecture in the city centre (Borgo Teresiano) and some elegant later Art Nouveau buildings. It occupies an idyllic setting on a promontory with Miramare castle and the nearby resorts of Sistiana and Duino Castle (which hosted Dante). The poet Rilke, the exiled James Joyce and Svevo were the initiators of Trieste's literary tradition, which continues to this day with contemporary Italian writers and poets. Trieste is also an international centre for scientific research.

The Friuli-Venezia-Giuila region is noted for its S. Daniele ham, wine production (Pinot and Refosco), grain, fruit orchards, dairy products and livestock. Industries include shipyards at Monfalcone and Trieste, textiles, chemicals, cutlery, forestry, furniture, and lead and zinc mining. The aftermath of the 1988 earthquake gave a huge boost to the local economy and the reconstruction funds were wisely used to modernise industry. Unemployment is low at around 7 per cent. Udine has the highest rainfall in Italy and winters in Trieste are noted for some very cold days with strong winds known as *bora*. In contrast, summers are mild and pleasant without the very high temperatures found in many other regions.

Property is reasonably priced and in the towns often features pretty Venetian architecture, while stone chalets with slate roofs are common in the mountains. On the Lagoon of Marano there are traditional fishermen's houses built of reeds with cone-shaped roofs, which are sometimes let for rustic holidays. The region's communications are good and ferries leave from Trieste for the southern Adriatic and Greece. *Autostrade* link Trieste with Milan, Turin and Venice and there's a rail link with Austria via the Tarvisio Pass and an international airport in Trieste.

Lazio (Latium): The region of Lazio contains the provinces of Frosinone, Latina, Rieti, Rome (Roma) and Viterbo, covering an area of 17,224km² (6,651mi²) with a population of some 5.2 million. The regional capital (and capital of Italy) is Rome, where half of Lazio's population is concentrated. Situated in the centre of the peninsula, Lazio has borders with all five regions of central Italy plus Campania. Its coastline is washed by the Tyrrhenian Sea and crossed by the River Tiber, while to the east are the high peaks of the Abruzzi. Lazio has a good road network (all of which lead to Rome!), pretty rolling hills, gracious villas, walled hill towns, vineyards, olive groves and hazlenut orchards. Some three-quarters of the population is employed in the service sector, particularly tourism and work connected with the central government. Unemployment is around 13 per cent. Agriculture also thrives and is an important industry in the hinterland around Rome and the south towards Latina.

Rome (the eternal city) is built on seven hills and was the capital of Christianity and the seat of the Papal States long before it became the capital of a united Italy in 1870. It's one of the world's great historic cities, which is reflected in the wealth of monuments and buildings from Roman times to the masterpieces of Renaissance and Baroque art and architecture. Other reasons for visiting Rome are its plethora of parks, fountains, and priceless art treasures, such as those housed in the Vatican museum. Romans have a familiarity with greatness, as much of the civilised world was once ruled from here, which is seen in their lifestyle and *joie de vivre*. A sage once said that 'every day you spend in Rome adds a year to your intellectual life' and the city attracts people from around the globe.

It has the second largest number of foreign residents in Italy after Milan, which is reflected in the number of schools, activities, and associations for foreigners. More hotels are being built for the Holy or Jubilee Year of 2000 and it's becoming increasingly difficult to find reasonably priced accommodation within easy reach of the centre. Unfortunately the days of *La Dolce Vita* (as portrayed in Fellini's celebrated film) are long gone and Rome has become heavily polluted by traffic fumes that have degraded the quality of the city's air and life. Rome is the only world capital with a double number of embassies and ambassadors, as most countries have an embassy to the Italian state and another to the Holy See (the Vatican City).

Hill towns in the Castelli area (where Romans go for Sunday excursions) include Castel Gandolfo (the Pope's summer residence), Frascati (famous for its wine), Genzano, Rocca di Papa and Tivoli (site of Hadrian's Villa and Villa d'Este with its famous fountains). Seaside resorts to the south include Anzio, Circeo, Gaeta, Sabaudia, San Felice, Sperlonga, Terracina and the island of Ponza (hydrofoil from Formia). The Pontine islands, Ponza and Ventotene lie 32km (20mi) off the coast and are served by a summer ferry service from Anzio (a city made famous by the Allied landings in 1943 during WWII). North of Rome are Santa Marinella and Santa Severa, and the inland lakes of Bolsena, Bracciano and Vico, much loved by English and German expatriates. In the Tuscia-Viterbese area north of Rome the towns of Cerveteri, Tarquinia and Tuscania, and the rupestre necropolis of Norchia near Vetralla are reminders of the mysterious Etruscan people who once inhabited this area. Viterbo's medieval quarter is the best preserved in Europe. The area is slowly but surely being discovered by foreigners (Tusciashire!) who prefer it to Tuscany due to its relatively low property prices and proximity to Rome (but far enough away to avoid the traffic and pollution). Other interesting towns include Agnani, Caprarola (with its magnificent Palazzo Farnese), Civitavecchia (the busy port of Rome), Ferentino and historic Palestrina.

The region's architecture is typified by the many fortified hill towns with their tall, narrow houses built of grey peperino stone and tufa rock. Property prices are relatively high in the areas surrounding Rome, as many Romans commute from the coast or have weekend retreats in the countryside. Prices in Rome are fairly stable with the exception of luxurious city centre properties. The Aventino, Cassia, EUR, Flaminia and Parioli areas are favoured by foreigners for their proximity to international schools, and quality apartments in these areas run from Lit. 3 to 5 million per m². As you would expect, Lazio (and Rome in particular) has excellent road, rail and air links with other regions and internationally.

Liguria: The region of Liguria contains the provinces of Genoa (Genova), Imperia, La Spezia and Savona, and has a population of some 1.7 million, 90 per cent of whom live on the coast (which puts a huge strain on the infrastructure). The capital is Genoa with a population of over 700,000. Liguria is one of Italy's smallest regions covering an area of 5,417km² (2,092mi²), extending the entire length of the coast of the Ligurian Sea, from the French border to Tuscany, with one of the steepest and most dramatic coastlines in Italy. It's noted for its mild year-round climate and natural beauty. Unemployment in the region is around 11 per cent.

The coastal area is known as the Italian Riviera and is an international holiday playground for the rich and famous. It actually consists of two Rivieras: the Riviera di Ponente to the west of Genoa and the Riviera di Levante to the east, which is the more cosmopolitan and glamorous. The Gulf of La Spezia (with Lerici and Portovenere) is known as the 'gulf of poets' in memory of Byron and Shelley who lived and died there. It's famous for the beautiful resorts of Cinque Terre and Sarzana, while further up the coast are Camogli (and its pastel houses), Chiavari, Portofino (with its perfect harbour), Rapallo, San Fruttuoso and S. Margherita. Few tourists venture into the interior, which abounds with beautifully preserved medieval villages that have maintained their charm and peaceful character. Among the many historic towns worth a visit are Albenga and Ventimiglia.

Agriculture is limited to olives groves, vineyards, and flowers particularly in the Riviera dei Fiori (Riviera of Flowers) area around Diano Marina, San Remo (famous for its song festival and casino) and Alassio, where flower nurseries are the major business and roses bloom all winter. These are favourite holiday destinations, both with summer visitors and retirees in winter. The coastal strip from Genoa to the French border is an area of great beauty, although it's overdeveloped and overrun with tourists in some parts. It was made popular by the British (who built the magnificent Hanbury Gardens) and Russian emigres in the 1920s, attracted by the best climate in northern Italy, sheltered from the cold eastern winds by the Maritime Alps and the Ligurian Appenines. Genoa is the largest industrial zone and port in Italy, and is flanked by Savona and La Spezia and their large commercial ports. Genoa is rich in culture and history and was the birthplace of Christopher Columbus and one of the five great maritime republics of Italy in the 13th century. The port area was recently renovated and new attractions constructed, including a magnificent aquarium, which has added a shine to what was a run down historic centre.

The architecture of Liguria is typified by attractive turn of the century villas, often with pastel plastered walls or painted with tromp l'oeil. Property is expensive along the coast, but homes in inland village are reasonably priced. The property market divides almost in two halves around Genoa, with the western part of Liguria offering much cheaper properties along the narrow coastal plain, while the eastern half has rocky coastal villages and sky high prices. Prices on the Italian Riviera have remained stable or have fallen in recent years and are between Lit. 8 and 11 million per m² for a quality apartment with a view in a top resort such as Portofino. In the Cinque Terre villages, apartments can be purchased for around Lit. 4 to 6 million per m². Liguria is served by Nice (France) and Genoa airports and also has excellent road and rail connections.

Lombardy (Lombardia): Lombardy is situated in the north of Italy (bordering Switzerland) and contains the provinces of Bergamo, Brescia, Como, Cremona, Mantua (Mantova), Milan (Milano, also the region's capital), Pavia, Sondrio and Varese. It's one of Italy's largest regions covering an area of 23,854km² (9,211mi²) with a population of almost 9 million. Lombardy is an important commercial region and the industrial heartland of Italy, with the area around Milan producing some 40 per cent of Italy's GDP. One of the main industries is textiles, particularly silk (Como) and wool (Biella), while Milan is the country's financial centre and it wealthiest city (with its most expensive property and highest cost of living). The region has a low unemployment rate of around 6 per cent.

Geographically Lombardy is the most varied region in Italy with the vast alluvial plain of the River Po (Italy's longest river) valley in the south and gently rolling hills rising to the dramatic peaks of the Alps in the north, interspersed with the lakes of Como, Garda, Maggiore and d'Iseo. The lakes area is popular for both principal and holiday homes and their stunning backdrop of mountains has inspired artists and writers for generations including Rossini, Shelley, Verdi and Wordsworth. Among the most attractive lake towns are Bellagio (which has a beautiful and breathtaking setting on Lake Como), Desenzano, Gardone Riviera, Limone sul Garda (where a special micro climate allows for winters mild enough for wine production and botanical gardens), Salò and Sirmione. It's a favourite area with retirees as the hills protect the lakefront from northern winds. With the opening of a new autostrada, the towns of Arona, Baveno, Stresa and Verbania are now within 45 minutes of Milan and have seen increasing numbers of Milanese buying principal homes. Prices here are around Lit. 1.5 million per m² for homes in need of restoration and Lit. 2.5 to 5 million per m² for restored properties. Tourists and residents alike are attracted to Stelvio National Park and popular mountain resorts such as Aprica, Bormio, Caspoggio, Chiesa, Livigno, Madesimo, Ponte di Legno, Santa Caterina, Stelvio and Valfurva.

Milan is the financial and economic centre of Italy and also the heart of its communications and fashion industry. It's renowned for its rich cultural life and numbers among its many attractions the Brera gallery, Leonardo's famous fresco of the Last Supper in the church of Santa Maria della Grazie, the La Scala opera house, Sforzesco Castle, and a myriad of museums and galleries. Milan is one of Italy's foremost shopping cities with a wealth of elegant (and expensive) shopping streets such as the Galleria and Via Montenapoleone. The symbol of Milan is the imposing Gothic cathedral (the third largest in Europe) with its Madonnina set amid a forest of spires, pinnacles and flying buttresses. Milan is also noted for its cuisine and boasts some of Italy's best restaurants where one can try the local *risotto alla milanese*. Other fine cities in Lombardy include Bergamo, Brescia, Crema, Mantova, Mantua, Monza (with a royal villa and it famous F1 racetrack) and Vigevano, each with its own unique character.

Property in Lombardy is among the most expensive in Italy, particularly in Milan (with its wealth of *palazzi* with elegant patio-courtyards) and the lakes area, and the more fashionable ski resorts. Lombardy is served by two international airports in Milan (Linate for European flights and Malpensa for intercontinental flights) and has superb road and rail connections, both nationally and internationally.

Marche: The region of Marche contains the provinces of Ancona (the regional capital), Ascoli Piceno, Macerata and Pesaro. The region's population is around 1.5 million, mostly concentrated along the coast and in the main valleys, in an area of 9,693km² (3,743mi²). Situated between Umbria and the Adriatic coast, Marche is little known to foreigners and one of Italy's best kept secrets. The landscape is reminiscent of Tuscany with lush vegetation, rolling hills and charming hill towns such as Urbino, home of the painter Raphael and the Ducal Palace of the Montefeltro dynasty. Other interesting towns include Ascoli Piceno (with a magnificent main square surrounded by porticos), Camerino, (a tiny university town), Fano, Fabriano (famous for its paper and salami), Fermo, Jesi, Loreto (with its famous sanctuary), Macerata, Pesaro (with a fine historic centre), Recanati (home of the poet Leopardi), San Leo and Tolentino.

Marche has a long Adriatic coastline with wide sandy beaches and many attractive resorts which include Civitanova, Fano, Gabicce, Pesaro, Porto Recanati, San Benedetto del Tronto, Senigallia and the high cliffs of the Conero Riviera. The region is famous for its excellent coastal fish restaurants, white Verdicchio wine and, in Ascoli Piceno, stuffed *olive all'ascolana*. With its friendly people, unhurried pace and stunning landscapes (the national park of Monti Sibillini is a walker's paradise), Marche is one of Italy's most attractive regions. Once poor, it now enjoy a relatively high standard of living due to recent industrialisation, low unemployment (around 8 per cent) and little crime.

The local architecture includes gracious *palazzi*, white stone farms and cottages, and a wealth of attractive villages with interesting architecture. Relatively expensive apartments are common on the coast, whereas prices for property in the remote hinterland are quite reasonable. It's possible to buy an inexpensive rural property (prices are much lower than in Tuscany or Umbria) in need of renovation, but access is often poor due to the dearth of sealed roads and other services. In the countryside of Camerino, Osimo or Urbino a farmhouse requiring restoration costs between Lit. 1 and 1.5 million per m², while on the coast you can expect to pay between Lit. 3 and 4 million per m² for an apartment in a popular resort such as Senigallia or Sirolo. Communications are good along the coast, which is served by the A14 *autostrada*, but poor inland due to the Appenine mountains and a series of parallel valleys that make the going slow. A railway line runs along the coast and there's a regional airport at Ancona.

Molise: Molise, which until 1963 was part of Abruzzo, contains the provinces of Campobasso (also the regional capital) and Isernia, which still bears the scars of a 1984 earthquake. Molise is a poor and backward area of 4,439km² (1,714mi²) with a population of around 325,000 and an unemployment rate of some 17 per cent, where the orderliness of the north and the poverty of the south meet. Its traditions, customs and dialects are influenced by Croatia and Albania, its neighbours across the Adriatic. Agriculture and livestock are the main industries in the wide river valleys which are cultivated with grains, cereals, grapes, fruit and potatoes, although most terrain is too steep for farming. There are some cottage and food processing industries near the port of Termoli and natural gas has recently been discovered in the region.

Molise is isolated from the main paths of communication and isn't a popular area among foreign property buyers, either for a permanent or holiday home. The only good road and rail links are along the coast, which is served by the Bologna-Taranto motorway and the Bologna-Lecce railway. The nearest international and domestic airport is Naples.

Piemonte (Piedmont): Piemonte (the name *pied mont* means the fertile land at the foot of the mountains) contains the provinces of Alessandria, Asti, Cuneo, Novara, Turin (Torino, the regional capital) and Vercelli. It's the largest region on the peninsula (Sicily is larger) with an area of 25,398km² (9,807mi²) and some 4.3 million inhabitants, mostly concentrated in the densely populated industrial plains.

Along with Valle d'Aosta, Piemonte is the least Italianate region of Italy, where the educated people traditionally spoke French. Most people also speak the Piedmontese dialect, which has a poetic tradition. Piemonte is part of the industrial triangle formed by Milan, Turin and Genoa and an important economic centre with relatively low unemployment of around 9 per cent. Historically, it was the fountain-head of Italian unity at the time of the Risorgimento under the Savoy family and boasts elegant baroque architecture, excellent cuisine, (Turin is also noted for its chocolate and sweets), and fine wines including Barolo, Barbera, Barbaresco, Asti Spumante, Cinzano and Martini. Langhe, a pretty hilly region south of the Po, is famous for its wines, truffles and gastronomy.

Piemonte is similar in character to its neighbour Lombardy, surrounded by the Alps with vast flat plains through which flows the River Po. It's a land-locked region but shares Lake Maggiore and its mild climate with Lombardy. Among the region's many resort towns are Arona, Stresa and Verbania, while Orta San Giulio on Lake Orta and Viverone on the lake of the same name are picture paradises. The southern zone includes the provinces of Alessandria, where Borsalino hats are made, and Vercelli, a rice-growing area. The region's major industry is car manufacturing in Turin (FIAT) plus textiles, wool and clothing (notably high fashion, particularly in the Biella area).

Turin (Torino) is a noble and elegant city with fine shops, important museums and a population of around one million, which is dominated by FIAT which has its headquarters here. It's a relatively wealthy, cosmopolitan city with wide boulevards reminiscent of Paris, although it lacks the charm and sophistication of many of Italy's other major cities. Turin's many historic palaces such as Superga and Stupinigi palaces, which Juvarra designed for the Savoy family, contrast with the Art Deco buildings and elegant modern villas with surrounding parklands. Turin is also a centre of pilgrimage, as it's the home of the Holy Shroud (*Sacra Sindone*), the cloth in which many believe Christ's body was wrapped when removed from the cross. Situated near the Alps, Switzerland and the Italian Riviera, Turin is less polluted than Milan.

Piemonte contains many winter sports resorts (mainly in the north-west) including Claviere, Sauze d'Oux and Sestriere, and the Gran Paradiso national park on the border with Valle d'Aosta where rare ibex are still found. The architecture is varied with grey stone houses with slate (*ardesia*) or stone tiled roofs in mountainous areas. A property at Sauze d'Oux costs around Lit. 3.5 million per m² while in Sestriere the same home may be as much Lit. 6.5million per m². The Langhe area is more reasonably priced. The region has excellent communications and is well served by international trains, autostrade and the international airports of Turin, Genoa and Milan.

Puglia (Apulia or Le Puglie): Puglia contains the provinces of Bari (the regional capital), Brindisi, Foggia, Lecce and Taranto. It covers an area of 19,356km² (7,474mi²) with a population of some four million people and has a high unemployment rate of around 22 per cent. Puglia forms the heel of the Italian boot in the south-east where it juts into the Ionian and Adriatic Seas towards Albania, forming the Gulf of Taranto. The original inhabitants were probably from Illyria and Greece and Hannibal and Frederick II were just two of the many invaders who passed through and left their mark (Puglia's ports were also jumping-off points for the Crusaders in the Middle Ages). More recent 'invaders' include Albanian and

Kurdistan refugees who frequently wash up on the shores of Puglia, which has led to an increase in crime in the region.

The region has low rainfall and chronic water shortages and therefore only crops resistant to drought are successful. The huge Tavoliere plateau near Foggia is a rich grain-growing plain producing around half of Italy's durum wheat (for pasta) and other important crops include olives (and olive oil), of which Puglia supplies around half the country's requirements, plus almonds and grapes (for wine). There'e some heavy industry at Bari, Barletta, Brindisi and Taranto. The Gargano peninsula in the north-east has a steep rocky coastline and peaks rising to around 1,000m (over 3,000ft) and encompasses a national park where wooded crags thrust into the sea towards the tiny Tremiti Islands. Here lies the historic sanctuary of Monte S. Angelo and the home of Padre Pio, S. Giovanni Rotondo, attractive towns such as Peschici and Vieste, and tourist amenities such as the holiday villages at Pugnochiuso. The impressive grottos or Caves at Castellana are a major tourist attraction, as are the 13th century fortress of Castel del Monte in Andria and the marine grotto of Polignano.

The cities of Bari (known for Fiera del Levante), Brindisi, Foggia, Lecce and Taranto contain superb examples of Baroque and Romanesque architecture. Unique local forms of architecture include white-washed houses with dark conical roofs known as *trulli,* which are found only in Alberobello, and isolated, walled country farmsteads (*masserie*). Traditional country and coastal properties include attractive, whitewashed cube-shaped houses. In general property is reasonably priced except in the centre of cities and a centrally-located property in Ostuni or Vieste costs from Lit. 1.5 to 2.5 per m². An autostrada and railway line run along the Adriatic coast, but connections with the Tyhrrenian coast are difficult due to the Appenine mountains. The region's main domestic airports are Bari and Brindisi. Regular ferries to Greece and the former Yugoslavia, operate from Brindisi and Otranto.

Sardinia (Sardegna): Sardinia contains the provinces of Cagliari (the regional capital), Nuoro, Oristano and Sassari. The island's rich and colourful history and its cultural heritage dates back to the time of the Phoenicians. It was later a Roman colony and then invaded in turn by Ostrogoths, Byzantines, Vandals, Saracens and Normans (1061), and was also a subject of the maritime republics of Pisa and Genoa and the Aragonese. Sardinia was then ruled by the house of Hohenstaufen, the Piedmontese house of Savoy (1718) and finally became part of a united Italy. Some of the towns reflecting this patchwork history are Iglesias (Pisa), Bosa (Spanish), Alghero (Catalan), Castelsardo (Genoa) and Carloforte (Piedmontese).

Sardinia is the second largest island in the Mediterranean (after Sicily), 267km (166mi) long and 120km (75mi) wide, and just 6.5km (4mi) from Corsica (France) across the Strait of Bonifacio. The island is noted for it's rugged mountainous terrain, which reaches a height of 1,833m (6,017ft) on Monti Gennargentu. Its inhabitants consider it to be a tiny continent rather than island, as it contains such a large variety of geography in such a small area. Within a few hours drive from Porto Cervo you can see landscapes similar to the Seychelles, an 'African' desert, 'Australian' beaches and can visit both prehistoric sites and modern areas reminiscent of North America.

It's Italy's most sparsely populated region with (unusually) the largest concentration of people in the interior, where the traditionally sheep-rearing communities have largely ignored the 1,287km (800mi) coastline until fairly recently. Sardinians are a proud and ancient people who speak five different dialects reflecting the varied history of the island. The island is largely undeveloped with problems resembling those of southern Italy such as low investment, poor services and communications, high unemployment (22 per cent), low incomes and a high crime rate (including frequent incidences of kidnapping). There's some industry in Cagliari, Nuoro and Porto Torres, but the economy is mainly based on sheep rearing and tourism.

Many foreigners purchase homes here for the breathtaking, mountainous landscape, the sea of varying colours, the beaches of fine white sand and rocky coves, and the excellent food. There are charming resorts in the south such as Santa Margherita di Pula, Capo Boi and Villasimius, where property prices range from Lit. 2 to 3 million per m². At the other end of the scale, the resorts on the Costa Smeralda in the north-east are among the most exclusive in the Mediterranean and a popular playground of Europe's rich and famous. This exclusive area with its golf courses, marinas and elegant villas was developed by the Aga Khan in the '70s and boasts prices in Porto Rotondo and Porto Cervo of around Lit. 10 million per m² for its elegant villas. Elsewhere the architecture is simple stone houses and the city and town architecture has little of the flair common on the mainland.

Sardinia is located 200km (124mi) from the mainland with which it has regular air connections and is served by ferries from Genoa, a fast, three-hour ferry from Civitavecchia (the port of Rome), Naples, Palermo, Tunisia and France. It's the only region of Italy without any *autostrade*, although most roads are of good quality.

Sicily (Sicilia): Sicily contains the provinces of Agrigento, Caltanissetta, Catania, Enna, Messina, Palermo, Ragusa, Syracuse (Siracusa) and Trapani. Sicily's rich and complex history is evident in the capital Palermo, a splendid city in the grand manner; opulent and vital, with a wealth of remarkable architecture, particularly Norman and Baroque. It was the most important Carthaginian colony in the Mediterranean for five centuries and there's a strong feeling for its ancient traditions among Palermo's 750,000 inhabitants. Other major cities include Catania with a population of around 350,000, Messina, a modern city entirely rebuilt after being destroyed by an earthquake in 1908, and the ancient city of Agrigento with its magnificent Greek temples.

The island has witnessed successive waves of invasion by Greeks, Cathaginians, Saracens and Romans (who made it their granary), Byzantines, Arabs, Normans, Angevins, Aragonese and Bourbons, all of whom left their mark and contributed to the unique quality of this extraordinary island. Among the rich Greek remains are the temple complexes of the Valley of the Temples, Agrigento, Syracuse (with its theatre), Segesta and Selinunte, all of which are better preserved than anything comparable in Greece. Roman relics are best seen in the villa of Piazza Armerina with its exceptional mosaics, which include women in bikinis! Sicily is a fascinating mixture of architectural styles including numerous Arab influences, while the cathedral of Monreale is the most significant Norman building in the whole of Italy.

Sicily is the largest and most densely populated island in the Mediterranean. It's a land of stark contrasts between the breathtaking coastal scenery and rundown resorts; the city slums and polluting industries and the interior's wealth of greenery including eucalyptus, citrus and olive trees, prickly pear cactus and vines; and the sparse population of the island's interior and teeming urban conurbation's on the coastal belt. Sicily has more autonomy than most other Italian regions for historical and ethnic reasons, although it's also synonymous with the mafia (*cosa nostra*), whose

GNP is reckoned to be around 12 per cent of Italy's! It's the most powerful and richest criminal organisation in the world and makes Sicily a dangerous place for police, magistrates and judges. Another problem is very high unemployment, which is around 26 per cent.

There are large sandy beaches on the southern coast, where Cefalu near Palermo is a favourite seaside resort, as are Acireale, Acitrezza, Mondello and Tindari. Other beautiful towns include Agrigento, Syracuse and Taormina, (overlooked by Mount Etna's still active volcano) and the attractive smaller centres of Monreale, Erice, Noto, Gela, Modia and Marsala, famous for its Marsala wine, a tradition begun by English families residing in the area. Many small islands surround Sicily, offering spectacular scenery and excellent facilities for scuba-diving and underwater fishing. These include the islands of Lipari plus Vulcano, Panarea and Stromboli, Ustica, Favignana, Levanzo, Marettimo, Pantelleria and Lampedusa.

Sicily has numerous foreign devotees, many of whom own holiday homes there. The island is noted for its typical cube-shaped houses with flat roofs and also for its flimsily-built modern buildings and concrete jungle resorts. Coastal homes may be purchased from around Lit. 1 to 1.5 million per m² in Syracuse up to Lit. 3.5million per m² for a good property on the coast at Taormina. Communications and road links are poor to adequate but improving. The railway journey from Rome is a tortuous 10 to 12 hours, although Palermo's international airport has good links with the rest of Italy and internationally, and there are regular ferries to the mainland. A bridge across the Strait of Messina between Villa San Giovanni and Messina has been planned for some 25 years and may actually be completed by the year 2006.

Tuscany (Toscana): Tuscany covers 22,990km² (8,877mi²) and contains the provinces of Arezzo, Florence (Firenze), Grosseto, Prato, Leghorn (Livorno), Lucca, Massa Carrara, Pisa, Pistoia and Siena. The regional capital is Florence. Tuscany's population of around 3.6 million is concentrated along the coast and between Florence and Pisa, an area where cultural tourism is the major industry (unemployment is relatively low at around 8 per cent). Florence, birthplace of the Renaissance, is one of the world's most beautiful cities. Cradle of Italian art and science, the city is a living museum and the most popular cultural site in Europe, containing a wealth of art, bridges, churches, palaces and statues (including Michelangelo's 'David' in the Uffizi gallery). Due to its popularity, Florence is in danger of being overwhelmed by tourists, which number some seven million a year. Siena is Florence's great historical rival, the largest surviving medieval town in Europe and home of the famous Palio horse race. Other notable Tuscan cities, each with its own remarkable cathedral (*duomo*), include Arezzo, Leghorn, Lucca, Pisa (and its famous 13th century leaning tower), Pistoia and Prato.

In few places in the world have man and nature blended so harmoniously than in Tuscany, with its combination of agreeable climate, stunning scenery, beautiful towns and cities, cultural heritage and culinary delights. The countryside has a unique charm with gently rolling hills, farmhouses, vineyards, olive and cypress groves, and soft colours. The countryside is criss-crossed with white roads (*strade bianche*) which inevitably lead to the region's famous stone farmhouses (*casali*) that many foreigners find so irresistible and romantic, particularly if they have seen the film 'Stealing Beauty' or read the book 'Under the Tuscan Sun'. The most famous area of Tuscany is Chianti, the oldest officially-designated, wine-growing area in the world. It's marvellous walking country and has been dubbed Chiantishire due to the large number of Anglo-Saxon visitors and summer residents. The world's most expensive wine is produced in the Montalcino area and it also boasts a DOC (*Denominazione di Origine Controllata*) olive oil. The finest olive oil and wine is to be found in the golden triangle bounded by Florence, Siena and Volterra, while truffles (*tartufi*) are found in Val d'Orcia and S. Giovanni val d'Arno. Among the region's best resorts are Forte dei Marmi, Lido di Camaiore, Marina di Castiglioncello, Marina di Pietrasanta and the Argentario peninsula. The resort of Viareggio is blessed with wide sandy beaches, while in nearby Torre del Lago Puccini, a music festival honors the composer Giacomo Puccini.

The island of Elba (where Napoleon lived from May 1814 to February 1815) has some excellent sandy beaches, although two-thirds of its 224km² (86mi²) is composed of woodland. It's Italy's third largest island (after Sicily and Sardinia) and is reached by ferry from Leghorn and Piombino. Other islands of the Tuscan archipelego include Capraia, Giannutri, Giglio, Gorgona, Montecristo (where Dumas set his classic tale) and Pianosa. On the Maremma coast is the Parco Regionale della Maremma and Uccellina, 25,000 acres of wild and beautiful unspoilt country. Nearby Monte Argentario, a peninsula attached to the mainland by three isthmuses containing the seaside towns of Orbetello, Porto Ercole and Porto Santo Stefano. The area is noted for it beautiful villas and marinas (such as Cala Galera) and is a fashionable summer holiday retreat among wealthy Romans and Florentines. Other popular holiday areas on this part of the Tuscan coast include Ansedonia, Punta Ala (with its marina and golf course) and Talamone. There are famous spas at Montecatini, Bagni di Lucca, Casciana, Terme, Chianciano and San Casciano Bagni.

Tuscany's architecture is typified by its stone farmhouses and stunning fortified hilltop towns with a profusion of towers and turrets, such as Cortona, Monteriggioni and San Gimignano. The region is noted for its fine villas and palazzi, painted in traditional Tuscan red, farmhouses (*casali*), stone village houses, and warm-coloured stone and terracotta roofs. Property in central Tuscany is among the most expensive in the country, particularly anywhere within an hour of the cities of Florence, Siena or Pisa. Less expensive properties can be found north of Lucca, in Lunigiana and around Arezzo. Tuscany boasts an excellent road and rail network and has major international airports at Florence and Pisa, while Leghorn is a busy port.

Trentino-Alto-Adige: Trentino-Alto-Adige contains the autonomous provinces of Bolzano and Trento, each with its own capital of the same name, which are also the regional capitals with equal status. The population of around 900,000 speaks Italian, German and Ladino, plus a variety of dialects. The region has one of the lowest population densities in the country, a third of whom live in small mountain villages, and it also boasts the country's lowest unemployment rate of just 3 per cent. This bilingual region was part of the Austro-Hungarian Empire until 1918 and German is still taught in the schools. The cuisine has a distinctly Austrian flavor with *knodel, krapfen* and *strudel* existing alongside polenta and spaghetti. There's a definite Austrian influence in the Baroque architecture, the painted palace façades, and the large wood and stone chalets.

Trentino-Alto-Adige is Italy's northernmost region and is dominated by the Alps which divide Italy from Austria. The Dolomite mountains are a heady mixture of dense forests, alpine lakes and fascinating rock formations, and a magnet for visitors from around the world. Tourism is the region's most important industry and important resorts include Bressanone, Brunico, Merano, Ortisei, San Candido, Santa Cristina, Selva di Val Gardena and Vipiteno. Tourists flock year round to the resorts of Canazei, Madonna di Campiglio, Moena, San Martino di Castrozza and Val di Fassa. Agriculture is also important, particularly in Val di Non, famous for its apple orchards, while the region's vineyards produce mostly white wines such as guwurztraminer, riesling, sylvaner and terlaner. Dairy farming is another important industry.

Trentino-Alto-Adige is noted for its fine estates and castles (*castelli*). Property in the most popular mountain resorts is in high demand and is relatively expensive. The region has a good road and rail network and is linked with Austria via the Brenner Pass.

Umbria: Umbria contains the provinces of Perugia (the regional capital) and Terni. It's one of Italy's smallest regions covering an area of 8,455km² (3,265mi²) with a population of less than 1 million and unemployment of around 9 per cent. Despite lying on a major earthquake fault line, Umbria is one of the few areas where the countryside hasn't been largely deserted by the population. River valleys such as those of the Tiber River are cultivated with grain, olive groves and terraced vineyards, and there's some industry around Foligno, Narni, Perugia and Terni. Umbria is the most quintessential Italian corner of the peninsula, known as the 'green heart of Italy' and the 'land of woods (it's mostly comprised of forest and farmland) and saints'. It's a landlocked region, less accessible, dramatic and glamorous than its neighbour Tuscany, but also with much lower property prices. It also has far fewer tourists and foreign property owners, although more people are discovering its unspoilt, backwater charms.

The spiritual loveliness of the countryside is reflected in its hilltop towns such as Todi, which has become a fashionable spot with a large enclave of foreign artists and writers since an American university voted it one of the world's most liveable towns. Perugia, the region's capital and largest city, is a fine old Etruscan town with a famous University for Foreign Students specialising in courses in Italian art, culture and language. Assisi is the home of St Francis (Italy's patron saint), whose life is commemorated in the immortal frescoes of Giotto (which were badly damaged in an earthquake in 1997) in the Basilica di San Francesco. Spoleto is famous for its annual arts (music, drama and dance) 'Festival of Two Worlds'. Other famous towns include Città della Pieve (the home of Perugino), Città di Castello, Deruta (famous for its ceramics), Foligno, Gubbio (a medieval 'film set'), Narni, Norcia, Orvieto (magnificent cathedral and fine wines) and Panicale.

The local architecture is sombre but attractive, featuring light-coloured stone and similar in style to Tuscany. Towers are a typical feature of the region's hilltop villages and farmhouses, which cost from around Lit. 2 million per m² near Bevagna to Lit. 4 million per m² near Assisi. Communications in the region are fair and improving. There's a domestic airport at Perugia and the E45 superstrada connects with the A1 autostrada and also the Civitavecchia-Rome autostrada, making it a fast journey to Rome and Fiumicino international airport. From Perugia it's also possible to make day trips to the sea and the sandy beaches of the Etruscan Riviera via the E45 superstrada to Orte and the Orte-Viterbo superstrada to Tarquinia.

Val D'Aosta: The autonomous region of Val D'Aosta contains only one province, Aosta, and is the smallest and most sparsely populated region in Italy with a population of just 100,000. It's also Italy's wealthiest area with a unemployment rate of around 7 per cent. The regional capital and only large city is Aosta, founded by the Romans in 25BC and named after Emperor Augustus, containing a wealth of Roman remains including the city walls, theatre and a triumphal arch. In the 11th century it came under the domination of the Savoy family, but was always considered autonomous. Officially bilingual Italian and French, there are also some dialects such as French-Provençal *patois* and *walser*, a German dialect.

Thanks to the region's landscapes and outstanding natural beauty, tourism is the largest industry, attracting over 700,000 visitors annually. The region's mountains include Monte Bianco (Mont Blanc), Europe's highest mountain at 4,810m/15,780ft, the Matterhorn (4,478m/14,691ft), Monte Rosa (4,633m/15,200ft) and Monte Cervino, which draw skiers year round, including glacier skiing in summer. The Gran Paradiso national park contains an abundance of forests and wild flowers, and many rare animals (lynx, stambecchi) and plants. The region is one of the favourite Italian winter sports areas and in winter people flock to the main resorts of Cervinia, Courmayeur (the best known), Breuil-Cervinia and Gressoney. Other industries include iron mining near Cogne, artisans workshops (e.g. wood sculpting) and livestock.

Sturdily built and well-designed wooden and stone chalets (*rascards*) are typical of the region. Property prices are generally higher than in neighbouring Piedmont, with top properties costing up to Lit. 9 million per m² in chic Courmayer, Lit. 6 million per m² in Cervinia, and around Lit. 4 million per m² in Saint Vincent (noted for its casino). The region has excellent autostrade connections with Milan and Turin and, through the Gran San Bernardo pass and the Monte Bianco tunnel, with Switzerland and France, and is also well served by international airports in neighbouring regions.

Veneto: The Veneto region contains the provinces of Belluno, Padua (Padova), Rovigo, Treviso, Venice (Venezia, the regional capital), Verona and Vicenza. It has a huge variety of terrain from the Eastern Alps to marshy plains and the Venice lagoon. The north-eastern area takes in the Dolomite mountains (including the fashionable winter resort of Cortina d'Ampezzo) and the seaside resorts of Bibione, Caorle, Lido di Jesolo and Sottomarina (near Chioggia). There are also a number of popular resorts (such as Sirmione) on the eastern bank of lake Garda near Verona. The vast alluvial plain in the south is formed by many rivers (including the Po) that empty into the Adriatic and is cultivated with vineyards, cereals, fruit trees, sugar beet, tobacco, and potatoes. Dairy farming and fishing are also important industries (the unemployment rate is low at around 6 per cent).

The regions many historic cities include Verona, best known for Romeo and Juliet and its Roman Arena (where opera is performed in summer during the Verona festival), and Padua (Padova) with its great basilica of St. Anthony. The Marca Trevigiana ('marca gioisa et amorosa') boasts the beautiful towns of Conegliano and Asolo, the ancient hill town where Elizabeth Barret Browning and Eleanora Duse once lived, and famous for its frescoed façades. *Urbs Picta* is a nickname for Treviso

in the foothills of the Dolomites, containing a plethora of Rennaisance palaces and arcades. Local culinary specialities include radicchio (red salad), risotto, polenta and local cheeses, and the wines of Cartizze, Merlot, Prosecco and Recioto.

The pearl of Veneto is, of course, Venice, considered by many to be the most beautiful and romantic city in the world, with its traffic-free streets and plethora of enchanting canals, small squares and bridges. The city is a living museum with its many splendid sites including the Doges' Palace, St. Mark's Square and the Bridge of Sighs. However, Venice is a victim of its own popularity and is inundated with some nine million tourists a year (although there's talk of limiting their numbers). Other problems include the winter flooding (*acqua alta*) that's a constant threat to the city's buildings, many of which are decaying and in danger of sinking into the sea. Venice is the most expensive city in Italy, where the local population has fallen by around two-thirds in the last 20 years and the business community is shrinking due to the high cost (some 40 per cent higher than on the mainland) of transporting raw materials along the waterways.

The wonderful Venetian architecture and sumptious *palazzi* built of pink Verona or Istrian stone, has always been a strong attraction for wealthy foreigners who happily pay between Lit. 6 to 9 million per m² for a slice of paradise. However, less expensive properties can be found on the islands of the lagoon such as Burano, Murano, and Torcello. The region has good road and rail links with Milan and Central Europe, and Venice airport handles a number of international flights. Venice is also a port of call for cruise ships.

RESEARCH

There's an overwhelming choice of property for sale in Italy, which is a buyers' market in most areas and likely to remain that way for some years. As when buying property anywhere, it's never advisable to be in too much of a hurry. Have a good look around in the region(s) you have chosen and obtain an accurate picture of the kinds of property available, Their relative prices and what you can expect to get for your money. However, before doing this, you should make a comprehensive list of what you want (and don't want) from a home so that you can narrow the field and save time on wild goose chases.

Note that it's sometimes difficult to compare homes in different regions as they often vary considerably and few houses are exactly comparable. In most areas properties range from derelict farmhouses, barns and village homes to modern townhouses and apartments with all modern conveniences; from dilapidated *castelli* and mansions requiring complete restoration to luxury modern chalets and villas. You can also buy a plot of land and have an individually designed house built to your own specifications. If, however, after discussing it with your partner one of you insists on a brand new luxury apartment in Rome and the other on a 17th century *castello* in Lombardy, the easiest solution may be to get a divorce!

Although property in Italy is relatively inexpensive compared with many other European countries, the fees associated with the purchase of property are among the highest in Europe and add up to 15 per cent to the cost (more if you have an Italian mortgage). To reduce the chances of making an expensive error when buying in an unfamiliar region, it's often prudent to rent a home for a period (see **Renting** on page 141), taking in the worst part of the year (weather-wise). This allows you to become familiar with the region and weather, and gives you plenty of time to look for a home at your leisure. Wait until you find something you fall head over heels in love with and then think about it for another week or two before rushing headlong to the altar! One of the advantages of buying property in Italy is that there's usually another 'dream' home around the next corner – and the second or third dream home is often even better than the first. Better to miss the 'opportunity of a lifetime' than end up with an expensive pile of stones around your neck. **However, don't dally too long as good properties at the right price don't remain on the market for ever.**

One of the most common mistakes people make when buying a rural property in Italy is to buy a house that's much larger than they need with a large plot of land, simply because it appears to offer such good value. Don't, on the other hand, buy a property that's too small. Bear in mind that extra space can easily be swallowed up, and when you have a home in Italy you will invariably discover that you have many more relatives and friends than you ever thought possible! For many foreign buyers, Italy offers the opportunity to buy a size or style of home that they could never afford in their home countries.

Buying a huge house with a few acres may seem like a good investment, but bear in mind that should you need to sell, buyers may be thin on the ground, particularly when the price has doubled or trebled after adding the cost of renovation. In most areas there's a narrow market for renovated rural property. There are usually plenty of buyers in the lower Lit. 90 to 150 million price range, but they become much scarcer at around Lit. 300 million unless a property is exceptional, i.e. outstandingly attractive, in a popular area and with a superb situation. In some areas even desirable properties remain on the market for a number of years. Although it's tempting to buy a property with a lot of land, you should think about what you're going to do with it. After you've installed a swimming pool, tennis court and croquet lawn, you still have a lot of change left out of even a few acres. Do you like gardening or are you prepared to live in a jungle? Can you afford to hire a gardener? A large garden needs a lot of upkeep (i.e. work). Of course you can always plant an orchard or vineyard, create a lake or take up farming!

If you're looking for a holiday home (*secondo casa*), you may wish to investigate mobile homes or a scheme that restricts your occupancy of a property to a number of weeks each year. These include shared ownership, leaseback, time-sharing (*multiproprietaria*) and a holiday property bond (see page 159). Don't rush into any of these schemes without fully researching the market and before you're absolutely clear about what you want and what you can realistically expect to receive for your money.

Bear in mind that foreign buyers aren't welcome everywhere, particularly when they 'colonise' a town or area. Understandably, the Italians don't want property prices driven up by foreigners (particularly second home owners) to levels they can no longer afford. However, foreigners are generally welcomed by the local populace, not least because they boost the local economy, and in rural areas often buy derelict properties that Italians won't touch. Permanent residents in rural areas who take the time and trouble to integrate into the local community are invariably warmly received.

The more research you do before buying a property in Italy the better, which should (if possible) include advice from people who already own a house there, from whom you can usually obtain invaluable information (often based on their own mistakes). In many countries there are international property magazines that include homes for sale in Italy, such as *World of Property* and *International Property* in the UK (see **Appendix A** for a list). In Italy, property is advertised for sale in all major city newspapers (many of which contain real estate supplements on certain days), advertising journals such as *Seconda Mano* (Milan, Bologna and Florence) and many free publications. Homes are also advertised in local property newspapers such as *Panorama Casa* (Tuscany), *La Oulce* (Florence), *Più Case* (Milan) and *Porta Portese immobiliare* (Rome), and magazines such as the monthly *Case e Country* and *Ville & Casali* (mainly for up-market properties). Information about properties for sale in Italy is also available on the Internet.

AVOIDING PROBLEMS

The problems associated with buying property abroad have been highlighted in the last decade or so, during which the property market in some countries has gone from boom to bust and back again. From a legal point of view, Italy is one of the safest countries in Europe in which to buy a home and buyers have a high degree of protection under Italian law. However, you should take the usual precautions regarding contracts, deposits and obtaining proper title. Many people have had their fingers burnt by rushing into property deals without proper care and consideration. It's all too easy to fall in love with the beauty and ambience of Italy and to sign a contract without giving it sufficient thought. If you're uncertain, don't allow yourself to be rushed into making a hasty decision, e.g. by fears of an imminent price rise or because someone else is interested in a property. Although many people dream of buying a holiday or retirement home in Italy, it's vital to do your homework thoroughly and avoid the 'dream sellers' (often fellow countrymen) who will happily prey on your ignorance and tell you anything in order to sell you a property.

The vast majority of people buying a home in Italy don't obtain independent legal advice and most of those who experience problems take no precautions whatsoever. Of those that do take legal advice, many do so only after having paid a deposit and signed a contract or, more commonly, after they have run into problems. The most important point to bear in mind when buying property in Italy (or anywhere) is to obtain expert legal advice from someone who's familiar with Italian law. As when buying property in any country, you should never pay any money or sign anything without first taking legal advice. You'll find the relatively small cost (in comparison with the cost of a home) of obtaining legal advice to be excellent value for money, if only for the peace of mind it affords. Trying to cut corners to save a few lire on legal costs is foolhardy in the extreme when a large sum of money is at stake. You may be able to obtain a list of lawyers who speak your national language and are experienced in handling Italian property sales, either in Italy or in your home country, e.g. British buyers can obtain a list from the Law Society in Britain.

There are professionals speaking English and other languages in most areas of Italy, and many expatriate professionals (e.g. architects, builders and surveyors) also practise there. However, don't assume that because you're dealing with a fellow countryman that he'll offer you a better deal or do a better job than an Italian (the contrary may be true). It's wise to check the credentials of all professionals you employ, whether Italian or foreign. Note that it's *never* advisable to rely solely on advice proffered by those with a financial interest in selling you a property, such as a builder or estate agent, although their advice may be excellent and totally unbiased.

Declared Value: Don't be tempted by the 'quaint' Italian custom of tax evasion, where the 'official' sale price declared to the authorities is reduced by an 'under the table' cash payment. It's possible when buying a property direct from the vendor that he may suggest this, particularly if he's selling a second home and must pay capital gains tax on the profit. Obviously if the vendor can show a smaller profit, he pays less tax. You will also save money on taxes and fees, but will have a higher capital gains tax bill when you sell if it's a second home. **You should steer well clear of this practice, which is naturally strictly illegal (although widespread).** If you under-declare the price, the authorities can revalue the property and demand that you pay the shortfall in tax plus interest and fines. If you're selling a property, you should bear in mind that if the buyer refuses to make the illicit payment after the contract has been signed, there's nothing (legally) you can do about it!

Among the most common problems experienced by buyers in Italy are buying in the wrong area (**rent first!**); buying a home that's unsaleable; buying too large a property and grossly underestimating restoration and modernisation costs; not having a survey done on an old property; not taking legal advice; not including the necessary conditional clauses in the contract; buying a property for business, e.g. to convert to self-catering accommodation, and being too optimistic about the income; overcharging by vendors and agents (particularly when selling to foreigners); taking on too large a mortgage; and property management companies going bust or doing a moonlight flit with owners' rental receipts.

Other problems, although rare, include buying a property without a legal title; properties built or extended illegally without planning permission; properties sold that are subject to embargoes; properties sold by a bankrupt builder or company (which are part of the assets of that company); undischarged mortgages from the previous owner; builders absconding with the buyer's money before completing a property; claims by relatives after a property has been purchased; properties sold to more than one buyer; and people selling properties that they don't own. Note that if an Italian company or builder goes bankrupt (*fallito*) within two years of selling a property, the liquidator can issue a 'revocation' (*revocatoria*) of the sale and include the buyer as one of the company's creditors. Always beware when a property is offered at a seemingly bargain price by a builder, developer or other businessman (*imprenditore*) and run a thorough credit check on the vendor and his business.

One Italian law that property buyers should be aware of is the law of subrogation, whereby property debts, including mortgages, local taxes, utility bills and community charges, remain with a property and are inherited by the buyer. This is an open invitation to dishonest sellers to 'cut and run'. It is, of course, possible to check whether there are any outstanding debts on a property and this must be done by your legal advisor a few days before completion.

Illegal Building: Building illegally (called *abusivismo*) is a common practice in Italy, where it's estimated that around 150 houses a day are built illegally somewhere on the peninsula. Some 17,500 illegal homeowners in Italy have received demolition orders, although it's rare for demolition to actually be carried out. However, in one incident alone in 1998, the authorities demolished 72 villas that had been built illegally along a three kilometre stretch of the Salerno coastline. The land was owned by the state and had been expropriated by the *mafia* (the army had to be employed to carry out the demolition as no builder would do it). Many coastal areas are in danger of being ruined by uncontrolled development and of Italy's 8,000km (5,000mi) of coastline, only some 800km (500mi) remain undeveloped. The Galasso law of the '70s declared that there were to be no new buildings within 250 metres of the sea, but it has been ignored almost everywhere. In contrast, many inland towns and villages are almost totally unspoilt, and some regions have strict building regulations and have hardly changed in centuries. New development in Tuscany and some other areas is prohibited and renovation is strictly regulated, e.g. existing buildings must be replaced with properties built in the same style and of the same size.

It's advisable to have your finance in place before you start looking for a property in Italy and if you need a mortgage, to obtain a mortgage guarantee certificate from a bank that guarantees you a mortgage at a certain rate, which is usually subject to a valuation (see **Mortgages** on page 90). Note, however, that under Italian law a buyer can withdraw from a contract and have his deposit returned if he's unable to obtain a mortgage. You will need to pay a deposit when signing a contract (see page 169) and must pay fees and taxes (see **Fees** on page 147) of between 10 and 20 per cent of the purchase price on completion.

Summary: It's important to deal only with a qualified and licensed agent, and to engage a local lawyer (*avvocato*), before signing anything or paying a deposit. A surveyor may also be necessary, particularly if you're buying an old property or a property with a large plot of land. Your lawyer or surveyor will carry out the necessary searches regarding such matters as ownership, debts and rights of way. Enquiries must be made to ensure that the vendor has a registered title and that there are no debts against a property. It's also important to check that a property has the relevant building licences, conforms to local planning conditions and that any changes (alterations, additions or renovations) have been approved by the local town hall. If a property is owned by several members of a family, which is common in Italy, all owners must give their consent before it can be sold. With regard to a rural property, it's important to ensure that it has a reliable water supply.

Finally, if there's any chance that you will need to sell (and recoup your investment) in the foreseeable future, it's important to buy a home that will be saleable. A property with broad appeal in a popular area will usually fit the bill, although it will need to be very special to sell quickly in some areas. A modest, reasonably priced property is usually likely to be much more saleable than a large expensive home, particularly one requiring restoration or modernisation.

ITALIAN HOMES

Italian homes and living standards used to very basic, particularly in rural areas, where many homes had no bathroom or toilet. However, with the huge rise in the standard (and cost) of living in the last few decades, Italian homes have been transformed and today's average Italian is better housed than many other Europeans. In cities, people generally live in apartments, houses being rare and prohibitively expensive. Italian apartments are usually surprisingly small and it's unusual to find apartments with four or more bedrooms and even three-bedroom apartments aren't easy to find. Most do, however, have two bathrooms. New detached homes (called villas) are generally luxurious internally, but often have bland or even ugly exteriors. In contrast to modern homes, old buildings are an architectural delight and contain a wealth of attractive period features. Whether old or new, Italians take great pride in their homes and no expense is spared to make them comfortable and beautiful.

Homes in Italy are as varied as the climate and people, but one thing they all have in common is sturdy building materials. The exterior may be made of wood, stone, brick or other (usually fire resistant) materials. Interior walls are usually white *stucco* plaster (*intonaco*), which may be painted in pastel colours and makes a perfect backdrop for paintings and tapestries, while bedroom walls are often covered with wallpaper. Wood floors (*parquet*) are common in northern Italian homes and are considered a luxury in the rest of Italy and therefore generally reserved for the master bedroom. Marble or travertino is often used in entrance halls (*ingressi*), corridors (*corridoi*) and living rooms (*saloni*), while kitchens (*cucine*) and baths (*bagni*) are generally enhanced by beautiful ceramic tiles (for which Italy is famous). Bathrooms are fitted with a toilet, washbasin (*lavandino*), bidet and a shower (*doccia*) or bath (*vasca*), or perhaps a bath with a shower attachment. Luxury homes often sport a Jacuzzi (*idromassaggio*). When there's no separate utility or laundry room (*lavanderia*), the hotwater heater (*scaldabagno*) and washing machine (*lavatrice*) are usually stored in the main 'service' (*servizio*) bathroom.

Italian homes are completely empty when purchased, except perhaps for the bathroom porcelain and the kitchen sink. All the furnishings, appliances and white goods are chosen and bought by the new owner, who can have the kitchen fitted by a local carpenter-artisan or buy factory-produced kitchen cabinets. Ovens can be electric or mains gas (which is available in most urban areas) and country properties may also have an outside pizza/bread oven (*forno a legna*) and sometimes a *tinello* or *taverna* that acts as family room or a summer kitchen/dining room. Very few Italians use clothes dryers (the sun and wind suffice), but washing machines are as common as televisions. If you live in a rural area you may find a public washhouse (*lavatoio*), which is good for washing voluminous things such as curtains in addition to being a good place to catch up on local gossip and for summer swimming for children.

Unrestored country properties rarely have any kind of heating ('What you don't spend in wood, you spend in wool' is an old Italian saying), except for numerous fireplaces which mean lots of atmosphere and a well-stacked wood pile. The thick stone walls (which in old buildings may be over one metre) of older homes keep out the cold in winter thus reducing heating (*riscaldamento*) costs, while in summer they act as insulation against the heat. In northern Italy and mountainous areas, double-glazing is necessary. Heating systems may consist of an oil fired furnace, mains gas or gas bottles in rural areas (see page 185). In apartments (*condominio*), hot water and heating are centralised and paid for along with other *condominio* fees that may include cleaning of common areas, (*pulizia scale*), the porter (*portiere*) and gardener (*giardiniere*).

In old rural homes, the fireplace (*camino*) plays an important role, being used for heating and cooking as well as for atmosphere. (Most city dwellers dream of having a fireplace, while many country homeowners would like to have central heating!) Sometimes the fireplace surround is missing as old buildings are often 'stripped' of architectural detail, although replacements can be bought from architectural salvage dealers. However, an old fireplace surround in marble or peperino will cost between Lit. 3 and 10 million, although a local artisan can make a new one to order for much less. If you suspect that a room once had a fireplace, you can 'sound' the walls to find the flue, which can then be reopened. Windows are usually protected with shutters, which are usually closed at night to keep heat in and prying eyes out. In city apartments they are known as *tapparelle* or *avvolgenti* (rolling shutters) and are made of metal, wood or plastic slats. They are raised and lowered manually with cords (that break frequently) or with an electric motor.

CHOOSING THE LOCATION

The most important consideration when buying a home is usually its location – or as the old adage goes, the *three* most important points are location, location and location! A property in a reasonable condition in a popular area is likely to be a better investment than an exceptional property in a less attractive location. There's no point in buying a dream property in a terrible location. Italy offers almost anything that anyone could want, but you must choose the right property in the right spot. The wrong decision regarding location is one of the main causes of disenchantment among foreigners who have purchased property in Italy.

Where you buy a property will depend on a range of factors including your personal preferences, your financial resources and, not least, whether you plan to work in Italy. If you already have a job in Italy, the location of your home will probably be determined by the proximity to your place of employment. However, if you intend to look for employment or start a business, you must live in an area that allows you the maximum scope. Unless you have reason to believe otherwise, you would be foolish to rely on finding employment in a particular area. If, on the other hand, you're looking for a holiday or retirement home, you can live virtually anywhere. When seeking a permanent home, don't be too influenced by where you have spent an enjoyable holiday or two. A town or area that was acceptable for a few weeks holiday may be far from suitable, for example, for a retirement home, particularly regarding the proximity to shops, medical facilities and other amenities.

If you have little idea about where you wish to live, read as much as you can about the different regions of Italy (see page 113) and spend some time looking around your areas of interest. Note that the climate, lifestyle and cost of living can vary considerably from region to region (and even within a particular region). Before looking at properties it's important to have a good idea of the type of property you're looking for and the price you wish to pay, and to draw up a shortlist of the areas or towns of interest. If you don't do this, you're likely to be overwhelmed by the number of properties to be viewed. Real estate agents usually expect serious buyers to know where they want to buy within a 30 to 40km (19 to 25mi) radius and some even expect clients to narrow it down to specific towns and villages.

The 'best' area in which to live depends on a range of considerations, including the proximity to your place of work, schools, bar, country or town, shops, public transport, bar, sports facilities, beach, bar, etc. There are beautiful areas to choose from throughout Italy, most within easy travelling distance of a town or city (and a bar). Don't, however, believe the times and distances stated in adverts and by estate agents. According to some agents' magical mystery maps everywhere in the north is handy for the ski slopes or the Italian lakes and anywhere in the south is a stone's throw from a beach or airport.

When looking for a home, bear in mind travelling times and costs to your place of work, shops and local amenities (such as restaurants and bars!). If you buy a remote country property, the distance to local amenities and services could become a problem, particularly if you plan to retire to Italy. If you live in a remote rural area you will need to be much more self-sufficient than if you live in a town and you will need to use the car for everything, which will add significantly to the cost of living. **The cost of motoring is high in Italy and is an important consideration when buying a home there.**

If possible you should visit an area a number of times over a period of a few weeks, both on weekdays and at weekends, in order to get a feel for the neighbourhood (walk, don't just drive around!). A property seen on a balmy summer's day after a delicious lunch and a few glasses of *vino* may not be nearly so attractive on a subsequent visit *senza* sunshine and the warm inner glow. If possible, you should also visit an area at different times of the year, e.g. in both summer and winter, as somewhere that's wonderful in summer can be forbidding and inhospitable in winter. On the other hand, if you're planning to buy a winter holiday home, you should also view it in the summer, as snow can hide a multitude of sins! In any case, you should view a property a number of times before making up your mind to buy it. If you're unfamiliar with an area, most experts recommend that you rent for a period before deciding to buy (see **Renting** on page 113). This is particularly important if you're planning to buy a permanent or retirement home in an unfamiliar area. Many people change their minds after a period and it isn't unusual for families to move once or twice before settling down permanently.

If you will be working in Italy, obtain a map of the area and decide the maximum distance you wish to travel to work, e.g. by drawing a circle with your workplace in the middle. Obtain large scale maps of the area where you're looking, which may even show individual buildings, thus allowing you to mark the places that you've seen. You could do this using a grading system to denote your impressions. If you use an estate agent, he will usually drive you around and you can then return later to those that you like most at your leisure (providing that you've marked them on your map!).

There are many points to consider regarding the location of a home, which can roughly be divided into the local vicinity, i.e. the immediate surroundings and neighbourhood, and the general area or region. Take into account the present and future needs of all members of your family, including the following:

- For most people the climate (see page 48) is one of the most important factors when buying a home in Italy, particularly a holiday or retirement home. Bear in mind both the winter and summer climate, the position of the sun, the average daily sunshine, plus the rainfall and wind conditions. The orientation or aspect of a building is vital; if you want morning or afternoon sun (or both) you must ensure that balconies, terraces and gardens are facing the right direction.

• Check whether an area is particularly prone to natural disasters such as floods, storms or forest fires. If a property is located near a coast or waterway, it may be expensive to insure against floods, which are a constant threat in some areas. Note also that many areas of Italy are prone to earthquakes (see page 48). In areas with little rainfall, which includes most of Italy in summer, there are often severe water restrictions and high water bills.

• Noise can be a problem in some cities, resorts and developments. Although you cannot choose your neighbours, you can at least ensure that a property isn't located next to a busy road, railway line, airport, industrial plant, commercial area, discotheque, night club, bar or restaurant (where revelries may continue into the early hours). Look out for objectionable properties which may be too close to the one you're considering and check whether nearby vacant land has been 'zoned' for commercial activities or tower blocks. In community developments (e.g. apartment blocks) many properties are second homes and are let short term, which means you may have to tolerate boisterous holidaymakers as neighbours throughout the year (or at least during the summer months). In estate agents' speak, a popular (*popolare*) area may be cheap and run down, while a residential (*residenziale*) area is usually a pleasant, quiet residential area.

• Bear in mind that if you live in a popular tourist area you will be inundated with tourists in summer. They won't only jam the roads and pack the public transport, but may also occupy your favourite table at your local café or restaurant (heaven forbid!). Although a 'front-line' property on the beach or in a marina development may sound attractive and be ideal for short holidays, it isn't always the best choice for permanent residents. Many beaches are hopelessly crowded in the high season, streets may be smelly from restaurants and fast food joints, parking impossible, services stretched to breaking point, and the incessant noise may drive you crazy. Some people prefer to move inland or to higher ground, where it's less humid, more peaceful and you can enjoy panoramic views. On the other hand, getting to and from hillside properties is often precarious and the often poorly maintained roads (usually narrow and unguarded) are for sober, confident drivers only. Note also that many country roads are suited only to four-wheel-drive vehicles.

• Do you wish to live in an area with many of your fellow countrymen and other expatriates or as far away from them as possible? If you wish to integrate with the local community, avoid foreign 'ghettos' and choose an area or development with mainly local inhabitants. However, unless you speak fluent Italian or intend to learn, you should think twice before buying a property in a village. The locals in some villages resent 'outsiders' buying up prime properties, particularly holiday homeowners, although those who take the time and trouble to integrate into the local community are usually warmly welcomed. If you're buying a permanent home, it's important to check your prospective neighbours, particularly when buying an apartment. For example, are they noisy, sociable or absent for long periods? Do you think you will get on with them? **Good neighbours are invaluable, particularly when buying a second home.**

Do you wish to be in a town or do you prefer the country? Inland or on the coast? How about living on an island? Bear in mind that if you buy a property in the country, you will probably have to tolerate poor public transport (or none at all), long travelling distances to a town of any size, solitude and remoteness. You won't be able to pop along to the local *panetteria*, drop into the local bar for a glass of your favourite tipple with the locals or have a choice of restaurants on your doorstep. In a town or large village, the market will be just around the corner, the doctor and pharmacy close at hand, and if you need help or run into any problems, your neighbours will be close by.

In the country you will be closer to nature, will have more freedom (e.g. to make as much noise as you wish) and possibly complete privacy, e.g. to sunbathe or swim *au naturel*. Living in a remote area in the country will suit nature lovers looking for solitude who don't want to involve themselves in the 'hustle and bustle' of town life (not that there's much of this in Italian rural towns). If you're after peace and quiet, make sure that there isn't a busy road or railway line nearby or a local church within 'DONGING!' distance. Note, however, that many people who buy a remote country home find that the peace of the countryside palls after a time and they yearn for the more exciting city or coastal nightlife. If you have never lived in the country, it's advisable to rent first before buying. Note also that while it's cheaper to buy in a remote or unpopular location, it's usually much more difficult to find a buyer when you want to sell.

● If you're planning to buy a large country property with an extensive garden or plot of land, bear in mind the high cost and amount of work involved in its upkeep. If it's to be a second home, who will look after the house and garden when you're away? Do you want to spend your holidays mowing the lawn and cutting back the undergrowth? Do you want a home with a lot of outbuildings? What are you going to do with them? Can you afford to convert them into extra rooms or guest or self-catering accommodation?

● How secure is your job or business and are you likely to move to another area in the near future? Can you find other work in the same area, if necessary? If there's a possibility that you may need to move in a few years' time, you should rent or at least buy a property that will be relatively easy to sell and recoup the cost.

● What about your partner's and children's jobs or your children's present and future schooling? What is the quality of local schools? Even if your family has no need or plans to use local schools, the value of a home is often influenced by the their quality and location.

● What local health and social services are provided? How far is the nearest hospital with an emergency department?

● What shopping facilities are provided in the local neighbourhood? How far is it to the nearest sizeable town with good shopping facilities, e.g. a super/hypermarket? How would you get there if your car was out of commission? Note that many rural villages are dying and have few shops or facilities, and aren't necessarily a good choice for a retirement home.

- What is the range and quality of local leisure, sports, community and cultural facilities? What is the proximity to sports facilities such as a beach, golf course, ski resort or waterway? Bear in mind that properties in or close to ski and coastal resorts are usually considerably more expensive, although they also have the best letting potential. If you're interested in a winter holiday home, which area should you choose? While properties in the Alps are relatively expensive, they tend to appreciate faster than properties in many other areas and generally maintain their value in bad times.

- Is the proximity to public transport, e.g. an international airport, port or railway station, or access to an *autostrada* important? Don't, however, believe all you're told about the distance or travelling times to the nearest *autostrada*, airport, railway station, port, beach or town, but check for yourself.

- If you're planning to buy in a town or city, is there adequate private or free on-street parking for your family and visitors? Is it safe to park in the street? In some areas it's important to have secure off-street parking if you value your car. Parking is a problem in many towns and most cities, where private garages or parking spaces are rare and can be very expensive. Bear in mind that an apartment or townhouse in a town or community development may be some distance from the nearest road or car park. How do you feel about carrying heavy shopping hundreds of metres to your home and possibly up several flights of stairs? Traffic congestion is also a problem in many towns and tourist resorts, particularly during the high season.

- What is the local crime rate? In some areas, the incidence of housebreaking and burglary is extremely high. Due to the higher than average crime rate, home insurance is higher in major cities and some resort areas. Check the crime rate in the local area, e.g. burglaries, house breaking, stolen cars and crimes of violence. Is crime increasing or decreasing? Bear in mind that professional crooks like isolated houses, particularly those full of expensive furniture and other belongings, that they can strip bare at their leisure. You're much less likely to be a victim of theft if you live in a village, where crime is usually virtually unknown (strangers stand out like sore thumbs in villages, where their every move is monitored by the local populace).

- Do houses sell well in the area, e.g. in less than six months? Generally you should avoid neighbourhoods where desirable houses routinely remain on the market for six months or longer (unless the property market is in a severe slump and nothing is selling).

- A final consideration when choosing the location of your property is the likelihood of it being affected by radon. Radon is a naturally occurring radioactive gas formed underground by the radioactive decay of uranium, which is present in small quantities in rocks and soils and is particularly prevalent in some areas of Italy. For the majority of people the radiation dose received from radon isn't high enough to be a cause for concern and after surfacing in the open air it's quickly diluted to harmless concentrations. However, when it enters an enclosed space, such as a house, it can sometimes build up to potentially dangerous concentrations. The acceptable limit for radon concentration (known as the 'reference level') is 200 becquerels per cubic metre of air ($200Bq/m^3$). It has been shown that prolonged exposure to concentrations of radon above this level increases the chance of contracting lung cancer, and in a minority of homes and other buildings in Italy with very high radon levels there's a significant health risk for occupants. **You can have a test carried out to check the level of radon in a building or on a plot of land.**

RENTING

If you're uncertain about exactly what sort of home you want and where you wish to live, it's advisable to rent a property for a period in order to reduce the chances of making a costly error. Renting long-term before buying is particularly prudent for anyone planning to live in Italy permanently. If possible, you should rent a similar property to that which you're planning to buy, during the time of year when you intend to occupy it. Renting allows you to become familiar with the weather, the amenities and the local people; to meet other foreigners who have made their homes in Italy and share their experiences; and not least, to discover the cost of living for yourself. Providing you still find Italy alluring, renting 'buys' you time to find your dream home at your leisure. You may even wish to consider renting a home in Italy long-term (or 'permanently'), as it saves tying up your capital and can be surprisingly inexpensive in many regions. Some people let their family homes abroad and rent one in Italy for a period (you may even make a profit!).

Long-Term Unfurnished Rentals: Italy has a strong rental market and it's possible to rent every kind of property, from a tiny studio apartment (bedsitter) to a huge rambling *castello*. Most rental properties in Italy are let unfurnished (*non-ammobiliato*), particularly for lets longer than one year, and long-term furnished (*ammobiliato*) properties are difficult to find. If you're looking for a home for less than a year, then you're better off looking for a furnished apartment or house. Long-term contracts (*patti in deroga*) are usually for four years with an automatic renewal for a second four-year period. Owners must give notice (*disdetta*) to tenants in writing six months prior to the expiration of a lease (three months for annual contracts) in order to terminate a contract. Luxury apartments (*di lusso*), public housing and tourist apartments are exempt from four-year contracts and they don't affect contracts agreed before they came into force. Contracts for apartments must usually be approved by a tenants' and owners' association.

Rental costs vary considerably depending on the size (number of bedrooms) and quality of a property, its age and the facilities provided. However, the most significant factor affecting rents is the region of Italy, the city and the particular neighbourhood. Italy recently had a fair rent (*equo canone*) law that limited rents to those set by the local authorities rather than market levels. This resulted in a shortage of rental properties in some areas and owners are now permitted to set market level rents, which has encouraged more owners to rent their properties. Most rents are negotiable and you should try to obtain a reduction. Sometimes an agent will even suggest offering a reduced rent and will even tell you what to offer. Italian landlords (*padroni*) often prefer renting to non-residents foreigners, who pay higher rents and are easier to evict! Note that rent is tax deductible for residents. Long-term rents are roughly as follows:

Size of Property	Monthly Rental
Studio (bedsitter)	Lit. 500,000 to 1.5 million
1 bedroom	Lit. 750,000 to 2 million
2 bedrooms	Lit. 1 to 2.5 million
3 bedrooms	Lit. 1.5 to 3 million

The above rents are for unfurnished, good quality, new or renovated properties in most rural and suburban areas. They don't include properties in major city centres and popular resort areas (such as the Alps, Italian lakes and resorts), exclusive residential areas or furnished accommodation, for which the sky's the limit.

Short Term Furnished Rentals: Italy has an abundance of self-catering accommodation and the widest possible choice. You can choose from literally thousands of cottages, apartments, villas, bungalows, mobile homes, chalets, and even *castelli* and *palazzi*. Most property is available for short holiday lets only, particularly during the peak summer season, and little furnished property is let long-term. However, some foreign owners let their homes long-term, particularly outside the peak summer period. Note that when the rental period includes the peak letting months of July and August, the rent may be prohibitive. If you rent for a short period from an agent, you should negotiate a lower commission than the usual one month's rent, e.g. 10 per cent of the total rent payable. You can make agreements by fax when renting from abroad.

Standards vary considerably, from dilapidated ill-equipped cottages to luxury villas with every modern convenience. A typical holiday rental is a small cottage or self-contained apartment with one or two bedrooms (sleeping 4 to 8 and usually including a sofa bed in the living-room), a large living-room/kitchen with an open fire or stove, and a toilet and bathroom. Always check whether a property is fully equipped (which should mean whatever you want it to mean!) and whether it has central heating if you're planning to rent in winter.

For short-term lets the cost is calculated on a weekly basis (Saturday to Saturday) and depends on the standard, location, number of beds and the facilities provided. For holiday rentals, the year is generally split into three rental periods: low (October to April), mid (May and September) and peak (July and August). A rural property sleeping two costs from around Lit. 450,000 a week in the low season to Lit. 750,000 a week in the peak season, while a property sleeping four costs from Lit. 750,000 a week in the low season to Lit. 1.2 million in the high season. At the other end of the scale, you can easily pay Lit. 6 to 12 million a week for a farmhouse with a swimming pool in Tuscany in summer.

If you're looking for a rental property for say three to six months, it's best not to rent unseen, but to rent a holiday apartment for a week or two to allow yourself time to look around for a long-term rental. Properties for rent are advertised in Italian newspapers and magazines, including expatriate publications, and can also be found through property publications in many countries (see **Appendix A** for a list). Many real estate agents offer short-term rentals and builders and developers may also rent properties to potential buyers. Short-term rentals can be found through local tourist offices in Italy and the Italian State Tourist Offices abroad, travel agents, the Internet and many overseas newspapers. The best newspapers in the UK are the Sunday

Times, Sunday Telegraph and Observer, all of which contain holiday rental classifieds from British homeowners in Italy.

Note that rental laws and protection for tenants doesn't extend to holiday lettings, furnished lettings or sub-lettings. For holiday letting, the parties are free to agree such terms as they see fit concerning the period, rent, deposit and the number of occupants permitted, and there's no legal obligation for the landlord to provide a written agreement. However, you shouldn't rent a furnished property long-term without a written contract, which is imperative if you wish to get a deposit returned.

Hotels, etc. Hotel rates in Italy vary depending on the time of year, the exact location and the individual establishment, although you may be able to haggle over rates outside the high season and for long stays. In most rural towns, a single room costs from around Lit. 30,000 and double rooms from Lit. 50,000 per night. You should expect to pay at least double or treble these rates in a major city, where cheap hotels are often used as permanent accommodation. Hotels aren't a cost-effective solution for home hunters, although there's often little choice if you need accommodation for a short period only. Bed and breakfast accommodation is also available in Italy, although it isn't usually budget accommodation (see the books listed in **Appendix B**). For budget accommodation you need to choose a hostel or residence, which is similar to a hotel but contains self-catering apartments or studios. There are also apartment hotels, listed in yellow pages under *Residence e Appartamenti Ammobiliati*.

Home Exchange: An alternative to renting is to exchange your home abroad with one in Italy for a period. This way you can experience home living in Italy for a relatively small cost and may save yourself the expense of a long-term rental. Although there's an element of risk involved in exchanging your home with another family (depending on whether your swap is made in heaven or hell!), most agencies thoroughly vet clients and have a track record of successful swaps. There are home exchange agencies in most countries, many of which are members of the International Home Exchange Association (IHEA).

There are many home exchange companies in the USA including HomeLink International (16,500 members in around 50 countries), Box 650, Key West, FL 33041, USA (☎ 305-294 7766 or 800-638 3841). Two long-established home exchange companies in Britain are HomeLink International, Linfield House, Gorse Hill Road, Virginia Water, Surrey GU25 4AS, UK (☎ 01344-842642), who publish a Directory of homes and holiday homes for exchange, and Home Base Holidays, 7 Park Avenue, London N13 5PG, UK (☎ 0181-886 8752). In Italy there's Homelink International, Casa Vacanze, Via San Francesco 170, 35121 Padua and Intervac International Home Exchange, Via Oreglia 18, 40047 Riola (BO).

COST

Property prices in Italy rose considerably in the '80s in most areas, driven by the high demand for second homes from both foreigners and Italians. However, as the recession hit Italy in the late '80s and early '90s, property prices fell as buyers disappeared, although Italy didn't experience the dramatic falls that many other European countries and North America did. During the recession most Italians simply refused to accept the lower market prices and only sold if they were forced to do so. Foreign buyers in Italy also tend to be well-off middle class families or the very rich, who are cushioned to a large extent from economic downturns. Prices were also maintained by the cautious lending policies of Italian banks, which leads to fewer repossessions than in some other countries. The relative weakness of the lira against the sterling and $US in the last few years has also helped attract buyers, although this benefit will be lost when Italy converts to the Euro. On the plus side, mortgages are likely to be easier to find as foreign lenders enter the market. Nevertheless, there has been a sluggish property market in recent years and astute buyers can pick up a bargain.

Property prices in Italy generally rise slowly and steadily and are fairly stable, without the unpredictable swings experienced in some other countries. In rural areas where there's no strong local demand, prices are unlikely to rise or fall dramatically. As in most countries, property is at its cheapest in rural areas where the exodus in the last 30 years has left the countryside with a surfeit of empty properties. Italy is a buyers' market in most regions and there are still bargains to be found in many areas, although they are becoming scarcer. Property in Italy remains excellent value for money compared with many other countries, particularly rural properties with a large plot of land.

Property prices in Italy vary considerably and are generally high in cities and towns and relatively low in rural areas (except where high demand from foreign buyers has driven up prices). Prices were flat or fell in Italy's major cities during the recession, in contrast to the most popular areas for second homes where they remained stable or even appreciated. Although you can spend Lit. billions on a luxurious *palazzo* or a large country estate, it's also possible to buy a small one or two-bedroom apartment or a renovated village house from around Lit. 90 million. In many areas, old village houses in need of complete restoration can be purchased from as little as Lit. 30 to 45 million, although you should expect to pay two or even three times the purchase price in restoration costs. In many rural areas, Lit. 150 to 200 million will buy a restored two-bedroom farmhouse and a bit of land. However, you can easily pay over Lit. 600 million for a small farmhouse in a fashionable area of Tuscany or an apartment with a view on the Italian Riviera.

Among the most popular areas are the Italian lakes, which is reflected in the above average prices, e.g. Lit. 150 to 200 million for a new or restored one-bedroom apartment on Lake Como or Maggiore, and Lit. 200 to 300 million for a two-bedroom apartment. If you dream of living in Venice, a studio on the Grand Canal will set you back around Lit. 600 million (if you can find one)! Homes on the Italian Riviera are also highly prized and expensive, but a good investment. Here a studio apartment will set you back Lit. 150 million and a two-bedroom, sea-front apartment can easily cost Lit. 600 million or more. However, further inland, traditional unrestored village houses can be bought for as little as Lit. 60 million. Properties in ski resorts and on most islands are also expensive due to the shortage of building land and high demand, but are a good investment and have excellent rental potential. In a top ski resort such as Cortina, you will pay around Lit. 150 to 225 million for a studio, Lit. 225 to 300 million for a one-bedroom apartment and up to Lit. 450 million for a two-bedroom apartment. For those with somewhat smaller bank balances, holiday apartments in many coastal resorts and Sicily start at around Lit. 90 million.

Tuscany is one of the most popular (and expensive) regions for country homes among foreigners, particularly the so-called golden triangle bounded by Florence,

Siena and Volterra. So many Britons have purchased homes in Tuscany that the Chianti region has been dubbed 'Chiantishire' by expatriate Brits ('a corner of Italy that's forever England'). Much of Tuscany is too expensive and poor value for money, although it remains a good investment (providing you don't pay over the odds). However, in areas such as Lunigiana, Mugello, north of Lucca and around Arezzo, prices are around half those in the more expensive areas. If you're looking for a country property, you will find prices much more reasonable in Manche and Umbria, where property costs around a third to a half less than the most expensive areas of Tuscany and comes with up to ten times the amount of land.

The most expensive property of all is found in Italy's major cities, such as Milan and Rome, where a three-bedroom apartment can easily cost Lit. 600 million. Prime properties can cost up to Lit. 20 million a square metre in central Rome and Venice, and Lit. 10 to 15 million in other major cities and resort areas. However, property in most cities is typically around Lit. 2 million per square metre for old unrenovated properties and up to Lit. 6 million a square metre for new or renovated properties. In cities and towns, garages and external parking places are usually sold separately and may cost around Lit. 50 and 20 million respectively. Rural properties generally cost from Lit. 1 to 2 million a square metre. With the exception of properties within commuting distance of Rome and other major cities, the further south you go the cheaper rural property becomes.

Although there has been evidence of dual pricing in the past, the practice of quoting higher prices to foreigners is rare. The prices advertised abroad are invariably identical to those advertised in Italy. However, Italians drive a much harder bargain than most foreigners when buying a property, particularly an old property. They are often astonished at the prices foreign buyers are prepared to pay for nondescript homes in uninspiring areas, although they *never* complain about foreigners pushing up prices when they are on the receiving end! Many Italians think the British are particularly insane for buying up their tumbled down farmhouses and crumbling *castelli*. Few foreigners share the British passion for renovating old homes, although they have a grudging admiration for their painstaking and sensitive restorations.

To get an idea of property prices in different regions of Italy, check the prices of properties advertised in English-language property magazines and Italian newspapers, magazines and property journals (see **Appendix A**). Property price indexes for various regions are published by some Italian property magazines (e.g. *Ville & Casali*), although these should be taken as a rough guide only. **Before deciding on the price, make sure you know <u>exactly</u> what's included, as it isn't unusual for Italians to strip a house or apartment bare when selling and even remove the kitchen sink, toilets, light fittings and even the light switches!** If applicable, have fixtures and fittings listed in the contract.

Negotiating the Price

When buying a property in Italy it pays to barter over the price, even if you think it's a bargain – but don't show too much enthusiasm or it's likely to increase suddenly! Don't be put off by a high asking price as most sellers are willing to negotiate. In recent years many properties have sold for a lot less than their original asking prices, particularly luxury properties priced at over Lit. 500 million. Sellers generally presume buyers will bargain and rarely expect to receive the asking price, although some vendors ask an unrealistic price and won't budge one lira! In popular areas (e.g. the Italian Riviera and Tuscany), asking prices may be unrealistically high particularly to snare the unsuspecting and ignorant foreign buyer. It may be worthwhile obtaining an independent valuation (appraisal) to determine a property's market value.

If you're using an agent you should ask him what to offer, although he may not tell you (and indeed shouldn't if he's also acting for the seller). Note that if you make an offer that's too low you can always raise it, but it's usually impossible to lower an offer once it has been accepted (if your first offer is accepted without discussion, you will never know how low you could have gone). If an offer is rejected it may be worth waiting a week or two before making a higher offer, depending on the market and how keen you are to buy a particular property. If you make a low offer, it's advisable to indicate to the owner a few points of weakness (without being too critical) that merit a reduction in price. If you make a very low offer, an owner may feel insulted and refuse to do business with you! If a property has been realistically priced, you shouldn't expect to obtain more than a 5 or 10 per cent reduction, although cash buyers in some areas may be able to negotiate a considerable price reduction for a quick sale, depending on the state of the local property market and how urgent the sale. An offer should be made in writing, as it's likely to be taken more seriously than a verbal offer. **Always be prepared to walk away from a deal rather than pay too high a price.**

If you simply want to buy a property at the best possible price as an investment, then shopping around and buying a 'distress sale' from an owner who simply must sell is likely to result in the best deal. Obviously you will be in a better position if you're a cash buyer and are able to close quickly. Note, however, that if you're seeking an investment property, it's advisable to buy in an area that's in high demand, preferably with both buyers and renters. For the best resale opportunities it's usually best to buy in an area or community (and style) that's attractive to Italian buyers. You should find out as much as possible about a property before making an offer, such as when it was built; how long the owners have lived there; whether it's a permanent or holiday home; why they are selling (they may not tell you outright, but may offer clues); how keen they are to sell; how long it has been on the market; the condition of the property; the neighbours and neighbourhood; local property taxes and insurance rates; and not least, whether the asking price is realistic.

Timing is of the essence in the bargaining process and it's essential to find out how long a property has been on the market (generally the longer it has been for sale, the more likely a lower offer will be accepted) and how desperate the vendor is to sell. Some people will tell you outright that they must sell by a certain date and that they will accept any reasonable offer. You may be able to find out from neighbours why someone is selling, which may help you decide whether an offer would be accepted. If a property has been on the market for a long time, e.g. longer than six months in a popular area, it may be overpriced (unless it has obvious problems). If there are many desirable properties for sale in a particular area or development that have been on the market a long time, you should find out why. For your part you must ensure that you keep any sensitive information from a seller and give the impression that you have all the time in the world (even if you're desperate to buy immediately). All this 'cloak and dagger' stuff may seem unethical, but you can be assured that if you were selling and a prospective buyer knew you were desperate and would accept a low offer, he certainly wouldn't be in a hurry to pay you any more!

FEES

A variety of fees (also called closing or completion costs) are payable when you buy a property in Italy, which vary considerably depending on the price, whether you're buying via an agent or privately, and whether you have employed a lawyer or other professionals. Most property fees are based on the 'declared' value of a property, which is usually less than the actual purchase price or its 'market' value. The declared sale's figure must agree with the official value in the land registry (*catasto*), which is usually around 50 to 60 per cent of the purchase price. You should never be tempted to flagrantly under-declare the sale price in order to pay lower fees as it can have serious consequences if it's discovered.

The mandatory fees associated with buying a property in Italy are among the highest in Europe and include registration tax (*imposta di registro*), land registry and cadastral tax (*imposte ipotecarie e catastali*), the notary's (*notaio*) fees and real estate agent's fees. Fees are usually payable on the completion of a sale and range from around 8 to 15 per cent for an old property (with the average around 12 per cent), although they can be as high as 20 per cent for non-residents. This compares with just 3 per cent in the UK and 5 per cent in the USA! Value added tax (IVA) of 20 per cent is levied on all fees. Before signing a preliminary contract check exactly what fees are payable and have them confirmed in writing. The various fees and costs associated with a property purchase in Italy are shown below:

Registration tax (*imposta di registro*): Registration tax is the main tax on real property and is levied at 4 to 19 per cent of the declared value. The amount payable (on completion) depends on whether it's your first and only home or a second home, whether it's a new home and whether you're a resident. On your first home you're eligible for a reduced tax of 4 per cent plus a fixed Lit. 300,000 for mortgage and cadastral taxes. The property must be your principal home for residential use and be located in your present or future *comune* of residence (or in the *comune* where you have or plan to have your main place of business) and it mustn't be classified as a 'luxury' home. This concession is supposedly available once only, although this isn't always the case in practice. Registration tax is also 4 per cent on new properties purchased from a builder or developer.

The registration tax for non-residents buying second homes is 11 per cent, therefore if you're planning to become a resident in Italy it will pay to do so before buying a home there. If you're buying an agricultural property it may be possible to have it 'derauralised' (*deruralizzato*) before the sale, thus reducing the tax payable from 18 to 11 per cent (or to 4 per cent for a resident), although agricultural land is still taxed at 18 per cent. When a property comprises both an urban building and agricultural land, a notional contract is calculated separately for the building and the land. Registration tax rates are shown below:

Tax Rate	Description	+ Fixed Fee
4%	New property or property purchased during construction and first-time resident buyers.	Lit. 300,000
4%	Resale homes purchased by residents.	Lit. 200,000
11%	Second homes.	None
18%	Agricultural property or farming land.	None
19%	Luxury homes, commercial property or land zoned as 'commercial'.	Lit. 300,000

VAT: Value added tax (IVA) is levied at 10 per cent on new, non-luxury properties and at 20 per cent on luxury homes (with a rating of A1 in the property register), and is included in the price by the builder or developer. If you build your own home you pay a reduced rate of IVA at 4 per cent, although if you buy from a company or entity you must pay VAT at 20 per cent.

Notary's Fees: The notary's (*notaio*) fees are usually between 2 and 4 per cent of the cost of a property, with a minimum fee of Lit. 2 million. Notary fees depend on the price of a property and are higher (as a percentage of the price) on cheaper properties. There's also a fee for each page and each copy of a contract, plus fees for extra services such as taxes (e.g. tax stamps), expenses, legal advice and any payments made on your behalf. Notary's fees vary, although there are minimum and maximum fees for each service, e.g. if you buy or sell a property for Lit. 200 million the minimum basic fee is around Lit. 3.3 million and the maximum Lit. 4 million. You can obtain an estimate in writing, although the fees will vary depending on the actual work involved. All fees are itemised in the notary's bill (*parcella*), which will also contain a surcharge (*rimborso delle spese generali di studio*) for 'overheads' that's levied by all professionals in Italy.

Selling Agent's Commission: Real estate agents' fees (see page 159) in Italy vary considerably (e.g. from 3 to 8 per cent) and are usually shared between the vendor and buyer, e.g. a buyer may pay 3 per cent of the purchase price and the vendor about the same. Some agents levy a fixed fees, e.g. Lit. 4 million on properties costing up to Lit. 80 million, a maximum of Lit. 15 million on properties costing up to Lit. 500 million and 3 per cent on properties over Lit. 500 million. Note that fees may be payable when the preliminary sales contract is signed and not on completion! Before signing a purchase contract, check the agent's fees.

Conveyancing: The fees for conveyancing, which is usually performed by a *geometra* (surveyor) in Italy, is usually around 2 per cent of the declared price of a property or between Lit. 500,000 and 2,500,000, depending on the amount of work involved.

Mortgage Fees: Mortgage fees may include a commitment fee, an arrangement fee, an administration fee (e.g. 1 per cent), and an appraisal or valuation fee. There's also a fee payable to the notary for registration of the mortgage at the land registry (*catasto*).

Miscellaneous Fees: Other fees may include legal fees, surveyor's or inspection fees (e.g. between Lit. 400,000 and 900,000 depending on the work involved), architect's fees, utility connection and registration fees, and the cost of moving house.

Running Costs: In addition to the fees associated with buying a property, you must also take into account the running costs. These may include local property taxes (rates); buildings insurance (required by a lender); contents insurance (see page 58); standing charges for utilities (electricity, gas, telephone, water); community fees for a community property (see page 153); garbage tax (*tassa communale dei rifiuti*), garden and pool maintenance; and a caretaker's or management fees if you leave a home empty or let it. Annual running costs usually average around 2 to 3 per cent of the cost of a property. When you buy a home in Italy you should go to the town hall (*municipio*) to register your ownership, after which all bills for local services will be sent automatically.

If you're a resident, the fees associated with buying a property in Italy can be offset against income tax.

BUYING A NEW HOME

Italy's wealth of stunning historic architecture sadly isn't reflected in many of its modern buildings, particularly apartment blocks, although at its best Italy's modern home design is among the most beautiful and innovative in the world. Although new properties may lack the charm and character of older buildings, they offer attractive financial and other advantages. There are no costs or problems associated with renovation or modernisation and they are cheaper to heat and maintain due to the modern building methods and materials employed. It's often cheaper to buy a new home than restore a derelict property as the price is fixed, unlike the cost of renovation which can soar way beyond original estimates (as many people have discovered to their cost!). If required, a new property can usually be let immediately and modern homes have good resale potential and are considered a good investment by Italian buyers. On the other hand, new homes are usually smaller than old properties and rarely come with a large plot of land.

The standard of new buildings in Italy is strictly regulated (with the exception of illegally built homes!) and houses are built to official quality standards. They are built to higher specifications than old houses and usually include good insulation, double glazing, cavity and under-floor insulation, central heating, and a ventilation and dehumidifying system. Most new buildings use low maintenance materials and must have good insulation and ventilation, providing lower heating bills and keeping homes cooler in summer. New properties are covered by a 10-year warranty (*responsibilità della ditta*) against structural defects, and systems and equipment are also guaranteed for a limited period.

A huge variety of new properties are available in Italy including coastal and city apartments, sports developments (e.g. skiing or golf), and a wide range of individually designed detached houses. Many new properties are part of purpose-built developments, often located near the coast or in the mountains, and offer a range of sports facilities which may include a golf course, swimming pool, tennis and squash courts, a gymnasium or fitness club and a restaurant. Note, however, that many purpose-built developments are planned as holiday homes and may not be attractive as permanent homes (they are also generally expensive). If you're buying an apartment or a house that's part of a development, check whether your neighbours will be mainly Italian or other foreigners. Some people don't wish to live in a *comune* of their fellow countrymen and this will also deter Italian buyers when you want to sell. Prices of new properties vary considerably depending on their location and quality, from around Lit. 90 million for a studio or one-bedroom apartment in a resort, Lit. 120 to 150 million for a two-bedroom cottage or townhouse, and from around Lit. 180 million for a four-bedroom house. The cost of land is usually extra when buying a detached house on its own plot.

Most new properties are sold by property developers (*construttore*) or builders, although they are also marketed by estate agents. Note, however, that unlike many other countries, developers and builders aren't required to be underwritten by a bank, therefore it's possible for buyers to lose their money or end up with an unfinished property. It's possible to check a developer's or builder's financial status, although your best insurance when buying a new property is the reputation of the developer or builder. New developments have a sales office and may have a show house or apartment.

When buying a new property in a development, you're usually obliged to buy it off-plan (*acquistare su carta*), i.e. before it's built. In fact, if a development is built and largely unsold, particularly a quality development in a popular area, it usually means that there's something wrong with it! The contract contains the timetable for the property's completion; payment dates; the completion date and penalties for non-completion; guarantees for building work; and a copy of the plans and drawings. The floor plan and technical specifications are signed by both parties to ensure that the standard and size of construction is adhered to. Payments are spread over 12 to 18 months, although the actual payment schedule can vary considerably. A typical payment schedule may consist of a 20 per cent deposit; 20 per cent on completion of the roof; 20 per cent on tiling the bathroom and kitchen (or when the doors and window frames are installed); 20 per cent when the building is complete; 10 per cent when the exterior work is completed (such as the patio, pool and landscaping); with the remaining 10 per cent being withheld for a period (e.g. six months) as an insurance against defects. If a property is already partly built, the builder may ask for a higher initial payment, depending on its stage of completion.

If you're buying a property off-plan, you can usually choose your bathroom suite, kitchen, fireplace, wallpaper and paint, wall and floor tiles, and carpet in bedrooms, some of which may be included in the price. You may also be able to alter the interior room layout, although this will increase the price. Note, however, that new homes in Italy don't usually contain a high level of 'luxury' features, such as are common in many other countries. Some developers will negotiate over the price or include extras free of charge (such as a fitted kitchen when it isn't included in the price), particularly if a development isn't selling well. Note that it's advisable to make any changes or additions to a property during the design stage, such as including a chimney or additional shower room, which will cost much more to install later.

If you want to be far from the madding crowd, you can buy a plot of land (see **Buying Land** below) and have a house built to your own design or to a standard design provided by an Italian builder. Builders may also have a selection of building plots for sale. Although Italian builders have a range of standard designs, they will accommodate almost any interior or exterior variations (for a price), providing they are permitted under local building laws. If you decide to build your own home, you must ensure that the proposed size and style of house is legal by checking with the local town hall. Don't rely on the builder or developer to do it for you, but check yourself or have your architect or surveyor do it for you. If a mistake is made a building may need to be demolished!

Resale Homes: Buying new doesn't always mean buying a brand new home where you're the first occupant. There are many advantages in buying a modern resale home which may include better value for money; an established development with a range of local services and facilities in place; more individual design and style (than an old home); the eradication of 'teething troubles'; furniture and other extras included in the price; a mature garden and trees; and a larger plot of land. With a resale property you can see exactly what you will get for your money (unlike when buying off-plan), most problems will have been resolved, and the previous owners may have made improvements or added extras such as an extension or swimming pool, which may not be fully reflected in the asking price. The disadvantages of buying a resale home depend on its age and how well it has been maintained. They may include a poor state of repair and the need for refurbishment; few benefits of a brand new home unless it has been modernised; the need for redecorating and new carpets; poorer build quality and inferior design; no warranty; termite or other infestations; and the possibility of incurring high assessments for repairs in community properties.

Buying Land

You must take the same care when buying land as you would when buying a home. The most important point when buying land is to ensure that it has been approved for building and that the plot is large enough and suitable for the house you plan to build. When a plot of land has planning permission, the maximum size of building (in square metres) that can be built is usually stated and depends on the density permitted by the local *comune* and possible also the province or region. If you buy land from an agent, it will usually already have planning permission, but if it doesn't it should be made a condition of purchase. Some plots are unsuitable for building as they are too steep or require prohibitively expensive foundations. Also check that there aren't any restrictions such as high-tension electricity lines, water pipes or rights of way that may restrict building. Note also that the cost of providing services to a property in a remote rural area may be prohibitively expensive and it must have a reliable water supply. Always obtain confirmation in writing from the local town hall that land can be built on and has been approved for road access.

Most builders offer package deals which include the land and the cost of building your home. However, it isn't always advisable to buy the building plot from the builder who's going to build your home, and you should shop around and compare separate land and building costs. If you do decide to buy a package deal from a builder, you *must* insist on separate contracts for the land and the building, and obtain the title deed for the land before signing a building contract. Obtain a receipt showing that the plot is correctly presented in the local property register and check for yourself that the correct planning permission has been obtained (don't simply leave it to the builder). If planning permission is flawed you may need to pay extra to improve the local infrastructure or the property may even have to be demolished! Note that it can take a long time to obtain planning permission in Italy.

BUYING AN OLD HOME

In Italy, the term 'old home' usually refers to a building that's pre-war and possibly hundreds of years old, that's either in need of restoration and modernisation or which has already been restored. If you want a property with abundant charm and character; a building for renovation or conversion; outbuildings or a large plot of land; then you must usually buy an old property. Italy has a wealth of beautiful historic buildings, particularly 17th to 19th century buildings, and is an architectural treasure house. When buying an old building you're buying a place of history, a piece of cultural heritage, and a unique building that represents the architects' and artisans' skills of a bygone age. Old homes in Italy cover the whole spectrum from village houses to *castelli*, farmhouses to mansions, *palazzi* to medieval towers. Note, however, that if an old building is listed (preserved) there may be limitations on its use and future sale.

In many rural areas it's still possible to buy old properties for as little as Lit. 60 million, although you will need to carry out major renovation work, which will double or treble the price. It costs Lit. 1 to 2 million per square metre to totally restore an old house, depending on the region and the quality of the workmanship and materials. Because the purchase price is often low, many foreign buyers are lulled into a false sense of security and believe they are getting a wonderful bargain, without fully investigating the renovation costs. **Bear in mind that renovation or modernisation costs will invariably be higher than you imagined or planned!** Although property is cheaper in Italy than in many other western European countries, most of the cheaper rural homes require complete renovation and modernisation. Some even lack basic services such as electricity, a reliable water supply and sanitation. If you're planning to buy a property that needs restoration or renovation, get an *accurate* estimate of the costs *before* signing a contract.

It isn't usually cheaper to buy and restore an old building than buy a new one and it can be much more expensive. However, old properties may provide better value than new homes, although you must check their quality and condition carefully. As with most things in life, you generally get what you pay for, so you shouldn't expect a fully restored property for Lit. 60 million. At the other end of the scale, for those who can afford them there's a wealth of beautiful *castelli*, *palazzi* and mansions, many costing no more than an average four-bedroom house in other countries. However, if you aspire to live the life of the landed gentry in your own *castello*, bear in mind that the reason they often seem such good value for money is that the cost of restoration and maintenance is *astronomical*. For this reason, many larger buildings such as *palazzi* and large farmhouses have been converted into luxury apartments.

Don't buy a derelict property unless you have the courage, determination and money to overcome the many problems you will certainly face. **Taking on too large a task in terms of restoration is a common mistake among foreign buyers in all price ranges.** Unless you're prepared to wait until you can occupy it or are willing to live in a caravan for a long time while you work on it, it's best to spend a bit more and buy something habitable but untidy, rather than a property that needs completely gutting before you can live in it. Note that although many old rural properties are described as *habitable*, this word should immediately set the alarm bells ringing as it has an infinite number of interpretations. The *Concise Oxford Dictionary* ventures 'that can be inhabited', which doesn't help much (a field can be inhabited if you have a tent). In Italian habitable can mean anything from derelict and unfit for pigs to something that only needs redecorating. When a property is described as habitable you should be prepared to ask a lot of questions and should ensure that it means exactly what you need it to mean.

Bear in mind that if you buy and restore a property with the intention of selling it for a profit, you must take into account not only the initial price and the restoration costs, but also the fees and taxes associated with its purchase. If you aren't into do-it-yourself in a big way, you're usually better off buying a property that has already been partly or wholly restored. This often works out cheaper in the long term as the cost of restoration (to say nothing of the sweat and toil) is rarely fully reflected in the sale price. If you need to pay for the whole cost of restoration it can be prohibitively expensive (see **Renovation & Restoration** on page 171). It's often difficult to sell an old renovated property at a higher than average market price, irrespective of its added value. Italians have little interest in old restored properties, which is an important point if you need to sell an old home in a hurry in an area that isn't popular with foreign buyers. If you want to make a profit you may be better off buying a new home.

COMMUNITY PROPERTIES

In Italy, properties with common elements (whether a building, amenities or land) shared with other properties are owned outright through a system of co-ownership, similar to owning a condominium in the USA. Community property (called a *condominio*) includes apartments, townhouses, and detached (single-family) homes on a private estate with communal areas and facilities. Almost all properties that are part of a development are community properties. In general, the only properties that don't belong to a community are detached houses built on individual plots in public streets or on rural land. Owners of community properties not only own their homes, but also own a share of the common elements of a building or development including foyers, hallways, passages, lifts, patios, gardens, roads, and leisure and sports facilities (such as swimming pools and tennis courts). When you buy a community property you automatically become a member of the community of owners.

Over half of all Italians live in apartments, which are common in cities and resorts (or anywhere building land is limited). Many community developments are located near coastal or mountain resorts and may offer a wide range of communal facilities including a golf course, swimming pools, tennis courts, a gymnasium or fitness club, and a restaurant. Most also have landscaped gardens, high security and a full-time caretaker (*custode*), and some even have their own 'village' and shops. At the other extreme, some developments consist of numerous cramped, tiny studio apartments. Note that community developments planned as holiday homes may not be attractive as permanent homes.

Advantages: The advantages of owning a community property include increased security; lower property taxes than detached homes; a range of community sports and leisure facilities; community living with lots of social contacts and the companionship of close neighbours; no garden, lawn or pool maintenance; fewer of the responsibilities of home ownership; ease of maintenance; and properties are often situated in locations where owning a detached home would be prohibitively expensive, e.g. a beach-front or town centre.

Disadvantages: The disadvantages of community properties may include excessively high community fees (owners may have no control over increases); restrictive rules and regulations; a confining living and social environment and possible lack of privacy; noisy neighbours (particularly if neighbouring apartments are rented to holiday-makers); limited living and storage space; expensive covered or secure parking (or no secure parking); and acrimonious owners' meetings, where management and factions may try to push through unpopular proposals (sometimes using proxy votes).

Before buying a *condominio* property it's advisable to ask the owners about the community. For example, do they like living there, what are the fees and restrictions, how noisy are other residents (Italians can be *very* noisy), are the recreational facilities easy to access, would they buy there again (why or why not), and, most importantly, is the community well managed. You may also wish to check on your prospective neighbours. An apartment that has other apartments above and below it is generally more noisy than a ground or top floor apartment. If you're planning to buy an apartment above the ground floor, you may wish to ensure that the building has a lift. The ground or garden level along with the penthouse *(attico, mansarda)* are more prone to thefts and an insurance company will insist that openings such as skylights, doors, and windows are protected with grilles or bars before they will insure a property. Note that upper floor apartments are both colder in winter and warmer in summer, and incur extra charges for the use of lifts. Under-roof apartments may also have temperature control problems (hot in summer, cold in winter), although they enjoy better views. Heating in new properties is usually independent and controlled by owners, but in older properties it's usually controlled by the *condominio* and switched on in October and off in the spring (irrespective of the outside temperature), which may result in higher heating bills.

Cost: Prices vary considerably depending on the location, for example from around Lit. 90 million for a studio or one-bedroom apartment in an average location to a billion lire or more for a luxury apartment or townhouse in a prime location. Generally the higher the floor the more expensive an apartment is (unless it's number 17, considered by many Italians to be an unlucky number), as it will have more light, less road noise, a better view (fewer obstructions) and be more secure. Garages and parking spaces must often be purchased separately in developments, with a lock-up garage usually costing Lit. 50 million or more and a parking space around Lit. 20 million. If you're buying a resale property, check the price paid for similar properties in the same area or development in recent months, but bear in mind that the price you pay may have more to do with the seller's circumstances than the price fetched by other properties. Find out how many properties are for sale in a particular development; if there are many on offer you should investigate why as there could be management or structural problems. If you're still keen to buy you can use any negative aspects to drive a hard bargain.

Management: The management and co-ownership of a *condominio* building is regulated by Italian law and the rules and regulations (*regolamento di condominio*) are contained in a document, a copy of which you should receive. If you don't understand it you should have it explained or get it translated. An apartment block containing five or more apartments must employ an administrator (*amministratore di condominio*), who's elected by the owners to manage the property on their behalf. He's responsible for the management, efficient daily running and the apportioning of charges (*spese*) relating to the building, e.g. insurance, repairs and maintenance. The administrator bills individual owners for service charges and management fees. A residents' meeting (*riunione di condominio* or *assemblea condominiale*) must be held at least once a year to approve the budget and discuss other matters of importance, such as capital expenditure and, if necessary, appoint a new administrator. Owners must be given at least seven days notice of a meeting and all decisions are made by a majority vote (a quorum of 51 per cent of owners is necessary). If you're unable to attend you should give someone a proxy to vote for you. Non-residents can give someone in Italy (such as a *commercialistà*) a 'permanent' proxy and have all communications sent to him.

Condominium Fees: Owners must pay service charges (*spese del condominio*) for the upkeep of communal areas and for communal services. Charges are calculated according to each owner's share of the development and not whether they are temporary or permanent residents. The proportion (*unità immobiliare*) of the common elements (*l'ente condominiale*) assigned to each apartment owner depends on the number and size of apartments (and balconies) in the block. It's expressed in fractions of thousandths (*millesimi*), e.g. ten apartments in a block of the same size would each own 100/1,000ths of the common elements. The size of your apartment also governs the proportion of the community fees (*conto consultivo*) you pay. Ground floor owners don't usually pay for lifts and the amount that other owners pay depends on the floor (those on the top floors pay the most because they use the lifts most).

General charges include such services as a caretaker, upkeep of the garden and surrounds, swimming pool maintenance and refuse collection. In addition to general charges, there may also be special charges for collective services and common equipment such as lifts, central heating and hot water, which may be divided according to the share of the utility allocated to each apartment. An apartment block in a city with a resident concierge will have much higher community fees than one without (nevertheless, it's preferable to buy in a block with a concierge). Fees vary considerably from around Lit. 500,000 a year for a modest two bedroom apartment up to Lit. 2 million or more for a luxury development with a range of services and amenities such as a clubhouse, porter, swimming pool and tennis courts. However, high fees aren't necessarily a negative point (assuming you can afford them), providing you receive value for money and the community is well managed and maintained. The value of a community property depends to a large extent on how well it's maintained and managed. Some *condominio* expenses are tax deductible if you're a resident.

Always check the level of general and special charges before buying an apartment. Service charges are usually billed quarterly or half-yearly in advance (but can also be in arrears) and the amount paid is adjusted at the end of the year (which can be a nasty shock) when the annual accounts have been approved. If you're buying a resale apartment, ask to see a copy of the accounts and bills for previous years and the minutes of the last annual general meeting, as owners may be 'economical with the truth' when stating service charges, particularly if they are high.

Maintenance & Repairs: If necessary, owners can be assessed an additional amount to make up any shortfall of funds for maintenance or repairs. You should check the condition of the common areas (including all amenities) in an old development and whether any major maintenance or capital expense is planned for which you could be assessed. Beware of bargain apartments in buildings requiring a lot of maintenance work or refurbishment. Note, however, that under Italian law, disclosure of impending expenditure must be made to prospective buyers before they sign a contract. Owners' meetings can become rather heated when finances are discussed, particularly when assessments are being made to finance capital expenditure.

Restrictions: The rules and regulations governing a *condominio* development allow owners to run their community in accordance with the wishes of the majority, while at the same time safeguarding the rights of the minority. Rules usually include such things as noise levels; the keeping of pets (usually permitted); renting; exterior decoration and plants (e.g. the placement of shrubs); garbage disposal; the use of swimming pools and other recreational facilities; parking; business or professional use; and the hanging of laundry. Permanent residents should avoid buying in a development with a high percentage of rental units, i.e. units that aren't owner-occupied. Check the regulations and discuss any restrictions with residents.

Holiday Apartments: If you're buying a holiday apartment that will be vacant for long periods (particularly in winter), don't buy in an apartment block where heating and/or hot water charges are shared, otherwise you will be paying towards your co-owners' heating and hot water bills. You should also check whether there are any rules regarding short or long-term rentals, or leaving a property unoccupied for any length of time. Note that when buying in a large development, communal facilities may be inundated during peak periods, e.g. a large swimming pool won't look so big when 100 people are using it and getting a game of tennis or using a fitness room may be difficult.

TIMESHARE & PART-OWNERSHIP SCHEMES

If you're looking for a holiday home, you may wish to investigate a scheme that provides sole occupancy of a property for a number of weeks each year. These include co-ownership, leaseback, timesharing and a holiday property bond. Don't rush into any of these schemes without fully researching the market and before you're absolutely clear what you want and what you can realistically expect to get for your money.

Co-Ownership: Co-Ownership includes schemes such as a consortium of buyers owning shares in a property-owning company and co-ownership between family, friends or even strangers. Some developers offer a turn-key deal whereby a home is sold fully furnished and equipped. Co-ownership allows you to recoup your investment in savings on holiday costs and still retain your equity in the property. A common deal is a 'four-owner' scheme (which many consider to be the optimum number of co-owners), where you buy a quarter of a property and can occupy it for up to three months a year. However, there's no reason why there cannot be as many as 12 co-owners with a month's occupancy each per year (usually shared between high, medium and low seasons).

Co-ownership provides access to a size and quality of property that would otherwise be unimaginable, and it's even possible to have a share in a substantial *castello* or *palazzo*, where a number of families could live together simultaneously and hardly ever see each other if they didn't want to. Co-ownership can be a good choice for a family seeking a holiday home for a few weeks or months a year and has the added advantage that (because of the lower cost) a mortgage may be unnecessary. Note that it's cheaper to buy a property privately with friends than through a developer, when you may pay well above the market price for a share of a property (check the market value of a property to establish whether it's good value). **Co-ownership is much better value than a timeshare and needn't cost a lot more.** Note, however, that a water-tight contract must be drawn up by an experienced lawyer to protect the co-owners' interests.

One of the best ways to get into co-ownership (if you can afford it) is to buy a house yourself and offer shares to others. This overcomes the problem of getting together a consortium of would-be owners and trying to agree on a purchase in advance, which is difficult unless it's just a few friends or family members. Many people form an Italian company to buy and manage the property, which can in turn be owned by a company in the co-owners' home country, thus allowing disputes to be dealt with under local law. Each co-owner receives a number of shares according to how much he has paid, entitling him to so many weeks occupancy a year. Owners don't need to have equal shares and can all be made direct title holders. If a co-owner wishes to sell his shares, he must usually give first refusal to other co-owners. However, if they don't wish to buy them and a new co-owner cannot be found, the property must be sold (although unlikely).

Leaseback: Leaseback or sale-and-leaseback schemes are designed for those seeking a holiday home for a limited number of weeks each year. Properties sold under a leaseback scheme are located in popular resort areas, e.g. golf, ski or coastal resorts, where self-catering accommodation is in high demand. Buying a property through a leaseback scheme allows a purchaser to buy a new property at less than its true cost, e.g. 30 per cent less than the list price. In return for the discount, the property must be leased back to the developer, e.g. for around ten years, so that he can let it as self-catering holiday accommodation. The buyer owns the freehold of the property and the full price is shown in the title deed. The purchaser is also given the right to occupy the property for a period each year, usually six or eight weeks, spread over high, medium and low seasons. These weeks can usually be let to provide income or possibly even exchanged with accommodation in another resort (as with a timeshare scheme). The developer furnishes and manages the property and pays all the maintenance and bills (e.g. for utilities) during the term of the lease, even when the owner is in occupation. **Note that it's important to have a contract checked by your lawyer to ensure that you receive vacant possession at the end of the leaseback period, without having to pay an indemnity charge, otherwise you could end up paying more than a property is worth.**

Timesharing: Timesharing (*multiproprietà*), where you purchase the right to occupy a property at designated times, isn't as popular in Italy as in some other countries, notably Spain and the USA. The best timeshare developments are on a par with luxury hotels and offer a wide range of facilities including bars, restaurants, entertainment, shops, swimming pools, tennis courts, health clubs, and other leisure and sports facilities. If you don't wish to take a holiday in the same place each year, choose a timeshare development that's a member of an international organisation such as Resort Condominium International (RCI) or Interval International (II), which allows you (usually for a fee) to exchange your timeshare with one in another area or country. The highest rated RCI timeshares are classified as Gold Crown Resorts and allow you to exchange with any timeshare anywhere in the world (RCI has over 2,000 member resorts in some 70 countries).

Timesharing (also called 'holiday ownership', 'vacation ownership' and 'holidays for life') has earned a poor reputation in the last few decades, although things are slowly improving. In recent years the Organisation for Timeshare in Europe (OTE) has been trying to restore respectability to timesharing and its members (which include Italy) are bound by a code of conduct. This includes a requirement that buyers have secure occupancy rights and that their money is properly protected prior to the completion of a new property. Since April 1997, an EU Directive has required timeshare companies to disclose information about the vendor and the property, and allow prospective buyers a 'cooling off period' during which they may cancel any sales agreement they have signed without penalty. However, although the directive technically binds timeshare companies, if they flout it you'll need to seek redress in a court of law, which may not be something you want (or can afford) to do!

Italy isn't plagued by the timeshare touts common is some other countries such as Spain. However, you may be 'invited' to a presentation in a popular resort and should know what to expect. If you're tempted to attend a sales pitch (usually lasting at least two hours), you should be aware that you may be subjected to some of the most persuasive, high-pressure sales methods employed anywhere on earth and many people are simply unable to resist (the sales staff are experts). If you do attend, don't take any cash, credit cards or cheque books with you so that you won't be pressured into paying a deposit without thinking it over. Although it's illegal for a timeshare company to accept a deposit during the 10-day cooling-off period, many companies will try to get you to pay one. Don't rely on being able to get your money back if you pay by credit card. If you pay a deposit your chances of getting it back are slim and if it's repaid, it's likely to take a long time. Bear in mind that of those who agree to buy a timeshare, around half cancel within the cooling-off period.

A personal guarantee must be provided by a timeshare company that the property is as advertised and, where applicable, the contract must be in the language of the EU country where the buyer is resident or the language of the buyer's choice (you cannot sign away any of your rights irrespective of what's written in the contract). If you're an EU citizen and get into a dispute, you can take legal action in your home country for a sale made in Italy. There are so many scams associated with timeshares that it would take a dedicated book to recount them all (and you would need to update it every few months!). An added problem is that timeshare companies occasionally go bust, as one did in Italy in 1997 with losses of Lit. 60 billion leaving some 8,500 owners with nothing to show for their money. **Suffice to say that many people bitterly regret the day they signed up for a timeshare!**

It isn't difficult to understand why there are so many timeshare companies and why salespersons often employ such intimidating, hard-sell methods. A week's timeshare in an apartment worth around Lit. 150 million can be sold for Lit. 15 million or more, making a total income of some Lit. 750 million for the timeshare company if they sell 50 weeks (at least five times the market value of the property!), plus management and other fees. **Most experts believe that there's little or no advantage in a timeshare over a normal holiday rental and that it's simply an expensive way to pay for your holidays in advance.** It doesn't make any sense to tie up your money for what amounts to a long-term reservation on an annual holiday. Top-quality timeshares usually cost around Lit. 15 million or more for one week in a one or two-bedroom apartment in a top-rated resort at a peak period, to which must be added annual management fees, e.g. Lit. 300,000 to 450,000 or more for each week, plus other miscellaneous charges. Timeshare owners can also be hit by hefty levies which can run into millions of lire per owner.

Most financial advisers believe that you're better off putting your money into a long-term investment, where you retain your capital and may even earn sufficient interest to pay for a few weeks holiday each year. If you wish to buy a timeshare, it's best to buy a resale privately from an existing owner or a timeshare resale broker, which sell for a fraction of their original cost. When buying privately you can usually drive a hard bargain and may even get a timeshare 'free' simply by assuming the current owner's maintenance contract.

Often timeshares are difficult or impossible to sell at any price and 'pledges' from timeshare companies to sell them for you or buy them back at the market price are usually just a sales ploy, as timeshare companies aren't interested once they have made a sale. **Note that there's no real resale market for timeshares and if you need to sell you're highly unlikely to get your money back.** Further information about timesharing can be obtained from the Timeshare Council (☎ UK 0171-821 8845) and the Timeshare Helpline (☎ UK 0181-296 0900) in Britain. The Timeshare Consumers Association (Hodsock, Worksop, Notts, S81 0TF, UK, ☎ 01909-591100, e-mail: tca@netcomuk.co.uk) publish a useful booklet entitled *Timeshare: Guide to Buying, Owning and Selling*.

A **Holiday Property Bond** is a good alternative to timesharing for those with a minimum of around GB£2,000 to invest. Holiday Property Bond (operated by Villa Owners Club Ltd., HPB House, Newmarket, Suffolk CB8 8EH, UK, ☎ 01638-660066) owns over 600 properties in some ten countries, including Italy. Each GB£1 invested is equal to one point and each week's stay in each property is assigned a points rating depending on its size, location and the time of year. There are no extra fees apart from a 'user' charge when occupying a property to cover cleaning and utility costs. Furthermore, there's a buy-back guarantee after two years, when an investment can be sold at the market value.

REAL ESTATE AGENTS

Unlike some other countries, where most property sales are handled by real estate agents (*agenzie immobiliari*), a large percentage of sales in Italy are private (directly between vendors and buyers) in order to avoid agent's fees. However, you will need to speak good Italian to buy privately or alternatively will need to use an Italian intermediary who speaks English or your mother tongue. Nationwide real estate chains in Italy include Grimaldi and Tecnocasa (who publish a monthly property magazine), which operate on a franchise basis and include some 500 agents (mostly in northern Italy and the Rome area). Bear in mind that most Italian agents are purely local and they don't have a nationwide listing of properties in other regions. If you wish to find an agent in a particular town or area, look under estate agents (*Agenzie Immobiliare*) in the local Italian yellow pages (available at main libraries in many countries). In Rome and Milan there are real estate 'exchanges' where you can buy and sell properties through agents. Buyers can list their details (name and telephone number and the type of property they are looking for or selling) which are accessed by real estate agents.

Where foreign buyers are concerned the vast majority of sales are made through agents. It's common for foreigners in many countries, particularly Britain, to use an agent in their own country who works with one or more Italian agents, or a British agent located in Italy. Italian agents aren't noted for their efficiency and you may receive a better service from a British or other foreign agent who speaks English and is used to dealing with foreigners and their particular requirements (such as old rural properties requiring renovation). On the downside, you may pay higher fees when dealing with a foreign agent as there may be more people involved and local property sellers may inflate the price when they think a 'rich' foreigner is interested in buying their home. A number of Italian agents advertise abroad, particularly in the publications listed in **Appendix A**, many of whom speak English or have English-speaking staff (so don't be discouraged if you don't speak Italian). Whoever you buy through, make sure that you know the market price of a property, as it's easy to pay over the odds in popular areas.

Qualifications: Italian estate agents are regulated by law and must be professionally qualified and licensed and hold indemnity insurance. To work in his own right in Italy, an agent must be registered with the local Chamber of Commerce (*Camera di Commercio*) and have a certificate issued by the local *comune* as proof of registration. An agent should also be registered with the Italian Association of Real Estate Agents (AICI, Via Nerino 5, 20123 Milan, ☎ 02-725 291) or the Italian Federation of Professional Estate Agents (FIAIP, Via Monte Zebio, 30, 00195 Rome, ☎ 06-321 9798). You shouldn't view properties with anyone who isn't a professional agent registered with one of the above bodies. There are a number of unlicensed illegal agents operating in Italy, who should be avoided.

Fees: Agents' fees vary considerably (e.g. from 3 to 8 per cent) depending on the agent and area, and are usually shared between the vendor and buyer. For example a buyer may pay 2 to 3 per cent of the purchase price and the vendor around the same. Some agents levy fixed fees for buyers, e.g. Lit. 4 million on properties costing up to Lit. 80 million, a maximum of Lit. 15 million on properties costing up to Lit. 500 million and 3 per cent on properties over Lit. 500 million. The cheaper the property, the higher the fee as a percentage of the sale, while on the most expensive properties fees may be negotiable. Note that fees may be payable at the time the preliminary sales contract is signed and not on completion! Before signing a purchase contract, check the agent's fees and when they must be paid. Many foreign agents work with Italian agents and share the standard commission, so buyers usually pay no more by using a foreign agent. **When buying, check in advance how much commission and other extras you're required to pay in addition to the sale price (apart from the normal fees and taxes associated with buying a property in Italy).**

Viewing: If possible, you should decide where you want to live, what sort of property you want and your budget *before* visiting Italy. Obtain details of as many properties as possible in your chosen area and make a shortlist of those you wish to view (it's also advisable to mark them on a map). Usually the details provided by Italian estate agents are sparse and few agents provide detailed descriptions of properties. Often there's no photograph and even when there is, it usually doesn't do a property justice. Obviously with regard to many old properties in need of renovation, there isn't a lot that can be said apart from stating the land area and the number and size of all buildings. Note that there are no national property listings in Italy, where agents jealously guard their list of properties, although many work with overseas agents in areas popular with foreign buyers. Italian agents who advertise in foreign journals or who work closely with overseas agents may provide colour photographs and a full description, particularly for the more expensive properties. The best agents provide an abundance of information. Agents vary enormously in their efficiency, enthusiasm and professionalism. If an agent shows little interest in finding out exactly what you want, you should go elsewhere.

If you have made an appointment to see particular properties, make a note of their reference numbers in case the Italian agent hasn't been informed (or has lost them). Note, however, that it isn't unusual for an Italian agent's reference numbers not to match those you're given by an agent abroad! Some agents, particularly outside Italy, don't update their records frequently and their lists may be way out of date. If you're using a foreign agent, confirm (and reconfirm) that a particular property is still for sale and the price before travelling to Italy to view it.

Note that an Italian agent may ask you to sign a document before showing you any properties, which is simply to protect his commission should you obtain details from another source or try to do a deal with the owner behind his back. Some Italian agents expect customers to know where they want to buy within a 30 to 40km (19 to 25mi) radius and may even expect you to narrow your choice down to certain towns or villages. If you cannot define where and what you're looking for, at least·tell the agent so that he will know that you're undecided. If you're 'just looking' (window shopping), say so. Most agents will still be pleased to show you properties, as they are well aware that many people fall in love with (and buy) a property on the spot. In Italy you're usually shown properties personally by agents and won't be given the keys (particularly to furnished properties) or be expected to deal with tenants or vendors directly. One reason is that many properties are almost impossible to find if you don't know the area and it isn't unknown even for agents to get lost when looking for properties! Many rural properties have no numbers and street names may be virtually non-existent (if someone invites you to dinner in Italy, make sure you have a telephone number for when you get lost).

You should make an appointment to see properties, as agents don't like people just turning up. **If you make an appointment, you should keep it or call and cancel it.** If you happen to be on holiday it's okay to drop in unannounced to have a look at what's on offer, but don't expect an agent to show you properties without an appointment. If you view properties during a holiday, it's advisable to do so at the beginning so that you can return later to inspect any you particularly like a second or third time. Italian real estate agents usually work on Saturdays and even on Sundays in holiday resorts during the peak season.

You should try to view as many properties as possible during the time available, but allow sufficient time to view each property thoroughly, to travel and get lost between houses, and for breaks for sustenance (it's *mandatory* to have a good lunch in Italy). Although it's important to see sufficient properties to form an accurate opinion of price and quality, don't see too many in one day (between six and eight is usually a manageable number) as it's easy to become confused as to the merits of each property. If you're shown properties that don't meet your specifications, tell the agent immediately. You can also help the agent narrow the field by telling him exactly what's wrong with the properties you reject.

It's advisable to make notes of both the good *and* bad features and take lots of photographs of the properties you like, so that you're able to compare them later at your leisure (but keep a record of which photos are of which house!). It's also wise to mark each property on a map so that should you wish to return, you can find them without getting lost (too often). The more a property appeals to you, the more you should look for faults and negative points; if you still like it after stressing all the negative points it must have special appeal!

INSPECTIONS & SURVEYS

When you have found a property that you like, you should make a close inspection of its condition. Obviously this will depend on whether it's a ruin in need of complete restoration, a property that has been partly or totally modernised, or a modern home. One of the problems with a property that has been restored is that you don't know how well the job has been done, particularly if the owner did it himself. Some simple checks you can do include testing the electrical system, plumbing, mains water, hot water boiler and central heating. Don't take someone else's word that these are functional, but check them yourself. If a property doesn't have electricity or mains water, check the nearest connection point and the cost of extending the service to the property, as it can be *very* expensive in remote rural areas. If a property has a well or septic tank, you should have it tested. An old property may show visible signs of damage and decay, such as bulging or cracked walls, rising damp, missing roof slates and rotten woodwork. Some areas are prone to flooding, storms and subsidence, and it's advisable to check an old property after a heavy rainfall, when any leaks should come to light. You may also wish to have a property checked for termites and other pests, which are found in many areas.

You should ensure that a property is structurally sound. Although building standards in Italy are generally high, you should never assume that a building is sound as even relatively new buildings can have serious faults (although rare). The cost of an inspection is a small price to pay for the peace of mind it affords. Some lenders insist on a 'survey' (*perizia*) before approving a loan, although this usually consists of a perfunctory valuation (*stima*) to confirm that a property is worth the purchase price.

Although a vendor must certify that a property is free from 'hidden defects', this provides little assurance as he can usually just plead ignorance and it's usually difficult or expensive to prove otherwise. An Italian wouldn't make an offer on a property before at least having it checked by a builder. A master builder will also be able to tell you whether the price is too high, given any work that needs to be done. If a property is pre-1945, then a builder or engineer (*ingegnere*) could be employed to check it for soundness, although an architect (*architetto*) is usually better qualified to check a modern house (unless he designed it himself!). Alternatively you can employ a professional valuer or surveyor (*geometra*). You can also have a full structural survey carried out, although this is rare in Italy (few Italians bother with a survey of any kind). However, if you would have a survey carried out if you were buying the same property in your home country, then you should have one done in Italy. You will usually need to pay around Lit. 300,000 for a 'rough' appraisal (*valutazione*) and around Lit. 900,000 (depending on the work involved) for a 'full' structural survey (*perizia strutturale*).

You may be able to make a 'satisfactory' survey a condition of the preliminary contract, although this isn't usual in Italy and a vendor may refuse or insist that you carry out a survey *before* signing the contract. If serious faults are revealed by the survey, a conditional clause should allow you to withdraw from the purchase and have your deposit returned. You may, however, be able to negotiate a satisfactory compromise with the vendor. If a property needs work doing on it to make it habitable, don't accept what you're told regarding the costs of repairs or restoration unless you have a binding quotation in writing from a local builder. One of the most common mistakes foreigners make when buying old properties in Italy is to underestimate the cost of restoration and modernisation (it bears repeating over and over again!). **You should obtain accurate estimates of renovation and modernisation costs before signing a contract** (see page 167).

Always discuss with a surveyor exactly what will be included in a survey, and most importantly, what will be excluded (you may need to pay extra to include certain checks and tests). A general inspection should include the structural condition of all buildings, particularly the foundations, roofs, walls and woodwork; plumbing, electricity and heating systems; and anything else you want inspected such as a swimming pool and its equipment, e.g. filter system or heating. You should receive a written report on the structural condition of a property, including anything that could become a problem in the future. Some surveyors will allow you to accompany them and they may even produce a video of their findings in addition to a written report. A home inspection can be limited to a few items or even a single system only, such as the wiring or plumbing in an old house. **You may also wish to have a radon test on a building or land situated in an area susceptible to radon (see page 140).**

You may prefer to employ a foreign (e.g. British) surveyor practising in Italy, who will write a report in English. However, an Italian surveyor (or other local expert) usually has an intimate knowledge of local properties and building methods. If you employ a foreign surveyor, you must ensure that he's experienced in the idiosyncrasies of Italian properties and that he has professional indemnity insurance covering Italy, which means you can happily sue him if he does a bad job!

Buying Land: Before buying a home on its own plot of land you should walk the boundaries and look for fences, driveways, roads, and the overhanging eaves of buildings that may be encroaching upon the property. If you're uncertain about the boundaries, you should have the land surveyed by a land surveyor (*perito agronomo*), which is advisable in any case when buying a property with a large plot of land. When buying a rural property in Italy, you may be able to negotiate the amount of land you want to be included in the purchase. If a property is part of a larger plot of land owned by the vendor or the boundaries must be redrawn, you will need to hire a surveyor to measure the land and draw up a new cadastral plan. You should also check the local land registry to find out what the land can be used for and any existing rights of way (*diretto di passaggio*).

GARAGES & PARKING

A garage or private parking space isn't usually included in the price when you buy a new apartment or townhouse in Italy, although secure parking may be available at an additional cost, possibly in an underground garage. Modern detached homes usually have a garage or a basement which can be used as a garage. Smaller homes usually have a single garage, while larger properties may have garaging for up to four cars. Parking isn't a usually a problem when buying an old home in a rural area, although there may not be a purpose-built garage.

When buying an apartment or townhouse in a modern development, a lock-up garage usually costs an additional around Lit. 50 million and even a reserved parking space can cost Lit. 20 million or more. Note that the cost of a garage or parking space isn't always recouped when selling, although it makes a property more attractive and may clinch a sale. The cost of parking is an important consideration when buying in a town or resort in Italy, particularly if you have a number of cars. It may be possible to rent a garage or parking space, although this can be prohibitively expensive in cities. Bear in mind that in a large development the nearest parking area may be some distance from your home. This may be an important factor, particularly if you aren't up to carrying heavy shopping hundreds of metres to your home and possibly up several flights of stairs.

Without a private garage or parking space, parking can be a nightmare, particularly in cities or during the summer in busy resorts or developments. Free on-street parking can be difficult or impossible to find in cities and large towns, and in any case may be inadvisable for anything but a wreck. A lock-up garage is important in areas with a high incidence of car theft and theft from cars (e.g. most cities), and is also useful to protect your car from climatic extremes such as ice, snow and extreme heat.

CONVEYANCING

Conveyancing (*pratica*), or more correctly 'conveyance', is the legal term for processing the paperwork involved in buying and selling real property and transferring the deeds of ownership. Conveyancing is strictly governed by Italian law and can be performed only by a public notary (*notaio*), who's a qualified legal professional (on a par with a lawyer) and a representative of the state. A *notaio* is responsible to the provincial authorities for the registration of land and property transfers at the local land registry (*catasto*). He (they are usually men) must follow a strict code of conduct and sign a personal insurance covering his professional responsibility and guaranteeing clients against any errors he may make. A *notaio* represents neither the seller nor the buyer, but the Italian government, and one of his main tasks is to ensure that all taxes are paid to the Ministry of Finance on completion of a sale.

There are two main stages when a *notaio* usually becomes involved in a property purchase. The first is the signing of the preliminary contract (*compromesso si vendita*), although this isn't mandatory, and the second is the completion when the deed of sale (*rogito*) is signed. The *notaio* is responsible for ensuring that the deed of sale is drawn up correctly and that the purchase price is paid to the vendor. He also witnesses the signing of the deed, arranges for its registration (in the name of the new owner) at the land registry, and collects any fees and taxes due. Note that the *notaio* doesn't verify or guarantee the accuracy of statements made in a contract or protect you against fraud. In Italy, a *notaio* usually acts for both the vendor and buyer, and must remain strictly impartial, although a buyer can insist on choosing the *notaio* as he usually pays his fee. Note that notarys' fees vary, so you should check what they will be in advance (see **Fees** on page 147). Don't expect a *notaio* to speak English (few do) or any language other than Italian, or to explain the intricacies of Italian property law. A *notaio* will rarely point out possible pitfalls in a contract, proffer advice or volunteer any information (as for example, a real estate agent usually will).

Anyone buying (or selling) property in Italy shouldn't even think about doing it without taking expert, independent legal advice. You should certainly never sign anything or pay any money before engaging a lawyer (*avvocato*). Your lawyer should also check that the notary does his job correctly, thus providing an extra safeguard. It isn't advisable to use the vendor's lawyer, even if this would save you money, as he's primarily concerned with protecting the interests of the vendor and not the buyer. You should employ an experienced lawyer, either locally or in your home country (who must naturally be fluent in Italian and an expert in Italian property law). He must also speak English or a language that you speak fluently.

Before hiring a lawyer, compare the fees charged by a number of practises and get quotations in writing. Always check what's included in the fee and whether it's 'full and binding' or just an estimate (a low basic rate may be supplemented by much more expensive 'extras'). A lawyer's fees may be calculated as an hourly rate (e.g. Lit. 300,000 an hour) or as a percentage of the purchase price of a property, e.g. 1 to 2 per cent, with a minimum fee of Lit. 1 to 2 million. You could employ a lawyer just to check the preliminary contract (see below) before signing it to ensure that it's correct and includes everything necessary, particularly regarding any necessary conditional clauses (see also **Avoiding Problems** on page 132).

Conveyancing includes ensuring that a proper title is obtained; arranging the necessary registration of the title; checking whether the land has been registered at the land registry; verifying that a property belongs to the vendor or that he has legal authority from the owner to sell it; checking that there isn't an outstanding loan larger than the selling price; verifying that there are no pre-emption rights or restrictive covenants over a property (such as rights of way); and checking that there are no plans to construct anything which would adversely affect the enjoyment or use of the property. Conveyancing should include the following (note, however, that this isn't intended to be a definitive list):

● Verifying that a property belongs to the vendor, as shown in the deed (*rogito*) and listed at the land registry (*catasto*) or that he has the legal authority to sell it. The owner should produce a certified notarial copy of the *rogito*. The description of the property at the land registry and on the deed should be identical.

● Checking that there are no pre-emption rights over a property and that there are no plans to construct anything which would adversely affect the value, enjoyment or use of the property such as roads, railway lines, airports, shops, factories or any other developments. Check whether there's a zoning policy (*piano regolatore*) in the town or area that may affect a property you're planning to buy.

● If you buy a rural property (*casa rurale*), it could be subject to compulsory purchase by a neighbouring farmer under a farmer's rights (*diretto del coltivatore*) law. This law allows farmers who earn over 70 per cent of their income from agriculture or agro-tourism to increase the size of their property by giving them the right to buy adjacent buildings or land for up to two years after it has been sold. To avoid this you can get your lawyer to draw up a document asking the farmer to confirm within 30 days whether he intends to exercise his right of purchase. If the farmer doesn't declare his intention to buy the land within this period, he automatically waives any right to buy it in future.

● You may wish to convert a *casa rurale* into a *casa urbana,* for example when buying an agricultural property which you wish to convert into a holiday home (although it isn't always possible). If done before purchase, this will reduce your registration tax (see **Fees** on page 147). The cost varies depending on the province, e.g. from Lit. 200,000 to 600,000 or more.

● Checking rights of way (*servitù di passagio*). Land may have a mandatory right of way (*servitù di necessità*) for a neighbour whose only access is via your land, which may be permanent or renewable.

● Ensuring that all building permits and planning permissions are in order (e.g. building licence, water and electricity supply, sewage connection) and are genuine, and that a property was built in accordance with the plans. Any modifications, renovations, extensions or additions (such as a swimming pool) must also be included on the plans and be authorised. These must be checked against the cadastral plan at the land registry. If you plan to make any changes or additions to a property, you should check whether this will be possible and if necessary make it a condition of purchase.

● If a property is an historic listed building (protected by the *Belle Arti*), of which there are thousands in Italy, there may be restrictions over its use and possible future sale. Note that if an historic building has been altered or restored illegally, it can be confiscated by the state.

● There are safety regulations for all domestic electrical and gas systems and appliances, which must be inspected annually. You should receive the certificates of inspection when you buy a property, which must be attached to the deed of sale (*rogito*).

● Before buying land for building, you should obtain a certificate from the local town hall stating what can be built on it and what a property or land can be used for. It's important to check the size of dwelling that can be built on a plot or how far an existing building can be extended.

● Checking that a property isn't part of a contested will, otherwise heirs may be able to claim all or part of it for up to five years after the death of the previous owner. Note that if a property was previously owned by a bankrupt company, the liquidator can reverse a sale and claim it for the creditors.

● Checking that there are no encumbrances, e.g. mortgages or loans, against a property or outstanding debts (see below). You *must* ensure that any debts against a property are cleared before you sign the deed of sale (*rogito*). **It's imperative for you or your lawyer to go to the land registry and check ALL entries <u>on the day of the completion</u> (this could be done a few days earlier and then you**

need only examine entries since the last check on the day of completion).
Other checks include:

– enquiring at the town hall whether there are any unpaid taxes such as property tax (see page 103) or other charges outstanding against a property;

– checking that there are no outstanding community (*condominio*) charges for the last five years (it may be possible for a vendor to pay the last year and ignore previous bills) and obtaining copies of the co-ownership rules and the latest accounts of the community of owners (which should state whether there are any impending levies for repairs for which you would be liable);

– checking that all bills for electricity, water, telephone and gas have been paid for the last few years. Receipts should be provided by the vendor for all taxes and services.

If you buy a property on which there's an outstanding loan or taxes, the lender or local authority has first claim on the property and has the right to take possession and sell it to repay the debt. All unpaid debts on a property in Italy are inherited by the buyer.

PURCHASE CONTRACTS

The first stage in buying a in Italy is the signing of a preliminary contract (*compromesso di vendita* or *contratto preliminare di vendita*), which may be drawn up by the vendor, agent, notary or a lawyer. Alternatives include a purchase proposal (*promessa d'acquisto*) or a promise of sale (*promesso di vendità*), although these are used only in special cases. The most common contract is the *compromesso di vendita*, usually referred to simply as the *compromesso*, which may be hand-written or a standard printed document (they are available from stationery stores). On signing the preliminary contract, both parties are bound to the transaction. Note that you should obtain a fiscal number (*codice fiscale*) as soon as possible after signing the *compromesso*, which is necessary for the completion (see page 169).

The *compromesso* contains the essential terms of the sale including full details of the property, details of the vendor and buyer; the purchase price, how it is to be financed, the closing date, and any other conditions (conditional clauses) that must be fulfilled prior to completion. Some agents provide an English translation of a contract, although translations are often so bad as to be meaningless or ARE misleading. You should ensure that you understand *every* clause in the preliminary contract. A sale must be completed within the period stipulated in the *compromesso*, usually six to eight weeks (although it can be from two weeks to three or four months).

Legal Advice: Note that the preliminary contract is binding on both parties and therefore it's important to obtain legal advice before signing it. Although it *isn't* necessary to employ a lawyer or notary when signing a preliminary contract, it's often advisable as he lends extra legal weight to a deal. **Most experts consider that you should have a preliminary contract checked by a lawyer before signing it.** One of the main reasons to engage a lawyer (*avvocato*) is to safeguard your interests through the inclusion of any necessary conditional clauses in the preliminary contract. If a real estate agent's commission is payable when the *compromesso* is signed, you must ensure that it's refundable if the sale doesn't go through and get it in writing! There are various other reasons to employ a lawyer, for example sometimes the best way to buy a property in Italy is through an Italian company (see below) or you may wish to make special provisions regarding inheritance (see **Inheritance & Gift Tax** on page 105). Note that the method of buying Italian property has important consequences, particularly regarding Italian inheritance laws and it can be difficult or expensive to correct any errors later.

Buying through a company: Buying a property in Italy through an Italian company can be beneficial, particularly when two or more people or families are buying between them or when you wish to avoid Italian inheritance laws. When a number of foreigners are buying a property together, the Italian company can in turn be owned by a company abroad, thus allowing legal disputes to be dealt with under local law. The principal advantages of a property owned by a company is that when it's sold or bequeathed, its shares can be simply transferred to the new owner. On the death of an owner, shares in the company are treated as movable assets and can be bequeathed in accordance with the owner's domicile. Owning Italian property through a company is of little or no benefit to residents as most of the advantages don't apply. If you plan to own a property through a company it should be done at the outset, as it will be more expensive to do it later. **Before buying a property through a company it's important to weigh up the long-term advantages and disadvantages and to obtain expert legal advice.**

Conditional Clauses (*clausola condizionale/resolutivo*): A preliminary contract, whether for an old or new property, may contain a number of conditional clauses that must be met to ensure the validity of the contract. Conditions usually apply to events out of control of the vendor or buyer, although almost anything the buyer agrees with the vendor can be included in a preliminary contract. If any of the conditions aren't met, the contract can be suspended or declared null and void, and the deposit returned. However, if you fail to go through with a purchase and aren't covered by a clause in the contract, you will forfeit your deposit or could be compelled to go through with a purchase. Note that if you're buying anything from the vendor such as carpets, curtains or furniture, which are included in the purchase price, you should have them listed and attached as an addendum to the contract. Any fixtures and fittings present in a property when you view it (and agree to buy it) should still be there when you take possession, unless otherwise stated in the contract (see also **Completion** on page 169). There are many possible conditional clauses concerning a range of subjects, including the following:

- being able to obtain a mortgage;

- obtaining planning permission and building permits, e.g. for a swimming pool or extension;

- plans to construct anything (e.g. roads, railways, etc.) which would adversely affect the enjoyment or use of the property;

- confirmation of the land area being purchased with a property;

- pre-emption rights or restrictive covenants over a property (such as rights of way);

- dependence on the sale of another property;

- subject to a satisfactory building survey or inspection.

Mortgage Clause: The most common conditional clause states that a buyer is released from the contract should he be unable to obtain a mortgage. This condition is compulsory for all property purchases in Italy. Even if you have no intention of obtaining a mortgage (you don't have to obtain a mortgage, even if you state that you're going to), it's advisable not to give up your right to do so. If you give up your right and later find that you need a mortgage but fail to obtain it, you will lose your deposit. The clause should state the amount, term and interest rate expected or already agreed with a lender, plus the lender's name (if known). If you cannot obtain a mortgage for the agreed amount and terms you won't lose your deposit. You must make an application for the loan within a certain time after signing the contract and have a specified period in which to secure it.

Deposit: A deposit (*caparra*) of around 10 per cent (but possibly up to 30 per cent) is paid to the vendor and is forfeited if the buyer doesn't go through with the purchase (if the vendor reneges he must pay the buyer double the amount of the deposit). **A deposit must be paid only to the vendor and not to a third party such as an agent or notary in Italy.** It's preferable that the deposit is described as *caparra penitenziale* and not as *caparra confirmatoria*. In the former the buyer 'simply' loses his deposit if he withdraws from a sale, while with the latter the vendor can take legal action to force a buyer to go through with a purchase. It's possible to pay a smaller nominal sum as a holding deposit (*anticipo di pagamento*) before the *compromesso* is signed as a sign of good faith.

A deposit is refundable under strict conditions only, notably relating to any conditional clauses such as the failure to obtain a mortgage, although it can also be forfeited if you don't complete the transaction within the period specified in the contract. Note that if you withdraw from a sale after all the conditions have been met, you won't only lose your deposit, but must also pay the real estate agent's commission. **Always make sure you know exactly what the conditions are regarding the return or forfeiture of a deposit.**

COMPLETION

Completion (closing or exchange of contracts), called *atto* in Italian, is the name for the signing of the final deed (*rogito*) or 'conveyance of transfer' (*atto di compravendita* or *scrittura privata*), which is drawn up by a notary. The date of completion is usually six to eight weeks after signing the preliminary contract (*compromesso*), as stated in the contract, although it may be 'moveable'. Completion involves the signing of the deed of sale, transferring legal ownership of a property, and the payment of the balance of the purchase price, plus any other payments due such as the *notaio's* fees, taxes and duties. When all the necessary documents concerning a purchase have been returned to the *notaio*, he will contact you and request the balance of the purchase price less the deposit and, if applicable, the amount of a mortgage. He will also give you a bill for his fees and all taxes, which must be paid on completion.

Final Checks: Property is sold subject to the condition that it's accepted in the state it's in at the time of completion, therefore you should be aware of anything that occurs between signing the preliminary contract and completion. Before signing the deed of sale, it's *imperative* to check that the property hasn't fallen down or been damaged in any way, e.g. by a storm or the previous owners. If you have employed a lawyer or are buying through an agent, he should accompany you on this visit. You should also do a final inventory immediately prior to completion (the previous owner should have already vacated the property) to ensure that the vendor hasn't absconded with anything that was included in the price.

You should have an inventory of the fixtures and fittings and anything that was included in the contract or purchased separately, e.g. carpets, light fittings, curtains or kitchen appliances, and check that they are present and in good working order. This is particularly important if furniture and furnishings (and major appliances) were included in the price. You should also ensure that expensive items (such as kitchen apparatus) haven't been substituted by inferior (possibly second-hand) items. Any fixtures and fittings (and garden plants and shrubs) present in a property when you viewed it should still be there when you take possession, unless otherwise stated in the contract. **Note that unless restrained, some vendors will go to amazing extremes, for example removing not just the bulbs, but the bulb-holders, flex and even the ceiling rose!**

If you find anything is missing, damaged or isn't in working order, you should make a note and insist on immediate restitution such as an appropriate reduction in the amount to be paid. In such cases it's normal for the *notaio* to withhold an appropriate amount in escrow from the vendor's proceeds to pay for repairs or replacements. **You should refuse to go through with the completion if you aren't completely satisfied, as it will be very difficult or impossible to obtain redress later.** If it isn't possible to complete the sale, you should consult your lawyer about your rights and the return of your deposit and any other funds already paid.

Declared Value: The deed of sale includes a declaration of the price paid by the buyer, which is usually less that the actual price paid. However, the declared figure mustn't be lower than the official value recorded at the local land registry (*catasto*). The value of a property is based on its notional letting value (*rendita catastale*), which is multiplied by a coefficient provided by the *comune* to arrive at the minimum value which should be declared in the *rogito*. You should never be tempted to flagrantly under-declare the sale price in order to pay lower fees, as it can have serious consequences if it's discovered. If you under declare (*sottodichiarazione*) the value too much, the tax authorities may make their own valuation and tax the parties accordingly, which may also result in a fine. The declared price is usually between 10 and 20 per cent of the actual price in cities, where property values are common knowledge and well documented, but in rural areas prices are often under-declared by 50 per cent or more. Note, however, that the authorities have been revising property values in recent years and fiscal values are now closer to actual values in many areas. **Take advice from your estate agent and/or lawyer when declaring the value.**

Signing: The final act of the sale is the signing of the deed of sale (*rogito*), which takes place in the *notaio's* office. Before the deed of sale is signed, the *notaio* checks that all the conditions contained in the preliminary contract have been fulfilled. It's normal for both parties to be present when the deed of sale is read, signed and witnessed by the *notaio*, although either party can give a representative power of attorney (*procura*). If you're married you will need to produce your marriage certificate so that it can be noted whether the property is to be owned jointly by both spouses or by one only. If the buyer doesn't understand Italian, an officially accredited interpreter must be present or a power of attorney must be given to the buyer's agent or lawyer. This is quite common among foreign buyers and sellers and can be arranged by your agent or lawyer in Italy. It can also be drawn up by an Italian agent or notary and authenticated by an Italian consulate in your home country, although this is more complicated and expensive.

Payment: The balance of the price after the deposit and any mortgages are subtracted must be paid by banker's draft or bank transfer. The money can be transferred directly to the *notaio's* bank account, which can be done by a bank-to-bank transfer. However, it's important to allow sufficient time for the funds to be transferred. Alternatively you can pay by banker's draft, which is probably the best method as you will have it in your possession (a bank cannot lose it!) and the *notaio* can confirm payment immediately. It also allows you to withhold payment if there's a last minute problem (see **Final Checks** above) that cannot be resolved. Note that when the vendor and buyer are of the same foreign nationality, they can agree that the balance is paid in a currency other than lire, although the *notaio* must also agree to this. In this case the money should be held by a lawyer or solicitor in the vendor's or buyer's home country. After paying the money and receiving a receipt, the *notaio* may not give you a document certifying that you're the owner of the property. You will also receive the keys!

Registration: There are no title deeds as such in Italy and proof of ownership is provided and guaranteed by registration of the property at the land registry (*catasto*). The land registry's stamp is placed on the deed of sale, a certified copy of which is given to the buyer by the *notaio* around two months after completion of the sale. If you have a mortgage, it's also recorded at the land registry. The original deed is retained indefinitely by the *notaio*. **Registration is of paramount importance, as until a property is registered you aren't the legal owner.** It's also important to check your copy of the deed of sale after registration to ensure that it's correct in every detail.

RENOVATION & RESTORATION

Many old properties purchased by foreigners in Italy are in need of restoration, renovation and modernisation. The most common examples are the many farmhouses that have been almost totally neglected since they were built in the 18th and 19th centuries and were often abandoned many years ago. In general the Italian attitude to old buildings is one of almost total neglect until they are literally in danger of falling down, when complete rebuilding is often necessary. A building sold as requiring renovation in Italy is usually in need of *substantial* work (rebuilding may be a more accurate description). Partly renovated usually means that part of a building is habitable, which means it at least has sanitation, but the rest is usually in need of restoration. The most dilapidated 'buildings' consist of just a few walls without a roof.

To be restored, partly restored or fully restored? Before buying a property requiring restoration or modernisation, you should consider the alternatives. An extra Lit. 30 to 60 million spent on a purchase may represent better value for money than spending the money on building work. It's often cheaper to buy a restored or partly restored property than a ruin in need of total restoration, unless you're going to do most of the work yourself. The price of most restored properties doesn't reflect the cost and amount of work that went into them, and many people who have restored a ruin would never do it again and advise others against it.

Condition: It's important to ensure that a property has sound walls. Properties that have walls with serious defects are best avoided as it's usually cheaper to erect a new building! Almost any other problem can be fixed or overcome at a price. A sound roof that doesn't leak is desirable and making a building waterproof is the most important priority if funds are scarce. Don't believe a vendor or agent who tells you that a roof or anything else can be repaired or patched up, but obtain expert advice from a local builder. Sound roof timbers are also desirable as they can be expensive to replace. Old buildings may also need a damp-proof course, timber treatment, new windows and doors, a modern kitchen and bathroom, re-wiring and central heating.

Electricity and mains water should preferably already be connected as they can be expensive to extend to a property in a rural area. **If a property doesn't have electricity or mains water, it's important to check the cost of extending these services to the property.** Many rural properties get their water from a spring or well, but you should check the reliability of the water supply as wells can run dry! If you buy a waterside property, you should ensure that it has been designed with floods in mind, e.g. with electrical installations above flood level and solid tiled floors. You should also check a building for leaks (e.g. after a rainstorm) before investing in expensive decoration. In earthquake-prone areas structural restorations can be done with a concept known as 'minimal intervention unit' (*Unità Minimo d'Intervento/UMI*). This choral reinforcement of walls and adjoining structures in historic centres means a 15 to 25 per cent increase in cost, but provides major resistance against seismic movements in old buildings.

Septic Tanks: The absence of a septic tank (*fossa settica*) or other waste water system isn't usually a problem, providing that the land size and elevation allows for its installation. If there's a stream running through a property it may mean that an expensive system needs to be installed to cope with the effluent, which costs three or four times that of a septic tank. If a property already has a septic tank, check that it's in good condition. An old style septic tank takes bathroom waste only, while new all-purpose septic tanks on a soak-away system can cope with a wide range of waste products. Make sure that a septic tank is large enough for the property in question, e.g. 2,500 litres for two bedrooms and up to 4,000 litres for five bedrooms. Note that you mustn't use cleaning agents such as ammonia in a septic tank, as it will destroy it. Specially formulated cleaners are available, including products that will extend its life-span.

Planning Permission & Building Permits: If modernisation of an old building involves making external alterations, such as building an extension or installing larger windows or new doorways, you will need planning permission (*permessi comunali* or *concessione edlizia*) from your local town hall and a building licence (*licenza*). Planning regulations may be decided by a *comune*, province or even a region. Check what you can and cannot alter as, for example, you may not be able to change the windows, doors, colour of exterior walls, entrances, staircases or build garden walls. Italian law also requires a ceiling height of 2.75 metres for living space (except for property located in villages, which are exempt) and you may need to raise the roof or lower the floor when converting a building. It's imperative to find out exactly what you can do before buying a property for restoration. The only foolproof way is to apply for and obtain planning permission before buying a property. Alternatively you should include a conditional clause in the preliminary contract (*compromesso*) stating that the purchase is contingent on obtaining planning permission. Sometimes a property already has planning permission, although you should check the period of validity (which should be at least two years) and whether it can be changed or extended if necessary.

A building contract must also be dependent on all necessary licences being issued. **Never start any building work before you have official permission.** It's also advisable to obtain permission from your local town hall before demolishing buildings on your land, irrespective of how dilapidated they are. You may be able to sell the building materials or get a builder to demolish them free of charge in exchange for the materials. Most people hire a *geometra* (who's actually a combination of architect and surveyor, for which there's no equivalent in English) to draw up the plans and make the planning application. Note that obtaining planning permission can take up to six months and usually costs at least Lit. 1 million for the simplest job and can cost Lit. 3 million or more for renovating a house.

When applying for planning permission, bear in mind possible future extensions and their likelihood of being granted, e.g. it's difficult to obtain planning permission if you live in an historic town or village or an area of great natural beauty. Restoration must usually be carried out with local materials and in the traditional style. In some regions, such as Tuscany and Marche, planning regulations are rigorously enforced to maintain the beauty of the countryside, and restorations must maintain the character of the building and wholesale alterations are likely to be refused planning permission. After restoring a ruin or building a new house, a certificate is required to confirm that building work has been carried out according to the planning application. You will also need a professional valuation of your home for insurance purposes.

Italians often resort to bribery (which is a way of life in Italy) when dealing with planning officials, rather than go through the tortuous planning procedures. If this fails many Italians simply build illegally (called *abusivo*) and wait to be fined. The government frequently has amnesties (*condono*) for people who have built or altered their homes illegally, which allows them to pay a fee rather than a much larger fine or even face demolition. However, a foreigner would be extremely unwise to follow their example and may not be treated so leniently by the authorities.

DIY or Builders? One of the first decisions you need to make regarding restoration or modernisation is whether to do all or most of the work yourself or have it done by professional builders or artisans. A working knowledge of Italian is essential for DIY (*fai da te*), particularly the words associated with building materials and measurements (renovating a house in Italy will also greatly improve your ability to swear in Italian!). If you're doing a lot of DIY or simply wish to confirm the cost of building materials, you can obtain price catalogues for each branch of the building trade from DEI Tipografia del Genio Civile, Via Nomentana 16, 00161 Tome (☎ 06-440 2046).

Note that when restoring a period property it's imperative to have a sensitive approach to restoration. You shouldn't tackle jobs by yourself or with friends unless you're sure you're doing it right (such as cleaning or restoring marble floors or tiles, which is a specialist job). In general you should aim to retain as many of a property's original features as possible and stick to local building materials such as wood, stone and tiles, reflecting the style of the property. In fact, this may be required by law. When renovations and 'improvements' have been botched, there's often little that can be done except to start again from scratch. It's important not to over-modernise an old property so that too much of its natural rustic charm and attraction is lost. Before starting work and as work is in progress, most people like to have a photographic record of their accomplishments, if only to justify the expense.

Italian or Foreign Builders: When it's a choice between using Italian craftsmen or foreign builders, most experts recommend using local labour for a number of excellent reasons. Italian artisans understand the materials and the traditional style of building, are familiar with local planning and building regulations, and usually do excellent work. There are no jobbing builders or jacks of all trades in Italy, where all artisans have a specialist trade such as a bricklayer, stonemason, joiner, roofer, plasterer, plumber or electrician. If you employ local builders you can virtually guarantee that the result will be authentic and it could also save you money. Italian builders' quotations are binding and their prices are usually reasonable. Finally, bringing in foreign labour won't endear you to the local populace and may even create friction. Never employ 'black' labour (Italian or foreign) as apart from their lack of insurance there are stiff penalties.

Finding a Builder (*muratore*)**:** When looking for a builder it's advisable to obtain recommendations from local people you can trust, e.g. a real estate agent, *notaio*, local mayor and neighbours. Note, however, that real estate agents or other professionals aren't always the best people to ask as they may receive a commission. Always obtain references from previous customers. Any tradesmen you employ should be registered at the local Chamber of Commerce in the requisite category and in the official list of artisans (*albo degli artigiani*) for his particular trade. Note that it's usually better to use a local building consortium or contractor rather than a number of independent tradesmen, particularly if you won't be around to supervise them (although it will cost you a bit more). On the other hand if you supervise it yourself using local hand-picked craftsmen you can save money and learn a great deal into the bargain.

Quotations: You should obtain a written quotation (*preventivo*) from at least two builders before employing anyone. It's advisable to get a few quotations and offer to pay a fee for a quotation for a large job, which should be reimbursed by the builder who gets the job. Builders usually provide an estimate per square metre (*misura*), which includes both labour and materials, although for jobs where it's difficult or impossible to provide an estimate, jobs are done at an hourly (*in economia*) or daily rate. For quotations to be accurate, you must detail exactly the work required, e.g. for electrical work this would include the number of lights, points and switches, and the quality of materials to be used. If you have only a vague idea of what you want, you will receive a vague and unreliable quotation. Make sure that a quotation includes everything you want done and that you fully understand it (if you don't, get it translated). Look out for any terms in a quotation allowing for the price to be increased for inflation or a general rise in prices, and check whether it's definitive or provisional, i.e. dependent on further exploratory work. You should fix a date for completion and if you can get a builder to agree to it, include a penalty for failing to meet it. It's difficult to get Italian builders to agree to this, but it's worth persevering. Always ask for start and finish dates in a quotation. After signing a contract it's usual to pay a deposit, e.g. 10 to 25 per cent, depending on the size of the job.

Supervision: If you aren't on the spot and able to supervise work, you should hire a 'clerk of works' such an architect (*architetto*) or surveyor (*geometra*) to oversee a job, either of whom can be employed to oversee an entire project or just one or two aspects of it. The fee is usually a percentage of the total cost, e.g. 10 per cent, and is usually worth every lira. A major building contract also needs a strict penalty clause, otherwise it could drag on for months (or years) or be left half-finished. Shop around and compare rates, but beware of expatriate project managers who have been known to rip-off their compatriots. Some Italian real estate agents will organise renovations and restoration and oversee a project for around 10 per cent of the total cost. Always obtain references from previous customers.

Many unsupervised Italian workmen are about as disciplined as Italian drivers and it isn't uncommon for artisans to work for a few days and then disappear for a few weeks or months on end! Italian artisans never like to turn down work, so tend to take on much more than they can handle and work a day here and a day there, thus annoying all their customers. Be extremely careful whom you employ if you have work done in your absence and ensure that your instructions are accurate in every detail. Always make absolutely certain that you understand exactly what has been agreed and if necessary get it in writing (with drawings). It isn't unusual for foreign owners to receive huge bills for work done in their absence that shouldn't have been done at all! **If you don't speak Italian, it's even more important to employ someone to oversee building works. Progressing on sign language and a few words of Italian is a recipe for disaster!**

Cost: All building work such as electrical work, masonry and plumbing is costed by the square metre (*misura*) or metre. The cost of total restoration by professional builders varies depending on the type of work involved, the quality of materials used and the region. You should expect to pay a minimum of Lit. 1 million per square metre (m2) to bring a ruin to a habitable condition and as much as Lit. 2 million per m² for a top quality job, e.g. insulated roofs, double glazing, full central heating, marble or top-quality ceramic tiles in kitchens and bathrooms, fully fitted kitchens, fireplace, etc. For a property of 100m2 you should reckon on a total bill of Lit. 100 to 200 million. As a rough guide you should expect the cost of fully renovating an old 'habitable' building to be at least equal to its purchase price and possibly much more. The cost must include VAT at 20 per cent, although a project may be eligible for a reduced rate of VAT (*l'abbatimento dell'IVA*) of 4 per cent on materials and labour (check with your local *comune*).

How much you spend on restoring a property will depend on your purpose and the depth of your pockets. If you're restoring a property as an investment, it's easy to spend more than you could ever hope to recoup when you sell it. On the other hand, if you're restoring a property as a holiday or permanent home, there's no limit to what you can do and how much money you can spend. Always keep an eye on your budget (which will inevitably be plus or minus 25 per cent — usually plus!) and don't be in too much of a hurry. Some people take many years to restore an Italian holiday home, particularly when they're doing most of the work themselves. In the last decade many foreigners have spent a fortune on renovations only to find it impossible to sell and recoup their investment. It isn't unusual for buyers to embark on a grandiose renovation scheme, only to run out of money before it's completed and be forced to sell at a huge loss. It's possible to obtain a mortgage that includes the cost of renovation work, but you must obtain detailed written quotations for a lender. It's also possible to obtain a grant to restore an historic property in some regions.

It's important to ensure that you pay for work on time, as if you get a reputation as a late payer (or not paying at all) you will soon find that you cannot get anyone local to work for you. However, you should make sure that a job's completely finished (including repairing any damage done by workmen) and passed by your architect or surveyor, before paying bills. Never pay a builder in advance (apart from a deposit), particularly a large sum, as it's possible that he will disappear with your money (it happens, particularly when employing foreign, non-registered builders). It's best to pay one month in arrears, which most builders will agree to. On the other hand, if you want a job doing while you're away you will need to pay a builder a sum in advance or get someone local to supervise his work and pay him regularly, otherwise he's unlikely to finish the job. Cash deals are often negotiated without IVA, although you should bear in mind if you don't have a legitimate bill you won't be able to offset the cost of work against rental income or capital gains tax when you sell.

Swimming Pools: It's common for foreign buyers to install a swimming pool at a home in Italy, which if you're letting, will greatly increase your rental prospects and the rent you can charge. Many self-catering holiday companies won't take on properties without a pool. However, before adding a pool you need to check whether there's sufficient water supply in the area and how it will affect your taxes, as having a pool automatically places a home in the luxury (A1) category. Note that you need planning permission to install a pool and this may be refused in areas with acute water shortages.

There are many swimming pool installation companies in Italy or you can even buy and install one yourself. Above ground pools are the cheapest but they are unsightly and are advisable only as a stop-gap or for those who cannot afford anything better. Expect to pay around Lit. 5 million for an 8 x 4m above ground pool. A better option is a liner pool, which can be installed by anyone with basic DIY skills, costing around Lit. 20 to 25 million fully installed. A conventional pool measuring 8 x 4 metres (with a simple but effective step/filter unit) can be purchased for around Lit. 25 million, including installation. A saline water option costs a bit more, but gives a better quality of water and offers lower maintenance costs. A concrete, fully tiled pool of 8 x 4 metres costs from around Lit. 35 to 40 million installed including filtration and heating, and can be almost any shape. Pools require regular maintenance and cleaning. If you have a holiday home in Italy or let a property, you will need to employ someone to maintain your pool (you may be able to get a local family to look after it in return for using it).

DIY & Building Supplies: There's a wide range of DIY equipment, tools and building supplies in Italy, although there's less choice than in some other European countries such as the UK and it's usually more expensive (Italians prefer to do other things with their spare time such as eat and chase women). Ask your neighbours about where to buy fittings and materials as they usually know the best places locally. There are many DIY hypermarkets and superstores in Italy, which in addition to stocking most DIY requirements also have a wide range of tools and machinery for hire. Most DIY stores stock a large selection of goods (and keep most items in stock), accept credit cards and have helpful staff. Always look out for special promotions and even if nothing appears to be on offer it's worth asking, as offers aren't always advertised. Most towns have a hardware store that's handy for tools and small items and there are building yards which are good for plumbing parts, porcelain, fireplaces and doors. It's also possible to buy reclaimed materials such as porcelain, tiles, doors and fireplaces from architectural salvage dealers.

See also **Buying an Old Home** on page 152, **Inspections & Surveys** on page 162, **Water** on page 186 and **Heating & Air-Conditioning** on page 189.

MOVING HOUSE

After finding a home in Italy it usually takes only a few weeks to have your belongings shipped from within continental Europe. From anywhere else it varies considerably, e.g. around four weeks from the east coast of America, six weeks from the US west coast and the Far East, and around eight weeks from Australasia. Customs clearance is no longer necessary when shipping your household effects from one European Union (EU) country to another. However, when shipping your effects from a non-EU country to Italy, you should enquire about customs formalities in advance. If you're moving to Italy from a non-EU country you must present an inventory (in English and Italian) of the things that you're planning to import at your local Italian consulate, which must be officially stamped. You will also need a 'stay permit' (*permesso di soggiorno*) from the local police station (*questura*) in Italy. If you fail to follow the correct procedure you can encounter problems and delays and may be charged duty or fined. The relevant forms to be completed by non-EU citizens depend on whether your Italian home will be your main residence or a second home. Removal companies usually take care of the paperwork and ensure that the correct documents are provided and properly completed (see **Customs** on page 203).

It's advisable to use a major shipping company with a good reputation. For international moves it's best to use a company that's a member of the International Federation of Furniture Removers (FIDI) or the Overseas Moving Network International (OMNI), with experience in Italy. Members of FIDI and OMNI usually subscribe to an advance payment scheme providing a guarantee. If a member company fails to fulfil its commitments to a client, the removal is completed at the agreed cost by another company or your money is refunded. Some removal companies have subsidiaries or affiliates in Italy, which may be more convenient if you encounter problems or need to make an insurance claim.

You should obtain at least three written quotations before choosing a company, as costs vary considerably. Moving companies should send a representative to provide a detailed quotation. Most companies will pack your belongings and provide packing cases and special containers, although this is naturally more expensive than packing them yourself. Ask a company how they pack fragile and valuable items, and whether the cost of packing cases, materials and insurance (see below) are included in a quotation. If you're doing your own packing, most shipping companies will provide packing crates and boxes. Shipments are charged by volume, e.g. the square metre in Europe and the square foot in the USA. You should expect to pay from Lit. 6 to 12 million to move the contents of a three to four-bedroom house within Western Europe, e.g. from London to the north of Italy. If you're flexible about the delivery date, shipping companies will quote a lower fee based on a 'part load', where the cost is shared with other deliveries. This can result in savings of 50 per cent or more compared with a individual delivery. Whether you have an individual or shared delivery, obtain the maximum transit period in writing, otherwise you may have to wait months for delivery!

Be sure to fully insure your belongings during removal with a well established insurance company. Don't insure with a shipping company that carries its own insurance as they will usually fight every lira of a claim. Insurance premiums are usually 1 to 2 per cent of the declared value of your goods, depending on the type of cover chosen. It's prudent to make a photographic or video record of valuables for insurance purposes. Most insurance policies cover for 'all-risks' on a replacement value basis. Note that china, glass and other breakables can usually only be included in an 'all-risks' policy when they're packed by the removal company. Insurance usually covers total loss or loss of a particular crate only, rather than individual items (unless they were packed by the shipping company). If there are any breakages or damaged items, they should be noted and listed before you sign the delivery bill (although it's obviously impractical to check everything on delivery). If you need to make a claim, be sure to read the small print as some companies require clients to make a claim within a few days, although seven is usual. Send a claim by registered mail. Some insurance companies apply an 'excess' of around 1 per cent of the total shipment value when assessing claims. This means that if your shipment is valued at Lit. 50 million and you make a claim for less than Lit. 500,000, you won't receive anything.

If you're unable to ship your belongings directly to Italy, most shipping companies will put them into storage and some allow a limited free storage period prior to shipment, e.g. 14 days. **If you need to put your household effects into storage, it's imperative to have them fully insured as warehouses have been known to burn down!** Make a complete list of everything to be moved and give a copy to the removal company. Don't include anything illegal (e.g. guns, bombs, drugs or pornographic videos) with your belongings as customs checks can be rigorous and penalties severe. Provide the shipping company with *detailed* instructions how to find your Italian home from the nearest *autostrada* (or main road) and a telephone number where you can be contacted.

After considering the shipping costs, you may decide to ship only selected items of furniture and personal effects and buy new furniture in Italy. If you're importing household goods from another European country, it's possible to rent a self-drive van or truck. Note, however, that if you rent a vehicle outside Italy you will need to return it to the country where it was hired. If you plan to transport your belongings to Italy personally, check the customs requirements in the countries you must pass through. Most people find it isn't advisable to do their own move unless it's a simple job, e.g. a few items of furniture and personal effects only. It's no fun heaving beds and wardrobes up stairs and squeezing them into impossible spaces. If you're taking pets with you, you may need to ask your vet to tranquillise them, as many pets are frightened (even more than people) by the chaos and stress of moving house.

Bear in mind when moving home that everything that can go wrong often does, therefore allow plenty of time and try not to arrange your move from your old home on the same day as the new owner is moving in. That's just asking for fate to intervene! **Last but not least, if your Italian home has poor or impossible access for a large truck you must inform the shipping company (the ground must also be firm enough to support a heavy vehicle).** Note also that if furniture needs to be taken in through an upstairs window, you may need to pay extra. See also **Customs** on page 203 and the **Checklists** on page 205.

MOVING IN

One of the most important tasks to perform after moving into a new home is to make an inventory of the fixtures and fittings and, if applicable, the furniture and furnishings. When you have purchased a property, you should check that the previous owner hasn't absconded with any fixtures and fittings which were included in the price or anything which you specifically paid for, e.g. carpets, light fittings, curtains, furniture, kitchen cupboards and appliances, garden ornaments, plants or doors (see **Completion** on page 169). It's common to do a final check or inventory when buying a new property, which is usually done a few weeks before completion.

When moving into a long-term rental property it's necessary to complete an inventory (*inventario*) of its contents and a report on its condition. This includes the condition of fixtures and fittings, the state of furniture and furnishings, the cleanliness and state of the decoration, and anything that's damaged, missing or in need of repair. An inventory should be provided by your landlord or agent and may include every single item in a furnished property (down to the number of teaspoons). The inventory check should be carried out in your presence, both when taking over and when terminating a rental agreement. If an inventory isn't provided, you should insist on one being prepared and annexed to the lease. If you find a serious fault after signing the inventory, send a registered letter to your landlord and ask for it to be attached to the inventory.

An inventory should be drawn up both when moving in and when vacating a rented property. If the two inventories don't correspond, you must make good any damages or deficiencies or the landlord can do so and deduct the cost from your deposit. Although Italian landlords are generally no worse than those in most other countries, some will do almost anything to avoid repaying a deposit. Note the reading on your utility meters (e.g. electricity, gas and water) and check that you aren't overcharged on your first bill. The meters should be read by utility companies before you move in, although you may need to organise it yourself.

It's advisable to obtain written instructions from the previous owner concerning the operation of appliances and heating and air-conditioning systems; maintenance of grounds, gardens and lawns; care of special surfaces such as wooden, marble or tiled floors; and the names of reliable local maintenance men who know a property and are familiar with its quirks. Check with your local town hall regarding local regulations about such things as rubbish collection, recycling and on-road parking.

HOME SECURITY

When moving into a new home it's often wise to replace the locks (or lock barrels) as soon as possible, as you have no idea how many keys are in circulation for the existing locks. This is true even for new homes, as builders often give keys to sub-contractors. In any case it's advisable to change the external locks or lock barrels regularly, e.g. annually, particularly if you let a home. If not already fitted, it's best to fit high security (double cylinder or dead bolt) locks. Modern properties may be fitted with high security locks that are individually numbered. Extra keys for these locks cannot be cut at a local hardware store and you will need to obtain details from the previous owner or your landlord. Many modern developments have security gates and caretakers.

In areas with a high risk of theft (e.g. most major cities and resorts), your insurance company will insist on extra security measures such as two locks on all external doors, internal locking shutters, security bars on windows less than 10m (33ft) from the ground and grilles on patio doors. An external door must usually be of the armoured (*porta blindata*) variety with a steel rod locking mechanism. An insurance policy may specify that all forms of protection must be employed when a property is unoccupied. If security precautions aren't adhered to, a claim may be reduced by half. It's usually necessary to have a safe for any insured valuables, which must be approved by your insurance company.

You may wish to have a security alarm fitted, which is usually the best way to deter thieves and may also reduce your household insurance (see page 58). It should include all external doors and windows, internal infra-red security beams, and may also include a coded entry keypad (which can be frequently changed and is useful for clients if you let a home) and 24-hour monitoring (with some systems it's even possible to monitor properties remotely from another country). With a monitored system, when a sensor (e.g. smoke or forced entry) detects an emergency or a panic button is pushed, a signal is sent automatically to a 24-hour monitoring station. The duty monitor will telephone to check whether it's a genuine alarm and if he cannot contact you someone will be sent to investigate.

You can deter thieves by ensuring that your house is always well lit and not conspicuously unoccupied. External security 'motion detector' lights (that switch on automatically when someone approaches); random timed switches for internal lights, radios and televisions; dummy security cameras; and tapes that play barking dogs (etc.) triggered by a light or heat detector may all help deter burglars. In remote areas it's common for owners to fit two or three locks on external doors, alarm systems, grills on doors and windows, window locks, security shutters and a safe for valuables. The advantage of grills is that they allow you to leave windows open without inviting criminals in (unless they are *very* slim). You can fit UPVC (toughened clear plastic) security windows and doors, which can survive an attack with a sledge-hammer without damage, and external steel security blinds (which can be electrically operated), although these are expensive. A dog can be useful to deter intruders, although he should be kept inside where he cannot be given poisoned food. Irrespective of whether you actually have a dog, a warning sign with a picture of a fierce dog may act as a deterrent. If not already present, you should have the front door of an apartment fitted with a spy-hole and chain so that you can check the identity of a visitor before opening the door. **Remember, prevention is better than cure as stolen property is rarely recovered.**

Holiday homes are particularly vulnerable to thieves and in some areas they are regularly ransacked. No matter how secure your door and window locks, a thief can usually obtain entry if he's sufficiently determined, often by simply smashing a window or even breaking in through the roof or by knocking a hole in a wall! In isolated areas thieves can strip a house bare at their leisure and an unmonitored alarm won't be a deterrent if there's no-one around to hear it. If you have a holiday home in Italy, it isn't advisable to leave anything of real value (monetary or sentimental) there.

If you vacate your home for an extended period, it may be obligatory to notify your caretaker, landlord or insurance company, and to leave a key with the caretaker or landlord in case of emergencies. If you have a robbery, you should report it immediately to your local police station, where you must make a statement (*dichiarazione*). You will receive a copy, which is required by your insurance company if you make a claim.

When closing up a property for an extended period, e.g. over the winter, you should ensure that everything is switched off and that it's secure (see **closing a property for the winter** on page 195). Another important aspect of home security is ensuring that you have early warning of a fire, which is easily accomplished by installing smoke detectors. Battery-operated smoke detectors can be purchased for around Lit. 15,000 (they should be tested weekly to ensure that the batteries aren't exhausted). You can also fit an electric-powered gas detector that activates an alarm when a gas leak is detected. See also **Crime** on page 75.

ELECTRICITY

Most electricity in Italy is imported from France and Switzerland and supplied by *Ente Nazionale per l'Energia Elettrica (ENEL)*, which had a monopoly on providing electricity before being privatised in 1998. In major cities, electricity may be controlled by a local municipal energy board, e.g. the *Azienda Energetica Municipale (AEM)* in Milan. Electricity and other utility offices are listed in the phone book under *Numeri di Pubblica Utilità*.

After buying or renting a property (unless utilities are included in the rent) in Italy, you must sign a contract at the local office of your electricity company. You need to take with you some identification (passport or residence card), a copy of the deeds, the registration number of the meter (*contatore*), the previous tenant's electricity contract or a bill paid by the previous owner (and a good book as queues can be long). If you have purchased a home in Italy, the real estate agent may arrange for the utilities to be transferred to your name or go with you to the office (no charge should be made for this service). Make sure all previous bills have been paid and that the contract is transferred to your name from the day you take over. If you're a non-resident owner, you should also give your foreign address or the address of your fiscal representative in Italy, in case there are any problems requiring your attention such as your bank refusing to pay the bills. You need to cancel (*disdire*) the contract when you move house.

Power Supply: The electricity supply in Italy is generally 220 volts AC with a frequency of 50 hertz (cycles) and either two or three phase, although in some areas older buildings may still use 125 volts. Not all appliances, e.g. TVs made for 240 volts, will function with a power supply of 220 volts. Power cuts are frequent in many areas of Italy (many lasting just a few microseconds or just long enough to crash a computer), particularly in rural areas, and the electricity supply is also unstable with power surges commonplace. If you use a computer you should have an uninterrupted power supply (UPS) with a battery backup, which allows you time to shut down your computer and save your work after a power failure. If you live in an area where cuts are frequent and rely on electricity for your livelihood, e.g. for operating a computer, fax machine and other equipment, you may need to install a backup generator. **Even more important than a battery backup is a power surge**

protector for appliances such as TVs, computers and fax machines, without which you risk equipment being damaged or destroyed. In remote areas you must install a generator or solar power system if you want electricity, as there's no mains electricity, although some people make do with gas and oil lamps (and without TVs and other modern conveniences).

Wiring Standards & Connection: Most modern properties (e.g. less than 20 years old) in Italy have good electrical installations. However, old rural homes may have no electricity or may need totally rewiring. You should ensure that the electricity installations are in good condition well in advance of moving house, as it can take some time to have a new meter installed or get the electricity reconnected. The wiring in a new or renovated house (that has been rewired) must be inspected and approved by an ENEL inspector before a contract is issued and connection (*allacciato*) is made. If you have any electrical work done in your home you should insure that you employ an electrician (*electtricista*) who's registered at the local chamber of commerce or a member of an official body such as Uane, who does work to ENEL's standards. Retain all bills for any installations or modifications as you will be able to offset the cost against a capital gain. There are safety regulations for all domestic electrical and gas systems and appliances, which must be inspected annually. Householders must have a certificate of inspection and there are fines of up to Lit. 10 million for offenders who break the law.

If you buy a rural property without electricity that's over 500 metres from the nearest electricity pylon, you must pay to have the service extended to the property. The cost of connecting a rural property to mains electricity may be prohibitively expensive or even be impossible, in which case you can install a generator or solar power system (see page 190). In this case wiring doesn't need to be installed to the high standard required by ENEL. Note that a generator should be powered by diesel and secured against theft.

Meters: In an old apartment block there may be a common meter, with the bill being shared among the apartment owners according to the size of their apartments. However, all new properties have their own meters, which for an apartment block or townhouse development may be installed in a basement in a special room or be housed in a meter 'cupboard' in a stair well or outside a group of properties. A meter should be located outside a home so that it can be read by electricity company staff when you aren't at home.

Plugs: Depending on the country you have come from, you will need new plugs (*spine*) or a lot of adapters. Plug adapters for most foreign electrical apparatus can be purchased in Italy, although it's wise to bring some adapters with you, plus extension cords and multi-plug extensions that can be fitted with Italian plugs. There's often a shortage of electricity points in Italian homes, with perhaps just one per room (including the kitchen), so multi-plug adapters may be essential. Electricity points don't usually have their own switches. Most Italian plugs have two or three round pins (when present, the middle pin of three is for the earth or ground) and come in various sizes depending on the power consumption of the appliance. Small low-wattage electrical appliances such as table lamps and small TVs don't require an earth. However, plugs with an earth must be used for high-wattage appliances such as fires, kettles, washing machines and refrigerators. These plugs must be used with earthed sockets. Electrical appliances that are earthed have a three-core wire and must never be used with a two-pin plug without an earth socket. **Always make sure that a plug is correctly and securely wired, as bad wiring can be fatal.**

Fuses: In modern properties, fuses (*fusibili*) are of the earth trip type. When there's a short circuit or the system has been overloaded, a circuit breaker is tripped and the power supply is cut. If your electricity fails, you should suspect a fuse of tripping off, particularly if you have just switched on an electrical appliance (usually you will hear the power switch off). Before reconnecting the power, switch off any high-power appliances such as a stove, washing machine or heater. Make sure you know where the trip switches are located and keep a torch handy so you can find them in the dark (see also **Power Rating** below).

Bulbs: Electric light bulbs in Italy are of the Edison type with a screw fitting. If you have lamps requiring bayonet bulbs you should bring some with you, as they cannot be readily purchased in Italy. You can, however, buy adapters to convert from bayonet to screw fitting (or vice versa). Bulbs for non-standard electrical appliances (i.e. appliances that aren't made for the Italian market) such as refrigerators and sewing machines may not be available in Italy, so bring some spares with you.

Power Rating: If the power keeps tripping off when you attempt to use a number of high-power appliances simultaneously, e.g. an electric kettle, heater and cooker, it means that the power rating of your property is too low. This is a common problem in Italy. If this is the case, you may need to contact your electricity company and ask them to uprate the power supply to your property (it can also be downgraded if the power supply is more than you require). Bear in mind that it can take some time to get your power rating changed. The power rating to a private dwelling in Italy can be 1.5kw, 3kw or 6kw (the maximum). The minimum rating is 1.5kw, which is sufficient for a few lights only and even with a 3kw rating you're unable to run more than two or three high-powered appliances simultaneously. Consequently many people are now switching to 6kw. The maximum is generally unrestricted, although is some remote areas (e.g. mountainous areas) you may be limited to just 3kw and to increase it you need to take out another contract for another 3kw (making a maximum of 6kw). If you have a low supply you can install a generator to increase it and use timers to ensure that no more than one high-powered apparatus is in operation simultaneously.

Your standing charge depends on the power rating of your supply, which is why owners tend to keep it as low as possible. A higher power rating will also increase the cost per unit of consumption. For example, changing from 3kw to 6kw can cost a million lire or more per year! Of the over 22 million electrical service contracts in Italy, over 18 million are for 3kw, including most apartments. The basic service cost depends on your power rating and whether your usage is low, medium or high, as shown in the table below:

Power Rating	Usage/Basic Service Cost (Lit.)		
	Low	Medium	High
1.5kw	6,450	17,250	28,650
3kw	12,900	34,500	57,300
6kw	25,800	69,000	114,600

Converters & Transformers: If you have electrical equipment rated at 110 volts AC (for example, from the USA) you will require a converter or a step-down transformer to convert it to 220 volts. However, some electrical appliances are fitted with a 110/220 volt switch. Check for the switch, which may be inside the casing, and make sure it's switched to 220 volts *before* connecting it to the power supply. Converters can be used for heating appliances, but transformers are required for motorised appliances. Total the wattage of the devices you intend to connect to a transformer and make sure that its power rating *exceeds* this sum. Generally all small, high-wattage, electrical appliances such as kettles, toasters, heaters and irons need large transformers. Motors in large appliances such as cookers, refrigerators, washing machines, dryers and dishwashers, will need replacing or fitting with a large transformer. In most cases it's simpler to buy new appliances in Italy, which are of good quality and reasonably priced (and sell them when you leave if you cannot take them with you). Note also that the dimensions of cookers, microwave ovens, refrigerators, washing machines, dryers and dishwashers purchased abroad may differ from those in Italy (and therefore may not fit into an Italian kitchen).

An additional problem with some electrical equipment is the frequency rating, which in some countries, e.g. the USA, is designed to run at 60Hertz (Hz) and not Europe's 50Hz. Electrical equipment *without* a motor is generally unaffected by the drop in frequency to 50Hz (except TVs). Equipment with a motor may run okay with a 20 per cent drop in speed; however, automatic washing machines, cookers, electric clocks, record players and tape recorders must be converted from the US 60Hz cycle to Italy's 50Hz cycle. To find out, look at the label on the back of the equipment. If it says 50/60Hz it should be okay; if it says 60Hz you can try it, **but first ensure that the voltage is correct as outlined above.** Bear in mind that the transformers and motors of electrical devices designed to run at 60Hz will run hotter at 50Hz, so make sure that apparatus has sufficient space around it to allow for cooling.

Tariffs: The cost of electricity in Italy is relatively high compared with many other EU countries. The tariff depends on your usage and power rating (see above), which is used to calculate your monthly standing charge, which is payable irrespective of whether you use any electricity during the billing period. Your actual consumption is charged per kwH and the cost depends on the amount of usage: Lit. 292.8 per kwH for low usage, Lit. 211.8 for medium usage and Lit. 177.8 for high usage. In other words, the basic cost (standing charge) increases with the power rating, but the actual cost of electricity consumption is reduced the more you use. Note that ENEL charges non-residents a higher rate and a residence certificate (*certificato di residenza*) is necessary to have a resident's contract. You can also buy energy friendly appliances that consume less energy than average and energy saving devices can be installed in appliances such as washing machines, dishwashers and dryers.

Bills: You're billed for electricity every two months. Bills (*conti* or *bolleta*) are based on estimated consumption and adjusted twice a year when meters have been read. Consumption is usually estimated for four months (two bills) and then adjusted (*conguaglio*) when a meter reading is taken. This may result in a larger than expected bill, therefore if you're a non-resident you should ensure that you have sufficient funds in your bank account. If you have overpaid you will receive a refund in the form of a postal order, which can be cashed at a post office. Half the bill contains account information and how to pay the bill and the other half a payment slip and a receipt for your records. Bills show the account number (*numero utente*), amount payable (*importo lire*), due date (*scadenza*) and the utility company's account number (*conto corrente*). Bills may be paid at banks, post offices and electricity company offices, although ENEL prefers to be paid by direct debit (*domiciliazione*) from a bank account (for which there's a small surcharge). Italian utility companies are notorious for over-charging, although customers rarely, if ever, get a refund. It's advisable to check that your meters remain static when services are turned off and to learn to read your electricity bill and meter and check your consumption to ensure that you aren't being overcharged.

GAS

Mains gas (*gas di città* or *mettano città*) in Italy is supplied by the *Societa Italiana per il Gas (ITALGAS or SIG)*. It's widely available in cities and large towns in the north of the country, but isn't available in the south or rural areas (e.g. in Tuscany and Umbria). When moving into a property with mains gas, you must contact SIG to have the gas switched on and the meter read, and have the account put into your name. You need to give the gas company the registration number of the meter and (if known) the name of the previous tenant. As with electricity, there are different contracts for residents and non-residents. The cost of mains gas is Lit. 65,710 per MCAL plus a standing charge of Lit. 3,000 per month. You're billed each two months and bills can be paid at banks, post offices and SIG offices, or by direct debit (*domiciliazione*) from a bank account.

Mains gas is mostly used for central heating and cooking. All gas appliances must be approved by SIG and installed by your local gas company; gas water heaters cannot be installed in bathrooms for safety reasons (although many people do so, often with fatal consequences). Old gas water heaters can leak carbon monoxide and have been the cause of a many deaths in Italy and other countries, although this is unlikely with a modern installation. Gas water heaters must be regularly serviced and descaled annually.

Bottled Gas: Bottled gas is mostly used for cooking, but can also be used to provide hot water and heating. The use of gas bottles (*bombolas*) is common in rural areas and they are also frequently used for portable gas fires in cities. You can have a combined gas hot water and heating system installed (providing background heat), which is relatively inexpensive to install and cheap to run. Cooking by bottled gas is cheaper than electricity and there's no standing charge (as with mains gas). Cookers often have a combination of electric and (bottled) gas rings (you can choose the mix). If your gas rings are sparked by electricity, keep some matches handy for use during power cuts.

You pay a deposit on the first bottle and thereafter exchange an empty bottle for a full one. The most common bottle size is 30kg, which costs around Lit. 40,000 plus a Lit. 5,000 delivery charge. Check when moving into a property that the gas bottle isn't empty. Keep a spare bottle or two handy and make sure you know how to change bottles (if necessary, ask the previous owner or your real estate agent to show you). Bottles are delivered in many areas and you can also buy them from agents and supermarkets. A bottle used just for cooking will last an average family around six weeks. Some people keep their gas bottles outside, often under a lean-to. If this is so, you must buy propane gas rather than butane, as it can withstand a greater range of temperatures than butane, which is for internal use only. Although bottled gas is very safe, if you use it you must inform your insurance company as there's an extra premium to pay.

If you live in a rural area you can have a gas tank (*bombolone*) installed. Tanks come in various sizes and can be installed (always above ground) by gas companies. It isn't necessary to buy the tank as it remains the property of the gas company who make their money through the sale of gas (although you can also buy your own tank and buy gas from which ever supplier is cheapest). When a tank is installed free, you must sign a contract to purchase a minimum amount of gas a year, e.g. to the value of Lit. 1 to 2 million. Gas can officially be used only for heating and hot water, although many people also use it for cooking and gas fires. A gas tank usually holds between 750 and 1,500 litres of liquid gas (1,000 litres is the most common size) and bulk gas costs around Lit. 1,000 per kg. The installation of gas tanks is strictly controlled and they must be at least 25m (82ft) from a house or road. If you have a gas tank installed on your property you must inform your insurance company as it will increase your home insurance.

WATER

In Italy, water is supplied by your *comune*, e.g. a local *Società d'Acquedotto (SADA)* or *Azienda Comunale Energia e Ambiente (ACEA)*. Each *comune* has its own rules concerning the use of water, which vary from area to area. Water, or rather the lack of it, is a major concern in many areas of Italy and the price paid for those long, hot summers. There's generally sufficient water in the north, but central and southern areas often experience acute shortages in summer.

Water is usually metered, with the meter being installed at the householder's expense. If water is metered, as in most of northern Italy, it's usual to have a contract for a limited number of cubic metres per household, per year, irrespective of the number of occupants. For example, 300 cubic metres (m³) per year, above which consumption you're charged at a high penal rate. Note that you cannot use this water for a garden or swimming pool, for which you need a special contract (called *uso vario*) and a separate meter. In rural areas, you may have access to 'agricultural' water for garden use. A *uso vario* contract can cost Lit. 1 to 2 million a year. In some regions the cost is prohibitive and therefore few residents have swimming pools, although you can recycle water for the garden and also have a pool filled by tanker (*autobotte*). In some areas, homeowners build an artificial water basin (*vasca*) that fills with rainwater during the winter and can also be fed by a spring or well. With a lining and filtering system, a *vasca* can double as a swimming pool in summer.

Cost: The price of water varies considerably from region to region, depending on its availability, and is among the most expensive in Europe. When moving into a new home, ask the local water company to read your meter. Where no water meter is installed, water is calculated on the size of a home (in square metres). Water bills (*acquedotto comunale*) are issued annually after your meter is read and should be paid within two months of receipt. Like other utility bills, water bills may be paid by direct debit (*domiciliazione*) from a bank account (unlike in some other countries, your water is unlikely to be summarily cut off if you're late paying a bill). Most apartment blocks (*condominios*) have a single meter for the whole block, where the cost is split equally between the owners and included in the fees or expenses (*spese*), which isn't a good idea if you have a holiday home in Italy.

Shortages: Water shortages are rare in towns, although they do occur occasionally, but are common in rural areas during the summer, when the water is periodically switched off (water is often switched off during the day and turned on at night). Water shortages are exacerbated in resort areas in summer, when the local population may swell tenfold and coincides with the hottest and driest period of the year. The use of sprinklers and hose-pipes is banned in many parts of Italy in summer. If you plan to maintain a garden in a region with low rainfall, you will need a reserve supply for dry periods (you can also use waste water). In some areas, water shortages create low water pressure, resulting in insufficient water to take a bath or shower. If you live in an area where cuts are common, you can have a storage tank (*cassone*) installed, which is topped up automatically when the water is switched on. A 500 litre tank is usually large enough for a family living in an apartment in a city or in a rural area that doesn't suffer water shortages. In a rural area without mains water it may be necessary to install an underground tank of 500,000 or one million litres (1,000m³) which is large enough to supply a family for up to six months. This is filled by tanker, but you should bear in mind that it's expensive.

Wells: Beware of the quaint well (*pozzo*) or spring (*sorgente*) as they can dry up, particularly in parts of central and southern Italy. Always confirm that a property has a reliable water source. If a property gets its water from a spring or well (possibly on a neighbour's land), make sure that there's no dispute over its ownership and your rights to use it, e.g. that it cannot be stopped or drained away by your neighbours. Note, however, that well water is usually excellent (and free), although you may need a pump (manual or electric) to bring it to the surface. You can also create your own well if land has water. Dowsing (finding water by holding a piece of forked wood) is as accurate as anything devised by modern science and has an 80 per cent success rate. A good dowser or water diviner (*rabdomante*) can estimate the water's yield and purity to within 10 or 20 per cent accuracy. Before buying rural land without a water supply, engage an experienced dowser with a successful track record to check it. Rural homes with their own well or spring are at a premium in Italy.

Mains Connection: If you own a property in or near a town or village, you can usually be connected to a mains water system. Note, however, that connection can be expensive as you must pay for digging the channels required for pipes. Obtain a quotation (*preventivo*) from the local water company for the connection of the supply and the installation of a water meter. Expect the connection to cost at least Lit. 1.5 million and possibly much more, depending on the type of terrain and soil (or rock!) which must be excavated to lay pipes. If you're thinking about buying a property and installing a mains water supply, get a quotation before signing the contract.

Water Heaters: If you need to install a hot water boiler or immersion heater, ensure that it's large enough for the size of property, e.g. one room studio (100 litres), two rooms (150 litres), three to four rooms (200 litres) and five to seven rooms or two bathrooms (300 litres). Many holiday homes have quite small water boilers that are often inadequate for more than two people. If you need to install a water heater or a larger water heater, you should consider the merits of both electric and bottled gas heaters. An electric water boiler with a capacity of 75 litres (sufficient for two people) usually takes between 75 to 125 minutes (in winter) to heat water to 40 degrees.

A (bottle) gas flow-through water heater is more expensive to purchase and install than an electric water boiler, but you get unlimited hot water immediately whenever you want it and there are no standing charges. A gas heater should have a capacity of 10 to 16 litres per minute if it's to be used for a shower. Note that there's usually little difference in quality between different priced heaters, although a gas water heater with a permanent flame may use up to 50 per cent more gas than one without it. A resident family with a constant consumption is usually better off with an electric heater, while non-residents using a property for short periods will find a self-igniting gas heater more economical. A solar power system can also be used to provide hot water (see page 190).

Security Measures: Before moving into a new home you should check where the main stop-valve or stopcock is located, so that you can turn off the water supply in an emergency. If the water stops flowing for any reason, you should ensure that all the taps are turned off to prevent flooding when the supply starts again. Note that in community (*condominio*) properties, the tap to turn the water on or off is usually located outside the building. When leaving a property empty for an extended period, particularly during the winter when there's the possibility of freezing, you should turn off the mains stopcock, switch off the system's controls and drain the pipes, toilets (you can leave salt in the toilet bowls to prevent freezing) and radiators. It's also advisable to have your cold water tank and the tank's ball valves checked periodically for corrosion, and to check the hosing on appliances such as washing machines and dishwashers. It can be very expensive if a pipe bursts and the leak goes undiscovered for a long time!

Quality: When water isn't drinkable it's usually marked 'non-drinking' (*acqua non potabile*). Note that water from wells and springs isn't always safe to drink. You can have well or spring water analysed by the public health department or the local water authority. It's possible to install filtering, cleansing and softening equipment to improve water quality, but you should obtain independent advice before installing a system as not all equipment is equally effective. Note that while boiling water will kill any bacteria, it won't remove any toxic substances contained in it. Although mains water in Italy is usually drinkable, it may be contaminated by industrial chemicals and nitrates, although supposedly not enough to harm your health. However, many Italians consider it undrinkable and drink bottled water (when not drinking wine!). In general, water is hard in Italy with a high calcium content. You can use a water softener to soften hard water and a filter to prevent the furring of pipes, radiators and appliances. Water in Italy may be fluoridated, depending on the area.

HEATING & AIR-CONDITIONING

Central heating systems in Italy may be powered by oil, gas, electricity, solid fuel (usually wood) or even solar power. Whatever form of heating you use, it's essential to have good insulation, without which up to 60 per cent of heating is lost through the walls and roof. Over half of Italian homes have central heating, which is essential in northern Italy if you plan to spend any time there outside the summer months. Many people keep their central heating on a low setting during short absences in winter (which can be controlled via a master thermostat) to prevent freezing. Heating requirements in winter vary from six hours a day for around 14 weeks a year in the south to over 14 hours a day for six months or longer in the north.

Apartment blocks (*condominios*) usually have central heating (*riscaldamento*) which can be either autonomous (*autonomo*) or central (*centrale*). With *riscaldamento autonomo* you can control the heating independently and are billed according to your use. With *riscaldamento centrale* the heating is turned on in autumn (October) and off in spring (March) and you have no control over this and must pay the same as other residents, even if you're a non-resident in winter. Note that aluminium radiators are preferable to cast-iron as they withstand extreme cold better and are less likely to leak or burst. More importantly, Italian insurance companies won't cover you for burst cast-iron radiators and the subsequent water damage.

Solid Fuel: Many people rely solely on wood-burning stoves or fireplaces for their heating and hot water, particularly in rural areas. Stoves come in a huge variety of sizes and styles, and may also heat radiators throughout a house and provide hot water. Most people burn wood (which should have been seasoned for at least two years), which is relatively inexpensive in Italy, rather than coal or coke. You can have it delivered cut and dried or can also collect it free if you live in the country. The main disadvantages are the chores of collecting and chopping wood, cleaning the grate and lighting fires. Smoke can also be a problem. Note that an open fireplace can be wasteful of heat and fuel. An enclosed hearth with a glass door is more effective and often has the advantage of a hot-air chamber that warms other parts of a home, plus less heat wastage, a reduced fire hazard, and less ash and dust.

Electric: Electric central heating isn't common in Italy as it's too expensive. However, many people with modern homes with good insulation and a permanent system of ventilation, use storage heaters. Electric central heating isn't recommended for old properties with poor insulation. If you install an electric central heating system you may need to increase your electricity rating (see **Power Rating** on page 183) to cope with the extra demand. Stand-alone electric (e.g. halogen) heaters are relatively expensive to run and are best suited to holiday homes.

Gas: Mains gas central heating is popular, relatively cheap to run and widely used in the north of Italy. Gas is clean, economical and efficient, and the boiler is usually fairly small and can be wall-mounted. In rural areas where there's no mains gas, you can have a gas tank (*bombolone*) installed on your property (see page 185). The cost of heating with methane (*metano*) gas is between Lit. 900 and Lit. 1,300 per square metre.

Oil: Oil-fired central heating isn't common in Italy due to the high cost of heating oil and the problems associated with storage and deliveries. Heating oil costs around Lit. 1,500 a litre (70 per cent of which is tax) and is among the most expensive in

Europe. An average family of four can expect to use around 1,700 litres a year over some 120 days at a cost of around Lit. 2.5 million. You also need space to install the storage tank. If you have a tank of 2,000 litre capacity or larger it must be buried in your garden or stored in a separate location sheltered from frost and away from the house. A smaller tank can be located in or near your home, but will need to be refilled more often.

Solar Power: A solar power system can be used to supply all your energy needs, although it's usually combined with an electric or gas heating system, as solar power cannot be relied upon year-round for heating and hot water. The main drawback is the high cost of installation, which varies considerably depending on the region and how much energy you require. A solar power system must be installed by an expert. The advantages are no running costs, silent operation, maintenance free and no electricity bills. A system should last 30 years (it's usually guaranteed for ten years) and can be uprated to provide more power in the future. Solar power can also be used to heat a swimming pool. Continuous advances in solar cell and battery technology are expected to dramatically increase the efficiency and reduce the cost of solar power, which is forecast to become the main source of energy world-wide in the next century. A solar power system can also be used to provide electricity in a remote rural home, where the cost of extending electricity is prohibitive.

The Costs: The cost of heating a property varies depending on a number of factors, not least the fuel used, the size of your home, and the length of time your heating is switched on. You can have your home inspected by a heating engineer who will assess its heating requirements and cost, taking into account the insulation and equipment installed. The engineer will produce a report detailing the most effective means of insulating and heating your home, and a number of cost estimates.

Humidifiers: Note that central heating dries the air and may cause your family to develop coughs. Those who find the dry air unpleasant can purchase a humidifier to add moisture to the air. Humidifiers that don't generate steam should be disinfected occasionally with a special liquid available from pharmacies, (to prevent nasty diseases). Humidifiers may range from simple water containers hanging from radiators to expensive electric or battery-operated devices.

Air-conditioning: Few homes in Italy have air-conditioning (*condizionamento d'aria*), despite the fact that summer temperatures reach over 40C (104F) in some areas. Although properties are built to withstand the heat, you may find it beneficial to install air-conditioning, although there can be negative effects if you suffer from asthma or respiratory problems. You can choose between a huge variety of air-conditioners, fixed or moveable, indoor or outdoor installation, and high or low power. Air-conditioning units cost from around Lit. 1.5 million (plus installation) for a unit that's sufficient to cool an average sized room. An air-conditioning system with a heat pump provides cooling in summer and heating in winter. Many people fit ceiling fans for extra cooling in the summer (costing from around Lit. 150,000), which are standard fixtures in some new homes.

PROPERTY INCOME

Many people planning to buy a holiday home in Italy are interested in owning a property that will provide them with an income to cover the running costs and help with mortgage payments. The most common examples are holiday letting for owners of second homes and self-catering or bed and breakfast accommodation for residents. Note, however, that you're highly unlikely to meet your mortgage payments and running costs from rental income. Buyers who over stretch their financial resources often find themselves on the rental treadmill, constantly struggling to find sufficient income to cover their running costs and mortgage payments. It's difficult to make a living providing holiday accommodation or bed & breakfast in most areas as the season is too short and there's simply too much competition (the market is saturated in most regions). If you're planning on holiday lets, don't overestimate the length of the season, which varies depending on the region. In some areas it's as long as 16 weeks, while in others it's ten weeks or less. The letting season is longest in southern Italy (e.g. on the Amalfi Coast and in Sicily) and the major cities and ski resorts, where properties have year-round letting potential. Bear in mind that tax must be paid on rental income earned in Italy and long-term rental properties must be registered with the authorities.

In the early '90s, some overseas buyers lost their Italian homes after they defaulted on their mortgage payments, often because rental income failed to meet expectations. Note that buying property in Italy (and in most other countries) isn't usually a good investment compared with the return on income that can be achieved by investing elsewhere. **Most experts recommend that you don't purchase a home in Italy if you need to rely on rental income to pay for it.**

Location/Swimming Pools: If an income from your Italian property has a high priority, you should buy a property with this in mind. To maximise rental income, a property should be located as close as possible to the main attractions, a major city and/or a beach, be suitably furnished and professionally managed. A swimming pool is obligatory, as properties with pools are much easier to let than those without (unless a property is situated on a beach, lake or river). It's usually necessary to have a private pool with a detached home, but a shared pool is sufficient with an apartment or townhouse. You can also charge a higher rent for a property with a pool and you may be able to extend the season even further by installing a heated or indoor pool. Some letting agencies won't handle properties without a pool. It's important to check the local regulations before installing a pool or letting a property with one.

Rents: Rental rates vary considerably depending on the time of year, area, size and quality. A house sleeping four to six people in an average area can be let for around Lit. 600,000 to 900,000 a week in high season. At the other extreme, a luxury property in a popular area with a pool and accommodation for 8 to 12 can be let for between Lit. 3 to 6 million or more a week in the high season, which generally includes the months of July and August and possibly the first two weeks of September. The mid season usually comprises June, September and October (and possibly Easter), when rents are around 20 to 25 per cent lower than the high season; the rest of the year is the low season. For long-term lets in the low season, a house sleeping four to six usually rents for around one million lire a month in most rural areas, with the tenant paying for all utilities.

Furnishings & Keys: If you let a property, don't fill it with expensive furnishings or valuable personal belongings. While theft is rare, items will certainly get damaged or broken over a period of time. When furnishing a property that you plan to let, you should choose hard wearing, dark coloured carpets which won't show the stains, and buy durable furniture and furnishings. Simple inexpensive furniture is best in a modest home, as it will need to stand up to hard wear. Small one or two-bedroom properties usually have a settee in the living room that converts into a double bed. Properties should be well equipped with cooking utensils, crockery and cutlery, and it's also advisable to provide bed linen and towels. You may also need a cot or high chair for young children. Depending on the price and quality of a property, your guests may also expect central heating, a washing machine, dishwasher, microwave, covered parking, a barbecue and garden furniture. Some owners provide bicycles, and badminton and table tennis equipment. It isn't usual to have a telephone in rental homes, although you could install a credit card telephone or a phone that will receive incoming calls only.

You will need several sets of spare keys, which will inevitably get lost at some time. If you employ a management company, their address should be on the key fob and not the address of the house. If you let a home yourself, you can use a 'keyfinder' service, whereby lost keys can be returned to the keyfinder company by anyone finding them. You should ensure that you get 'lost' keys returned, otherwise you may have to change the locks (in any case it's advisable to change the external locks annually if you let a home). You don't need to provide clients with keys to all external doors, only the front door (the others can be left in your home). If you arrange your own lets, you can mail keys to clients in your home country, otherwise they can be collected from a caretaker in Italy. It's also possible to install a security key-pad entry system.

Letting Agents: If you're letting a second home, the most important decision is whether to let it yourself or use a letting agent (or agents). If you don't have much spare time you're better off using an agent, who will take care of everything and save you the time and expense of advertising and finding clients. An agent will charge commission of between 20 and 40 per cent of gross rental income, although some of this can be recouped through higher rents. If you want your property to appear in an agent's catalogue, you must contact him the summer before you wish to let it (the deadline is usually September). Note that although self-catering holiday companies may fall over themselves to take on luxury properties in the most popular areas, top letting agents turn down as many as 9 out of every 10 properties they're offered.

Most agents don't permit owners to use a property during the peak letting season (July and August) and may also restrict their use at other times. There are numerous self-catering holiday companies, most of whom have agents in many countries (try your local travel agent). Some Italian real estate agents in resort areas and cities also act as agents for holiday lets and some specialise in long-term winter lets. Before buying a *condominio* you should check that letting is permitted. You may need to notify the *condominio's* administrator and your insurance company if a property is to be let.

Take care when selecting a letting agent, as a number have gone bust in recent years owing customers millions of lire. Make sure that your income is kept in an escrow account and paid regularly, or even better, choose an agent with a bonding scheme who pays you the rent *before* the arrival of guests (some do). It's absolutely essential to employ an efficient, reliable and honest company, preferably long-established. Note that anyone can set up a holiday letting agency and there are a number of 'cowboy' operators. Always ask a management company to substantiate rental income claims and occupancy rates by showing you examples of actual income received from other properties. Ask for the names of satisfied customers and check with them.

Other things to ask a letting agent include who they let to; where they advertise; whether they have contracts with holiday and travel companies; whether you're expected to contribute towards marketing costs; and whether you're free to let the property yourself and use it when you wish. The larger companies market homes via newspapers, magazines, overseas agents and colour brochures, and have representatives in many countries. Management contracts usually run for a year. A management company's services should include arranging routine and emergency repairs; reading meters (if electricity is charged as an extra); routine maintenance of house and garden, including lawn cutting and pool cleaning; arranging cleaning and linen changes between lets; advising guests on the use of equipment; and providing guest information and advice (24-hours in the case of emergencies). Agents may also provide someone to meet and greet clients, hand over the keys and check that everything is in order. The actual services provided usually depend on whether a property is a basic cottage or a luxury villa costing millions of lire a week. A letting agent's representative should also make periodic checks when a property is empty to ensure that it's secure and that everything is in order.

Doing Your Own Letting: Some owners prefer to let a property to family, friends, colleagues and acquaintances, which allows them more control (and *hopefully* the property will be better looked after). In fact, the best way to get a high volume of lets is usually to do it yourself, although many owners use a letting agency in addition to doing their own marketing in their home country. If you wish to let a property yourself, there's a wide range of Italian and foreign newspapers and magazines in which you can advertise, e.g. *Dalton's Weekly* and newspapers such as the *Sunday Times* and *Sunday Telegraph* in Britain. The English-language newspapers & magazines listed in **Appendix A** also accept advertisements from property owners. You will need to experiment to find the best publications and days of the week or months to advertise.

There are also companies which produce directories of properties let directly by owners. You pay for the advertisement but handle bookings yourself. Italian regional tourist agencies can put you in touch with Italian letting agents. You can also advertise among friends and colleagues, in company and club magazines (which may even be free), and on notice boards in company offices, stores and shopping centres. The more marketing you do, the more income you're likely to earn. It also pays to work with other local people in the same business and send surplus guests to competitors (they will usually reciprocate). It isn't necessary to just advertise locally or stick to your home country and you can also extend your marketing abroad (you can also advertise via the Internet). It's necessary to have a telephone answering machine and a fax machine.

Rents: To get an idea of the rent you should charge, simply ring a few letting agencies and ask them what it would cost to rent a property such as yours at the time of year you plan to let. They are likely to quote the highest possible rent you can charge. You should also check the advertisements in newspapers and magazines. Set a realistic rent as there's a lot of competition. Add a returnable deposit (Lit. 300,000) as security against loss of keys and breakages. A deposit should be refundable up to six weeks before the booking. It's normal to have a minimum two-week rental period in July and August. You will need to have a simple agreement form that includes the dates of arrival and departure and approximate times. Note that if you plan to let to non-English speaking clients, you must have a letting agreement in other languages.

If you plan to let a home yourself, you will need to decide how to handle enquiries about flights and car rentals. It's easier to let clients do it themselves, but you should be able to offer advice and put them in touch with airlines, ferry companies, travel agents and car rental companies (see page 44). You will also need to decide whether you want to let to smokers or accept pets or young children (some people don't let to families with children under five years of age due to the risks of bed-wetting). It's usual to provide linen (some agents provide a linen hire service), which is usually expected, although electricity may not be included in the rental fee.

It's advisable to produce a colour brochure containing external/internal pictures (or a single-colour brochure with coloured photographs affixed to it, although this doesn't look so professional), important details, the exact location, local attractions, details of how to get there (with a map), and the name, address and telephone number of your local caretaker or letting agent. You should enclose a stamped, addressed envelope when sending out leaflets. It's necessary to make a home look as attractive as possible in a brochure without distorting the facts or misrepresentation. Advertise honestly and don't over-sell your property.

Local Information: You should also provide an information pack for clients explaining how things work (such as heating and air-conditioning); what not to do; where to shop; recommended restaurants; local emergency numbers and health services such as doctors, hospitals and dentists; and assistance such as a general repairman, plumber, electrician and pool maintenance (although if you have an agent or local caretaker, he should take care of these). If you allow young children and pets, you should make a point of emphasising any dangers, such as falling into the pool. It's also beneficial to have a visitor's book where your clients can write their comments and recommendations. If you want to impress your guests you may wish to arrange for fresh flowers, fruit, a good bottle of wine and a grocery pack to greet them on their arrival. It's little touches like this that ensure repeat business and recommendations. If you go 'the extra mile' it will pay off in recommendations and you may find that you rarely need to advertise after your first year or two in business. Many people return to the same property each year and you should do an annual mail-shot to previous clients and send them some brochures. **Word-of-mouth advertising is the cheapest and always the best.**

Caretaker: If you have a second home in Italy, you will find it beneficial or even essential to employ a local caretaker, irrespective of whether you let it. You may also need to employ a gardener. You can have your caretaker prepare the house for your family and guests, in addition to looking after it when it isn't in use. If you have a holiday home in Italy it's advisable to have your caretaker check it periodically (e.g. weekly) and to give him authority to authorise minor repairs. If you let a property yourself, your caretaker can arrange for (or do) cleaning, linen changes, maintenance and repairs, gardening and the payment of bills.

Increasing Rental Income: It's possible to increase rental income outside the high season by offering special interest or package holidays, which can be organised in conjunction with other local businesses in order to broaden the appeal and cater for larger parties. These may include activity holidays such as golf, tennis, cycling or hiking; cooking, gastronomy and wine tours/tasting; and arts & crafts such as painting, sculpture, photography and writing courses. You don't need to be an expert or conduct courses yourself, but can employ someone to do it for you.

Long-term lets: Long-term lets can be anything from one to six months and usually exclude the high season. Most people who let year round have low, medium and high season rates. Rates are naturally much lower for winter lets, when you shouldn't expect to earn more than around one million lire a month in most regions for a property sleeping four to six. The tenant usually pays the running costs such as utilities. Note that central heating is essential if you want to let long-term. If you let a property long-term, you should be aware that there are separate laws governing unfurnished accommodation, furnished accommodation and holiday letting.

Closing a property for the winter: Before closing up a property for the winter, you should turn off the water at the mains and drain all pipes (see also **Security Measures** on page 188), remove all the fuses (except the one for a dehumidifier if you leave it on while you're away), empty the food cupboards and the refrigerator/freezer, disconnect gas cylinders and empty dustbins. You should also leave the interior doors and a few small windows with grills or secure shutters open to provide ventilation. Many people keep their central heating on a low setting during the winter (which can be controlled via a master thermostat) during absences to prevent freezing. Lock all the doors and shutters and secure anything of value against theft or leave it with a neighbour. Check whether any essential work is necessary before you leave and arrange for it to be done in your absence. Most importantly, leave a set of keys with a neighbour and have a caretaker check your home periodically. See also **Renting** on page 141.

SELLING A HOME

Although this book is primarily concerned with buying a home in Italy, you may wish to sell your Italian home at some time in the future. Before offering your Italian home for sale, it's advisable to investigate the state of the property market. For example, unless you're forced to sell, it definitely isn't advisable during a property slump when prices are depressed. It may be wiser to let your home long-term and wait until the market has recovered. It's also unwise to sell in the early years after purchase, when you will probably make a loss unless it was an absolute bargain. Having decided to sell, your first decision will be whether to try to sell it yourself or use the services of a real estate agent. Although the majority of properties in Italy are sold through real estate agents, a large number of owners also sell their own homes. If you need to sell a property before buying a new one, this must be included as a conditional clause (see page 167) in the purchase contract for a new home.

Price: It's important to bear in mind that (like everything) property has a market price and the best way of ensuring a quick sale (or any sale) is to ask a realistic price. In recent years prices have fallen and some properties have remained on the market for ages largely because owners have asked absurd prices. If your home's fairly standard for the area you can find out its value by comparing the prices of other homes on the market or those which have recently been sold. Most agents will provide a free appraisal of a home's value in the hope that you will sell it through them. However, don't believe everything they tell you as they may over-price it simply to encourage you. You can also hire a professional appraiser to determine the market value.

You should be prepared to drop the price slightly (e.g. 5 or 10 per cent) and should set it accordingly, but shouldn't grossly over-price a home as it will deter buyers. Don't reject an offer out of hand unless it's ridiculously low, as you may be able to get a prospective buyer to raise his offer. When selling a second home in Italy, you may wish to include the furnishings (plus major appliances) in the sale, particularly when selling a relatively inexpensive property with modest furnishings. You should add an appropriate amount to the price to cover the value of the furnishings, or alternatively you could use them as an inducement to a prospective buyer at a later stage (although this isn't usual in Italy). **Note that when selling a home in Italy, you may have to wait a number of weeks after completion before you receive payment.**

Presentation: The secret to selling a home quickly lies in its presentation, always assuming that it's competitively priced. First impressions (both exteriors and interiors) are vital when marketing your home and it's important to make every effort to present it in its best light and make it as attractive as possible to potential buyers. It may pay to invest in new interior decoration, new carpets, exterior paint and landscaping. A few plants and flowers can do wonders. Note that when decorating a home for resale, it's important to be conservative and not to do anything radical (such as install a red or black bathroom suite); white is a good neutral colour for walls, woodwork and porcelain.

It may also pay you to do some modernisation such as installing a new kitchen or bathroom, as these are of vital importance (particularly kitchens) when selling a home. Note, however, that although modernisation may be necessary to sell an old home, you shouldn't overdo it as it's easy to spend more than you could ever hope to recoup on its sale. If you're using an agent, you can ask him what you should do (or need to do) to help sell your home. If your home is in poor repair, this must be reflected in the asking price and if major work is needed which you cannot afford, you should obtain a quotation (or two) and offer to knock this off the asking price. Note that you have a duty under Italian law to inform a prospective buyer of any defects that aren't readily apparent and which materially affect the value of a property. There are also special disclosure requirements for apartments and other community properties (see page 153).

Selling Your Home Yourself: While certainly not for everyone, selling your own home is a viable option for many people and is particularly recommended when you're selling an attractive home at a *realistic* price in a favourable market. It may allow you to offer it at a more appealing price, which could be an important factor if you're seeking a quick sale. How you market your home will depend on the type of home, the price, and the country or area from where you expect your buyer to come. For example, if your property isn't of a type and style and in an area desirable to local inhabitants, it's usually a waste of time advertising it in the Italian press.

Advertising is the key to selling your home. The first step is to get a professional looking 'For Sale' (*vendisi*) sign made showing your telephone number and display it in the garden or a window. Do some market research into the best newspapers and magazines for advertising your property, and place an advertisement in those that look most promising. You could also have a leaflet printed (with pictures) extolling the virtues of your property, which you could drop into local letter boxes or have distributed with a local newspaper (many people buy a new home in the immediate vicinity of their present home). You may also need a 'fact sheet' printed if your home's vital statistics aren't included in the leaflet mentioned above and could offer a finder's fee (e.g. Lit. 1.5 million) to anyone finding you a buyer. Don't omit to market your home around local companies, schools and organisations, particularly if they have many itinerant or foreign employees. Finally, it may help to provide information about local financing sources for potential buyers. With a bit of effort and practice you may even make a better job of marketing your home than an agent! Unless you're in a hurry to sell, set yourself a realistic time limit for success, after which you can try an agent. When selling a home yourself, you will need to obtain legal advice regarding contracts and engage a *notaio* to complete the sale.

Using An Agent: Most vendors prefer to use the services of an agent, either in Italy or in their home country, particularly when selling a second home. If you purchased the property through an agent, it's often advisable to use the same agent when selling, as he will already be familiar with it and may still have the details on file. You should take particular care when selecting an agent as they vary considerably in their professionalism, expertise and experience (the best way to investigate agents is by posing as a buyer). Note that many agents cover a relatively small area, so you should take care to choose one who regularly sells properties in your area and price range. If you own a property in an area popular with foreign buyers, it may be worthwhile using an overseas agent or advertising in foreign newspapers and magazines, such as the English-language publications listed in **Appendix A**.

Agents' Contracts: Before offering a property for sale, an Italian agent must have a signed authorisation from the owner or his representative. There are generally two types of agreement, an ordinary or non-exclusive agreement, which means that you reserve the right to deal with other agents and to negotiate directly with private individuals, and an exclusive agreement. An exclusive agreement gives a single agent the exclusive right to sell a property, although you can reserve the right to find a private buyer. There are no multiple listings in Italy, so if you don't have an exclusive agreement you must contact a number of agents individually. An agent's fees are usually lower with an exclusive agreement than with a non-exclusive agreement. **If you sign a contract without reserving the right to find your own buyer, you must still pay the agent's commission even if you sell your home yourself.** Make sure that you don't sign two or more exclusive agreements to sell your home. Check the contract and make sure you understand what you're signing. Note that you must still pay an agent's fee if you sell to someone introduced by him within a certain period (e.g. one year) of the expiry of an agreement. Contracts state the agent's commission, what it includes, and most importantly, who must pay it. **Generally you shouldn't pay any fees unless you require extra services and you should never pay commission before a sale is completed.**

Agents' Fees: Agents' fees vary considerably (e.g. from 3 to 8 per cent) depending on the agent and area, and are usually shared between the vendor and buyer. For example a buyer may pay 2 to 3 per cent of the purchase price and the vendor about the same (see **Real Estate Agents** on page 159). When selling a property, the agent's commission is usually included in the purchase price. Foreign agents who work with Italian agents share the standard commission, so you should pay no more by using a foreign agent.

Capital Gains Tax: Capital gains tax (see page 104) has been abolished for property owners in Italy, although it's still payable on gains accrued before 1st January 1993 when a property is sold before 1st January 2003. Note, however, that you may be liable for CGT or income tax in another country. When CGT is payable, a percentage may be withheld from the proceeds of a sale by the *notaio*.

As when buying a home, you must be very, very careful who you deal with when selling a home. Never agree to accept part of the sale price 'under the table', which is illegal in any case, as if the buyer refuses to pay it there's nothing you can do about it. However, if you do decide to accept part of the price under the table, make sure that it's paid in cash *before* signing the final deed (see also **Avoiding Problems** on page 132). Note that when the buyer has a mortgage, it's usually a few weeks after completion when you receive payment.

5.

ARRIVAL & SETTLING IN

On arrival in Italy your first task will be to negotiate immigration and customs. Fortunately this presents few problems for most people, particularly European Union (EU) nationals after the establishment of 'open' EU borders on 1st January 1993. However, with the exception of EU nationals and visitors from a number of other countries, all others wishing to enter Italy require a visa (see page 18).

Italy is a signatory to the Schengen agreement (named after a Luxembourg village on the Moselle River where the agreement was signed) which came into effect in 1994 and introduced an open-border policy between member countries. Other Schengen members are Austria, Belgium, France, Germany, Greece, Iceland, Luxembourg, the Netherlands, Portugal, Spain and Sweden. Under the agreement, immigration checks and passport controls take place when you first arrive in a member country, after which you can travel freely between other Schengen countries. Italy has some 300 frontier crossing points, although entry to non-EU nationals requiring a visa is restricted to certain road/rail crossings and major airports only. A list is available from Italian consulates and embassies.

In addition to information about immigration and customs, this chapter contains checklists of tasks to be completed before or soon after arrival in Italy and when moving house, plus suggestions for finding local help and information.

IMMIGRATION

When you arrive in Italy from a country that's a signatory to the Schengen agreement (see above), there are usually no immigration checks or passport controls, which take place when you first arrive in a Schengen member country. Officially, Italian immigration officials should check the passports of EU arrivals from non-Schengen countries, although this doesn't always happen. If you're a non-EU national and arrive in Italy by air or sea from outside the EU, you must go through immigration (*immigrazione*) for non-EU citizens. If you have a single-entry visa it will be cancelled by the immigration official. If you require a visa to enter Italy and attempt to enter without one, you will be refused entry. Some people may wish to get a stamp in their passport as confirmation of their date of entry into Italy.

If you're a non-EU national coming to Italy to work, study or live, you may be asked to show documentary evidence. Immigration officials may ask non-EU visitors to produce a return ticket, proof of accommodation, health insurance and financial resources, e.g. cash, travellers' cheques and credit cards. The onus is on visitors to show that they are genuine and that they won't violate Italian immigration laws. Immigration officials aren't required to prove that you will break the immigration laws and can refuse you entry on the grounds of suspicion only. Young people may be liable to interrogation, particularly long-haired youths with 'strange' attire. It's advantageous to carry international credit and charge cards, a return or onward travel ticket, and if applicable, a student identity card, and a letter from an employer or college stating that you're on holiday.

Italian immigration officials are usually polite and efficient, although they are occasionally a little over zealous in their attempts to exclude illegal immigrants, and certain nationalities or racial groups (e.g. Africans and Albanians) may experience harassment or persecution.

CUSTOMS

The Single European Act, which came into effect on 1st January 1993, created a single trading market and changed the rules regarding customs (*dogana*) for EU nationals. The shipment of personal (household) effects to Italy from another EU country is no longer subject to customs formalities, although an inventory must be provided. Note, however, that all persons arriving in Italy from outside the EU (including EU citizens) are still subject to customs' checks and limitations on what may be imported duty-free. You may import or export up to Lit. 20 million in any combination of foreign and Italian currency and travellers' cheques without formality. Amounts over Lit. 20 million (e.g. to buy a home) must be declared in order to prevent money laundering and provide statistical data for the Bank of Italy (*Banca d'Italia*).

Information about duty-free allowances can be found on page 67 and pets on page 68.

Visitors

Your belongings aren't subject to duty or VAT when you visit Italy for up to six months (182 days). This applies to the import of private cars, camping vehicles (including trailers or caravans), motorcycles, aircraft, boats and personal effects. Goods may be imported without formality, providing their nature and quantity doesn't imply any commercial aim. All means of transport and personal effects imported duty-free mustn't be sold or given away in Italy, and must be exported when you leave the country. If you enter Italy by road, you may drive through a border post without stopping (most are now unmanned anyway). However, any goods and pets that you're carrying mustn't be subject to any prohibitions or restrictions. Customs' officials can still stop anyone for a spot check, e.g. to check for drugs or illegal immigrants, even within Italy.

If you arrive at a seaport by private boat there are no particular customs' formalities, although you must show the boat's registration papers on request. A vessel registered outside the EU may remain in Italy for a maximum of six months in any calendar year, after which it must be exported or imported (when duty and tax must be paid). Foreign-registered vehicles and boats mustn't be lent or rented to anyone while in Italy.

Non-EU Residents

If you're a non-EU resident planning to take up permanent or temporary residence in Italy, you're permitted to import your furniture and personal effects free of duty. These include vehicles, mobile homes, pleasure boats and aircraft. However, to qualify for duty-free importation, articles must have been owned and used for at least six months. Value Added Tax (VAT) must be paid on all items owned for less than six months that weren't purchased within the EU. If goods were purchased within the EU, a VAT receipt must be produced.

All items should be imported within six months of the date of your change of residence, although they may be imported in a number of consignments (but it's best to have one only). A complete inventory (in English and Italian) of all items to be imported must be approved by your local Italian consulate abroad (it will be stamped and a copy returned to you), together with proof of residence in your former country and proof of settlement in Italy (i.e. a *permesso di soggiorno*). If there's more than one shipment, subsequent consignments should be cleared through the same customs office. If you fail to follow the correct procedure you may encounter problems and delays. If you use a removal company to transport your belongings to Italy, they will usually provide all the necessary forms and take care of the paperwork. Always keep a copy of all forms and communications with customs officials, both with Italian customs officials and officials in your previous country of residence. You should have an official record of the export of valuables from any country in case you wish to re-import them later.

Prohibited & Restricted Goods

Certain goods are subject to special regulations and in some cases their import and export is prohibited or restricted. This applies in particular to animal products; plants; wild fauna and flora and products derived from them; live animals; medicines and medical products (except for prescribed drugs and medicines); firearms and ammunition; certain goods and technologies with a dual civil/military purpose; and works of art and collectors' items. If you're unsure whether any goods that you're planning to import fall into the above categories, you should check with Italian customs. Visitors arriving in Italy from 'exotic' regions, e.g. Africa, South America, and the Middle and Far East, may find themselves under close scrutiny from customs' and security officials looking for illegal drugs.

RESIDENCE PERMIT

All foreigners planning to reside in Italy for longer than 90 days are required to register with the local authorities and obtain a permit. Whether you're an employee, student, or a non-employed resident, you must apply at a local police headquarters (*questura*) for a permit to stay (*permesso di soggiorno*) within eight days of your arrival. The *permesso* can take up to three months to obtain. Note that a *permesso di soggiorno* certifies that you're permitted to live in the country and not that you're a resident. Once you have your *permesso* you can apply for a residence permit (*certificato di residenza*), which is necessary if you spend longer than 183 days a year in Italy.

FINDING HELP

One of the most important tasks facing new arrivals in Italy is how and where to obtain help with essential everyday tasks such as buying a car, obtaining medical help and insurance requirements. How successful you are at finding local help will depend on your employer (if applicable), the town or area where you live (those who live in major cities are usually better served than those who inhabit small towns), your nationality, Italian proficiency and sex (women are usually better served than men through numerous women's clubs).

There's an abundance of information available in Italian, but little in English and other foreign languages. An additional problem is that much of the available information isn't intended for foreigners and their particular needs. You may find that your friends and colleagues can help, as they can often offer advice based on their own experiences and mistakes. But take care! Although they mean well, you're likely to receive as much false and conflicting information as accurate (it may not necessarily be wrong, but may be invalid for your particular situation). Your local community is usually an excellent source of reliable information, but you need to speak Italian to benefit from it.

There's a wealth of valuable information and expatriate organisations in the major cities, particularly Rome and Milan, where foreigners are well-served by expatriate clubs and organisations. Contacts can also be found through many expatriate magazines and newspapers such as *Wanted in Rome* and *The Informer* (see **Appendix A** for a list). Some expatriate clubs and organisations (such as American Women's Clubs) run courses for newcomers that are designed to help foreigners adjust to life in Italy.

Note that it isn't necessarily what, but who you know in Italy, which can make the difference between success or failure. String-pulling or the use of contacts is widespread and is invaluable when it comes to breaking through the numerous layers of bureaucracy, when a telephone call on your behalf from a friend or colleague can work wonders. In fact any contacts can be of help, even a professional acquaintance, who may not even charge you for his time.

Most embassies (see page 212) and consulates in Italy provide their nationals with local information including the names of lawyers, interpreters, doctors, dentists, schools, and social and expatriate organisations.

CHECKLISTS

Before Arrival

The checklists on the following pages list tasks which you need (or may need) to complete before and after arrival in Italy, and when moving your home permanently to Italy.

- **Check that your and your family's passports are valid!**

- Obtain a visa, if necessary, for all your family members (see page 18). Obviously this *must* be done before arrival in Italy.

- Arrange health and travel insurance for yourself and your family (see pages 54 and 60 respectively). This is essential if you aren't covered by an international health insurance policy and won't be covered by Italian social security.

- If you don't already have one, it's advisable to obtain an international credit or charge card, which may prove invaluable in Italy.

- Obtain an international driver's licence, if necessary (see page 37).

- Open a bank account in Italy (see page 87) and transfer funds. You can open an account with many Italian banks while abroad, although it's best done in person in Italy.

- It's advisable to obtain some Italian lire before arriving in Italy, which will save you having to queue to change money on arrival (and you will probably receive a better exchange rate).

- If you plan to become a permanent resident you may also need to do the following:

  - Arrange schooling for your children.

  - Organise the shipment of your personal and household effects.

  - Obtain as many credit references as possible, for example from banks, mortgage companies, credit card companies, credit agencies, companies with which you have had accounts, and references from professionals such as lawyers and accountants. These will help you establish a credit rating in Italy.

If you're planning to become a permanent resident, you should take all your family's official documents with you. These may include birth certificates; driving licences; marriage certificate, divorce papers or death certificate (if a widow or widower); educational diplomas and professional certificates; employment references and curriculum vitaes; school records and student ID cards; medical and dental records; bank account and credit card details; insurance policies (plus records of no-claims' allowances); and receipts for any valuables. You also need the documents necessary to obtain a residence permit plus certified copies, official translations and numerous passport-size photographs (students should take at least a dozen).

After Arrival

The following checklist contains a summary of the tasks to be completed after arrival in Italy (if not done before arrival):

- On arrival at an Italian airport, port or border post, have your visa cancelled and your passport stamped, as applicable.

- If you aren't taking a car with you, you may wish to rent (see page 44) or buy one locally. Note that it's practically impossible to get around in rural areas without a car.

- Open a bank account (see page 87) at a local bank and give the details to any companies that you plan to pay by direct debit or standing order (such as utility and property management companies).

- Arrange whatever insurance is necessary such as health, car and home.

- Contact offices and organisations to obtain local information (see page 204).

- It's often a good idea to make courtesy calls on your neighbours and the local mayor within a few weeks of your arrival. This is particularly important in villages and rural areas if you want to be accepted and become part of the local community.

- If you plan to become a permanent resident in Italy, you may need to do the following within the next few weeks (if not done before your arrival):

- apply for a permit to stay (*permesso di soggiorno*) within eight days of your arrival.
- apply for a social security card from your local social security office;
- apply for an Italian driving licence (see page 37);
- register with a local doctor and dentist;
- arrange schooling for your children.

Moving House

When moving permanently to Italy there are many things to be considered and a 'million' people to be informed. Even if you plan to spend only a few months a year in Italy, it may still be necessary to inform a number of people and companies in your home country. The checklists below are designed to make the task easier and help prevent an ulcer or a nervous breakdown (providing of course you don't leave everything to the last minute). See also **Moving House** on page 177 and **Moving In** on page 179.

• If you live in rented accommodation you will need to give your landlord notice (check your contract).

• If you own your home, arrange to sell or rent it (if applicable) well in advance of your move to Italy.

• Inform the following:

 – Your employer, e.g. give notice or arrange leave of absence.

 – Your local town hall or municipality. You may be entitled to a refund of your local taxes.

 – If it was necessary to register with the police in your home country, you should inform them that you're moving abroad.

 – Your electricity, gas, water and telephone companies. Contact companies well in advance, particularly if you need to get a deposit refunded.

 – Your insurance companies (for example health, car, home contents and private pension); banks, post office (if you have a post office account), stockbroker and other financial institutions; credit card, charge card and hire purchase companies; lawyer and accountant; and local businesses where you have accounts.

 – Your family doctor, dentist and other health practitioners. Health records should be transferred to your new doctor and dentist in Italy.

 – Your children's schools. Try to give a term's notice and obtain a copy of any relevant school reports or records from your children's schools.

 – All regular correspondents, subscriptions, social and sports clubs, professional and trade journals, and friends and relatives. Give them your new address and telephone number and arrange to have your mail redirected by the post office or a friend.

- If you have a driving licence or car that you're taking to Italy, you will need to give the local vehicle registration office your new address abroad and, in some countries, return your car's registration plates.

• Return any library books or anything borrowed.

• Arrange shipment of your furniture and belongings by booking a shipping company well in advance (see page 177). International shipping companies usually provide a wealth of information and can advise on a wide range of matters concerning an international relocation. Find out the exact procedure for shipping your belongings to Italy from an Italian embassy or consulate.

• Arrange to sell anything you aren't taking with you (e.g. house, car and furniture). If you're selling a home or business, you should obtain expert legal advice as you may be able to save tax by establishing a trust or other legal vehicle. Note that if you own more than one property, you may need to pay capital gains tax on any profits from the sale of second and subsequent homes.

• If you have a car that you're exporting to Italy, you will need to complete the relevant paperwork in your home country and re-register it in Italy after your arrival. Contact an Italian embassy or consulate for information.

• Arrange inoculations and shipment for any pets that you're taking with you (see page 68).

• You may qualify for a rebate on your tax and social security contributions. If you're leaving a country permanently and have been a member of a company or state pension scheme, you may be entitled to a refund or may be able to continue payments to qualify for a full (or larger) pension when you retire. Contact your company personnel office, local tax office or pension company for information.

• It's advisable to arrange health, dental and optical checkups for your family before leaving your home country (see page 53). Obtain a copy of all health records and a statement from your private health insurance company stating your present level of cover.

• Terminate any outstanding loan, lease or hire purchase contracts and pay all bills (allow plenty of time as some companies may be slow to respond).

• Check whether you're entitled to a rebate on your road tax, car and other insurance. Obtain a letter from your motor insurance company stating your no-claims' discount.

• Check whether you need an international driving licence or a translation of your foreign driving licence(s) for Italy. Note that some foreign residents are required to take a driving test in order to drive in Italy (see page 37).

• Give friends and business associates an address and telephone number where you can be contacted in Italy.

• If you will be living in Italy for an extended period (but not permanently), you may wish to give someone 'power of attorney' over your financial affairs in your home country so that they can act for you in your absence. This can be for a fixed period or open-ended and can be for a specific purpose only. **Note, however, that you should take expert legal advice before doing this!**

- Allow plenty of time to get to the airport, register your luggage, and clear security and immigration.

Have a nice journey! (*Buon Viaggio!*)

Friends in Italy

Just what you need when looking for rented accommodation . . . whether an apartment in a princely Florentine palazzo, a secluded cottage on the Lucca hills, a farmhouse, B&B or cosy village apartment near Rome . . . live the Italian way, meet the people, explore the back roads . . . we organise airport pick-ups, cooking, photography and painting courses as well as Etruscan and Rome walks . . . all led by English-speaking experts . . . we've been doing it for friends and family for over 30 years . . . e-mail for our contacts in the UK, USA and Ireland (macryan@tin.it or paulacat@isa.it) or fax your requirements to us on +39-0761-485002. We look forward to showing you our Italy!

APPENDICES

APPENDIX A: USEFUL ADDRESSES

Embassies

Foreign embassies in Italy are located in Rome and many countries also have consulates in other major cities. Note that business hours vary considerably and all embassies close on their national holidays and on Italy's public holidays. Always telephone to check the business hours before visiting. Selected embassies are listed below:

Albania: Via Asmara 9, Rome (☎ 06-838 07 25).

Argentina: Piazza dell'Esquilino 2, 00185 Rome (☎ 06-474 25 51).

Australia: Via Alessandria 215, 00198 Rome (☎ 06-85 27 21).

Austria: Via G.B. Pergolesi 3, 00198 Rome (☎ 06-855 82 41).

Belgium: Via dei Monti Parioli 49, 00197 Rome (☎ 06-32 24 41).

Brazil: Piazza Navona 14, 00186 Rome (☎ 06-683 88 41).

Bulgaria: Via Rubens 21, Rome (☎ 06-322 46 43).

Canada: Via G.B. de Rossi 27, 00161 Rome (☎ 06-44 59 81).

China: Via Bruxelles 56, 00198 Rome (☎ 06-844 81 86).

Croatia: Via SS. Cosma e Damiano 26, Rome (☎ 06-332 502 42).

Czech Republic: Via Colli Farnesina 144, 00194 Rome (☎ 06-329 67 11).

Denmark: Via dei Monti Parioli 50, 00197 Rome (☎ 06-320 04 41).

Finland: Via Lisbona 3, 00198 Rome (☎ 06-854 83 29).

France: Piazza Farnese 67, 00186 Rome (☎ 06-68 60 11).

Germany: Via Po 25/c, 00198 Rome (☎ 06-88 47 41).

Greece: Via Mercadante 36, 00198 Rome (☎ 06-844 25 84).

Hungary: Via Villini 12/16, 00161 Rome (☎ 06-440 20 32).

Iceland: Via Donatello 21, Rome (☎ 06-706 385 15).

India: Via XX Settembre 5, 00187 Rome (☎ 06-46 46 42).

Ireland: Largo Nazareno 3, 00187 Rome (☎ 06-678 25 41).

Israel: Via Michele Mercati 14, 00197 Rome (☎ 06-36 19 81).

Japan: Via Sella 60, 00187 Rome (☎ 06-481 71 51).

Lithuania: Piazza Farnese 44, Rome (☎ 06-686 57 86).

Luxembourg: Via Ardeatina 134, 00153 Rome (☎ 06-518 08 85).

Malta: Lungotevere Marzio 12, Rome (☎ 06-689 26 87).

Monaco: Via Bertoloni 36, Rome (☎ 06-807 76 92).

Netherlands: Via Michele Mercati 8, 00197 Rome (☎ 06-322 11 41).

New Zealand: Via Zara 28, 00198 Rome (☎ 06-440 29 28).

Norway: Via Terme Deciane 7, 00153 Rome (☎ 06-575 58 53).

Pakistan: Via della Camilluccia 682, 00135 Rome (☎ 06-327 67 75).

Poland: Via Rubens 20, 00197 Rome (☎ 06-322 44 55).

Portugal: Via Pezzana 9, 00197 Rome (☎ 06-807 38 01).

Romania: Via Tartagelia 36, Rome (☎ 06-807 88 07).
Russia: Via Gaeta 5, 00185 Rome (☎ 06-494 16 49).
Slovak Republic: Via Colli Farnesina 144, Rome (☎ 06-363 086 17).
Slovenia: Via L. Pisano 10, Rome (☎ 06-808 10 75).
South Africa: Via Tanaro 14/16, 00198 Rome (☎ 06-841 97 94).
Spain: Largo Fontanella Borghese 19, 00186 Rome (☎ 06-580 01 44).
Sweden: Piazza Rio di Janeiro 3, 00161 Rome (☎ 06-442 314 59).
Switzerland: Via Barnaba Oriani 61, 00197 Rome (☎ 06-808 36 41).
Tunisia: Via Asmara 5-7, Rome (☎ 06-860 30 60).
Turkey: Via Palestro 28, 00185 Rome (☎ 06-446 99 32).
Ukraine: Via Castelfidardo 50, Rome (☎ 06-447 001 72).
United Kingdom: Via XX Settembre 80/a, 00187 Rome (☎ 06-482 54 41).
United States of America: Via Vittorio Veneto 119/A-121, 00187 Rome (☎ 06-4 67 41).
Yugoslavia: Via Monti Parioli 20, 00197 Rome (☎ 06-320 08 05).

British Provincial Consulates

Bari: Anglo Italian Shipping, Via Dalmazio 127 (☎ 080-554 36 68).
Brindisi: The British School, Via di Terrible 9 (☎ 0831-56 83 40).
Cagliari: Via San Lucifero 87 (☎ 070-66 27 50).
Florence: Piazzo Castelbarco, Lungarno Corsini 2 (☎ 055-28 41 33).
Genoa: Via XII Ottobre 2, 13th Floor (☎ 010-56 48 33).
Milan: Via San Paolo 7 (☎ 02-72 30 01).
Naples: Via Francesco Crispi 122 (☎ 081-66 35 11).
Trieste: Vicolo delle Ville 16 (☎ 040-76 47 52).
Turin: British Consul Trade Office, Corso Massimo D'Azeglio 60 (☎ 011-650 92 02).
Rome: Via XX Settembre 80a (☎ 06-482 54 41).
Venice: PO Box 679, Accademia Dorsoduro 1051 (☎ 041-522 72 07).

English-Language Newspapers & Magazines

Case e Country,Via Burigozzo 5, 20122 Milano. (☎ 02-58219). Glossy home decoration and country homes magazine with some property listings.
Dimore-Homes and Villas of Italy, Via Cristoforo Colombo 440,00145 Rome (☎ 06-542 251 28, fax 06-542 251 26, Internet: www.dimore.com). Magazine dedicated to luxury homes and properties for sale, with English/Italian text.
English Yellow Pages, Via Belisario 4/B, 00187 Rome (☎ 06-474 08 61, fax 06-474 45 16, e-mail: eyp@mondoweb.it).
Hello Milano, (☎ 02-295 205 70, fax 02-295 348 45, e-mail: jneuteb@tin.it). Free monthly entertainment magazine.

The Informer-Buroservice,Via dei Tigli 2, 20020 Arese (MI) (☎ 02-93581477, fax 02-93580280, Internet: www.mondoweb.it/informer). A useful monthly magazine for expatriates available by subscription only.

International Property Magazine, 2a Station Road, Gidea Park, Romford, Essex RM2 6DA, UK. Bi-monthly magazine.

Ville e Casali, Edizioni Living International, Via Anton Giulio Bragaglia 33, 00123 Rome (☎ 06/308 841 22, fax 06-308 899 44, e-mail: direzione@eli.it). Glossy monthly home magazine containing a catalogue of luxury properties with English summaries of articles and house descriptions.

Wanted in Rome, Via dei Delfini 17, 00186 Rome. (☎ 06-6790190, fax 06-6783798, e-mail: wantedinrome@compuserve.com). Rentals, properties for sale, holiday properties, Rome property guide.

World of Property, Outbound Publishing, 1 Commercial Road, Eastbourne, East Sussex BN21 3XQ, UK (☎ 01323-412001). Quarterly magazine.

Miscellaneous

British Association of Removers (BAR) Overseas, 3 Churchill Court, 58 Station Road, North Harrow, Middx. HA2 7SA, UK (☎ 0181-861 3331).

British Chamber of Commerce for Italy, Via Camperio, 9, 20123 Milan (☎ 02-877 798-805 6094).

British Italian Society, 24 Rutland Gate, London SW7 1BB, UK (☎ 0171-823 9204).

Federation of Overseas Property Developers, Agents and Consultants (FOPDAC), PO Box 3524, London NW5 1DQ, UK (☎ 0181-744 2362).

Italian Association of Real Estate Agents (AICI), Via Nerino 5, 20123 Milan (☎ 02-725291).

Italian Chamber of Commerce, Room 418-427 Walmar House, 296 Regent Street, London W1R 5HB, UK (☎ 0171-637 3153).

Italian Cultural Institute, 39 Belgrave Square, London SW1X 8NT, UK (☎ 0171-235 1461).

Italian Cultural Institute, 686 Park Avenue, New York, NY 10021, USA.

Italian Embassy, 1601 Fuller St., NW, Washington, DC 20009, USA (☎ 202-328-5500).

Italian Embassy, 14 Three Kings Yard, Davies Street, London W1Y 2EH, UK (☎ 0171-312 2200).

Italian Federation of Professional Estate Agents (FIAIP), Via Monte Zebio, 30, 00195 Rome (☎ 06-321 9798).

Italian Government Travel Office, 630 Fifth Avenue, Suite 1565, New York, NY 10111, USA (☎ 212-245-4822).

Italian State Tourist Office, 1 Princes Street, London W1R 8AY, UK (☎ 0171-408 1254).

Italian Trade Centre, 37 Sackville Street, London W1X 2DQ, UK (☎ 0171-734 2412).

APPENDIX B: FURTHER READING

The books listed below are just a small selection of the many books of interest to those planning to buy a home in Italy. Note that some titles may be out of print, but may still be obtainable from bookshops and libraries. Books prefixed with an asterisk (*) are recommended by the author.

Property & Business

*After Hannibal, Barry Unsworth (Penguin)
*Edith Wharton's Italian Gardens, Vivian Russell (Ecco Press)
*Gardens of the Italian Lakes, Judith Chatfield (Rizzoli)
Gardens of Tuscany, Ethne Clark (Weidenfeld & Nicolson)
*Great Houses of Tuscany: The Tuscan Villas (Viking)
The Hills of Tuscany - A New Life In An Old Land, F. Matè (Harper & Collins)
How To Rent & Buy Property in Italy, Amanda Hinton (How To Books)
Italian Country Style, Robert Fitzgerald & Peter Porter (Fairfax)
Italian Villas and Gardens, Paul van der Ree
*Italian Villas and Their Gardens, Edith Wharton (Da Capo)
Italy: The Hill Towns, James Bentley (Aurum)
North of Naples, South of Rome, Paolo Tullio (Lilliput Press)
*A Place in Italy, Simon Mawer (Sinclair Stevenson)
*A Small Place in Italy, Eric Newby (Picador)
*Traditional Houses of Rural Italy, Paul Duncan (Collins & Brown)
A Tuscan Childhood, Kinta Beevor (Penguin)
Urban Land and Property Markets in Italy, Gastone Ave (UCL Press)
*Under the Tuscan Sun, Frances Mayes (Broadway Books)
*A Valley in Italy: The Many Seasons of a Villa in Umbria, Lisa St. Aubin de Terán (Harper Collins)
Venice: the Most Triumphant City, George Bull
*Views from a Tuscan Vineyard, Carey More (Pavillion)
*Within Tuscany, Matthew Spender (Penguin)
*Your Home in Italy, F. Maxwell (Longman)

Living & Working in Italy

Getting it Right in Italy, William Ward (Bloomsbury)
Live & Work in Italy, Victoria Pybus (Vacation Work)
Living in Italy, Yve Menzies (Hale)
Living in Italy, Alvino E. Fantini (Pro Lingua)
Living, Studying & Working in Italy, Travis Neighbor & Monica Larner (Owl)
Setting Up in Italy, Sebation O'Kelly (Merehurst)

*Survival Guide to Milan, Jessica Halpern (Informer)

Travel

Blue Guide Northern Italy from the Alps to Bologna, Alta MacAdam (Blue Guides)
Blue Guide Tuscany, Alta MacAdam & John Flower (Blue Guides)
*Florence and Tuscany, Sheila Hale (Mitchell Beazley)
Fodor's Italy (Fodor)
*Fodor's Florence, Tuscany & Umbria, Fionn Davenport (Fodor)
*Frommer's Italy, Darwin Porter & Danforth Prince (Macmillan)
Frommer's Rome, Darwin Porter (Macmillan)
Frommer's Tuscany & Umbria, Reid Bramblett (Macmillan)
*Lombardy: The Italian Lakes, John Flower (Philip)
*Lonely Planet Italy, Helen Gillman, Damien Simonis & Stefano Cavedoni (Lonely Planet)
*Michelin Green Guide Italy (Michelin)
*The Rough Guide Italy, Ros Belford, Martin Dunford & Celia Woolfrey (The Rough Guides)
*Tuscany, Umbria and the Marche, Michael Pauls & Dana Facaros (Cadogan)
*Venice, Frail Barrier, Richard de Combray (Doubleday)
Venice and the Veneto, James Bentley (Aurum)

Food & Drink

The Best of Italy: A Cookbook, Evie Righter (Collins)
Cooking the Italian Way, Alphonse Bisignano (Lerner)
Eating in Italy: A Travelers Guide to the Gastronomic Pleasures of Northern Italy, Faith Heller Willinger & Faith Echtermeyer (William Morrow)
Eating Out in Italy, Dianne Seed & Robert Budwig (Ten Speed)
*Essentials of Classic Italian Cooking, Marcella Hazan (Knopf)
*Floyd on Italy, Keith Floyd (Penguin)
Food in Italy, Claudia Gaspari (Rourke)
*The Food of Italy, Waverly Root (Vintage)
*A Food Lover's Companion to Tuscany, Carla Capalbo (Chronicle)
Frommer's Food Lover's Companion to Italy, Marc & Kim Millon (Macmillan)
*Italian Food, Elizabeth David (Pengion)
*Italian Wine, Victor Hazan (Knopf)
Italy for the Gourmet Traveler, Fred Plotkin (Little, Brown & Co)
A Traveller's Wine Guide to Italy (Aurum Press)
Touring in Wine Country: Northwest Italy, Maureen Ashley (Mitchell Beazley)
Vino, Burton Anderson (Little Brown)

APPENDIX C: WEIGHTS & MEASURES

Italy uses the metric system of measurement. Nationals of a few countries (including the Americans and British) who are more familiar with the imperial system of measurement will find the tables on the following pages useful. Some comparisons shown are approximate only, but are close enough for most everyday uses. In addition to the variety of measurement systems used, clothes sizes often vary considerably depending on the manufacturer (as we all know only too well). Try all clothes on before buying and don't be afraid to return something if, when you try it on at home, you decide it doesn't fit (most shops will exchange goods or give a refund).

Women's Clothes

Continental	34	36	38	40	42	44	46	48	50	52
GB	8	10	12	14	16	18	20	22	24	26
USA	6	8	10	12	14	16	18	20	22	24

Pullovers:

	Women's						Men's					
Continental	40	42	44	46	48	50	44	46	48	50	52	54
GB	34	36	38	40	42	44	34	36	38	40	42	44
USA	34	36	38	40	42	44	sm	medium	Large	exl		

Note: sm = small, exl = extra large

Men's Shirts

Continental	36	37	38	39	40	41	42	43	44	46
GB/USA	14	14	15	15	16	16	17	17	18	

Men's Underwear

Continental	5	6	7	8	9	10
GB	34	36	38	40	42	44
USA	small	medium		Large	extra large	

Children's Clothes

Continental	92	104	116	128	140	152
GB	16/18	20/22	24/26	28/30	32/34	36/38
USA	24	6	8	10	12	

Children's Shoes

Continental	18	19	20	21	22	23	24	25	26	27	28
GB/USA	2	3	4	4	5	6	7	7	8	9	10

Continental	29	30	31	32	33	34	35	36	37	38
GB/USA	11	11	12	13	1	2	2	3	4	5

Shoes (Women's and Men's)

Continental	35	35	36	37	37	38	39	39	40	40
GB	2	3	3	4	4	5	5	6	6	7
USA	4	4	5	5	6	6	7	7	8	8

Continental	41	42	42	43	44	44
GB	7	8	8	9	9	10
USA	9	9	10	10	11	11

Weights

Avoirdupois	Metric	Metric	Avoirdupois
1 oz	28.35g	1g	0.035oz
1 pound*	454g	100g	3.5oz
1 cwt	50.8kg	250g	9oz
1 ton	1,016kg	1kg	2.2 pounds
1 tonne	2,205 pounds		

* A metric 'pound' is 500g, g = gramme, kg = kilogramme

Length

British/US	Metric	Metric	British/US
1 inch =	2.54 cm	1 cm	0.39 inch
1 foot =	30.48 cm	1 m3.	28 feet
1 yard =	91.44 cm	1 km	0.62 mile
1 mile =	1.6 km	8 km	5 miles

Note: cm = centimetre, m = metre, km = kilometre

Capacity

Imperial	Metric	Metric	Imperial
1 pint (USA)	0.47l	1 l	1.76 GB pints
1 pint (GB)	0.568l	1 l	0.265 US gallons
1 gallon (USA)	3.78l	1 l	0.22 GB gallons
1 gallon (GB)	4.54l	1 l	35.211 fluid oz

Note: l = litre

Square Measure

British/US	Metric	Metric	British/US
1 square inch	6.45 sq. cm	1 sq. cm	0.155 sq. inches
1 square foot	0.092 sq. m.	1 sq. m	10.764 sq. feet
1 square yard	0.836 sq. m.	1 sq. m.	1.196 sq. yards
1 acre	0.405 hect.	1 hectare	2.471 acres
1 square mile	259 hect.	1 sq. km	0.386 sq. mile

Temperature

° Celsius	° Fahrenheit	
0	32	freezing point of water
5	41	
10	50	
15	59	
20	68	
25	77	
30	86	
35	95	
40	104	

The Boiling point of water is 100°C / 212°F.

Oven temperature

Gas	Electric °F	°C
-	225-250	110-120
1	275	140
2	300	150
3	325	160
4	350	180
5	375	190
6	400	200
7	425	220
8	450	230
9	475	240

For a quick conversion, the Celsius temperature is approximately half the Fahrenheit temperature (in the range shown above).

Temperature Conversion

Celsius to Fahrenheit: multiply by 9, divide by 5 and add 32.
Fahrenheit to Celsius: subtract 32, multiply by 5 and divide by 9.

Body Temperature

Normal body temperature (if you're alive and well) is 98.4° Fahrenheit, which equals 37° Celsius.

APPENDIX D: SERVICE DIRECTORY

This **Service Directory** is to help you find local businesses and services in Italy, serving residents and visitors. Note that when calling Italy from abroad, you must dial the international access number (e.g. 00 from the UK) followed by 39 (the country code for Italy), the area code, including the leading zero (e.g. 06 for Rome), and the subscriber's number. Please mention *Buying a Home in Italy* when contacting companies.

AGENTS (PROPERTY)

Tuscany-Inside-Out, Diane Kilpatrick, Via Santa Lucia 6, 53047 Sarteano (SI), ☎ 0578-268 016, fax 0578-268 728, Internet www.tuscany-inside-out.com.

ROGIA Immobiliare, Giacomo Cilli & Roberto Satinelli, Via Cassia 36, 01019 Veteralla (VT), ☎/fax 0761-461 788.

BOOKSHOPS

The Anglo-American Bookshop, Via della Vite, 102, Rome (☎ 06-679 5222).

The English Bookshop,Via di Ripetta 248 , Rome (☎ 06-320 3301).

Louise McDermott, Via dei Giubbonari, 30, 00187 Rome (☎ 06-6880 5285). Produces a catalogue of out-of-print books about Italy.

FINANCIAL ADVISERS

Ing. Giovanni Mauvais, Prime Merrill Lynch Group (☎ 06-6830 7130).

HOLIDAY ACCOMMODATION

Friends in Italy (fax 0761-485002, e-mail: macryan@tin.it/paulacat@isa.it).

PROPERTY EXHIBITIONS

World of Property, Outbound Publishing, 1 Commercial Road, Eastbourne, East Sussex BN21 3XQ, UK (☎ 01323-412001).

RELOCATION AGENTS

Welcome Home S.a.S.,Yolanda Bernardini,Via Barbarano Romano, 15, 00189 Rome (☎ 06-3036 6936).

Theresa Morelli, Torsello & Partners, Corso di Porta Romana, 122, Milan, (☎ 02-5830 8737).

PROFESSIONAL & SUPPORT GROUPS

AWAR-American Women's Association, Hotel Savoia, Rome (☎ 06-4825 268). There are associated groups in Florence, Milan and other cities.

Women's International Networking, WIN Conferences, c/o Kristin Engvig, P.O. Box 130 , Corso C. Colombo 1, 20144 Milano.

APPENDIX E: MAP OF REGIONS OF ITALY

The map opposite shows the 20 regions of Italy, which are listed below with the 96 provinces. A map of Italy showing the major cities and geographical features is shown on page 6.

Region	Provinces
Abruzzo (Abruzzi)	Chieti, L'Aquila, Pescara, Teramo
Basilicata (Lucania)	Matera, Potenza
Calabria	Cantazaro, Cosenza, Reggio di Calabria
Campania	Avellino, Benevento, Caserta, Naples (Napoli), Salerno
Emilia Romagna	Bologna, Ferrara, Forli, Modena, Piacenza, Parma, Ravenna, Regio Emilia
Friuli-Venezia-Giuila	Gorizia, Pordenone, Trieste, Udine
Lazio (Latium)	Frosinone, Latina, Rieti, Rome (Roma), Viterbo
Liguria	Genova, Imperia, La Spezia, Savona
Lombardia (Lombardy)	Bergamo, Brescia, Como, Cremona, Mantua (Mantova), Milan (Milano), Pavia, Sondrio, Varese
Marche	Ancona, Ascoli Piceno, Macerata, Pesaro
Molise	Campobasso, Isernia
Piemonte (Piedmont)	Alessandria, Asti, Cuneo, Novara, Turin (Torino), Vercelli
Puglia (Apulia)	Bari, Brindisi, Foggia, Lecce, Taranto
Sardinia (Sardegna)	Cagliari, Nuoro, Oristano, Sassari
Sicily (Sicilia)	Agrigento, Caltanissetta, Cantania, Enna, Messina, Palermo, Ragusa, Syracuse (Siracusa), Trapini
Tuscany (Toscana)	Arezzo, Firenze (Florence), Grosseto, Leghorn (Livorno), Lucca, Massa Carrara, Pisa, Pistoia, Siena
Trentino-Alto-Adige	Bolzano, Trento
Umbria	Perugia, Terni
Val D'Aosta	Aosta
Veneto	Belluno, Padova (Padua), Rovigno, Treviso, Venice (Venezia), Verona, Vicenza

APPENDIX F: GLOSSARY

Abbonamento: Standing charge, e.g. for electricity, gas, telephone or water services. Also a subscription, e.g. to a magazine, or a season ticket for public transport.

Abitabile: Habitable.

Abitazione (tipo di): The housing category that determines the level of property and other taxes.

Abusivo: Abusive. The term used to denote building or alterations to a building that have been built or made illegally.

Acqua: Water.

Acqua (condotta d'acqua): Water piping.

Acqua di sorgente: Spring water.

Acquedotto comunale: Municipal water supply.

Acquistare su carta: Off-plan, i.e. buying a property before it has been built.

Affittacamere: Rooms for rent. Usually cheaper than a *pensione* and not part of the official classification system.

Affitasi: To let/for rent.

Affresco: Fresco. The painting method (favoured by the Renaissance masters) in which watercolour paint is applied to wet plaster.

Agenzia immobiliare: Real estate agency.

Agriturismo: A working farm with rooms for guests, a structure for rural tourism.

Albo degli artigiani: Official list of artisans (tradesmen).

Albergo: Hotel with up to five stars.

Alimentari: Grocery (food) shop.

Alloggio: Lodging. Usually cheaper than a *pensione* and not part of the official classification system.

Amministratore di condominio: Administrator of a condominium, e.g. an apartment block.

Ammobiliato: Furnished.

Ammortizzare: Amortisation. The gradual process of systematically reducing debt in equal payments (as in a mortgage) comprising both principal and interest, until the debt is paid in full.

Ampia metratura: Ample size.

Anagrafe/Ufficio di Stato Civile: Bureau of vital statistics or census office.

Anagrafe canina: Census office for dogs (where dogs are registered).

Angolo cottura: Cooking corner or small corner kitchen.

Annessi: Attached (usually small) out-buildings.

Annesso: Extension or enlargement.

Antico: Antique.

Anticipo di pagamento: Deposit sometimes paid before signing a preliminary contract.

Apparecchio: Appliance or machine.

Appartamento: Apartment, flat.

Appartamento ammobiliato: Furnished apartment.

Appartamento in affitto: Rented accommodation.

Appartamento (di lusso) nell'attico: Penthouse.

Appartamento su due piani: Duplex (apartment on two floors).

Appartamento vacanze: Holiday apartment.

Arcate: A row of free-standing arches, carried on columns or piers forming a covered walk.

Architetto: Architect.

Arco: Arch.

Arredamento: Furnishings.

Arredato: Furnished.

Ascensore: Elevator, lift.

Assicurazione: Insurance.

Assicurazione contro i terzi: Third-party insurance.

Astenersi agenzie: Without an agent (for rent/sale by owner).

Attaccate: Joined.

Attico: Top floor apartment or penthouse in a city or town. Attic in the country.

Atto di compravendita: Property conveyance document. (also called *atto notarile*).

Attrezzata: Equipped.

Autorimessa: Garage.

Autostrada: Motorway, freeway (usually a toll road).

Avvocato: Lawyer or solicitor.

Azienda agricola: Farm.

Bagno: Bathroom, also the toilet.

Balcone: Balcony or terrace.

Barocco: Baroque. Seventeenth century European art movement.

Bellissima: Beautiful.

Ben conservata: Well preserved.

Ben tenuto: Well maintained.

Bifamiliare: Semi-detached (two-family building).

Bilocale: Two rooms. 3-locale (three rooms), 4-locale (four rooms), etc.

Bolletta: Bill.

Bollo: State tax stamp.

Bombola: Gas bottle.

Bombolone: Gas tank (used to store liquid gas).

Borgo/Borghi: An ancient town or village, often walled.

Borgo: A suburb (or city neighbourhood) or a street leading into a suburb from the centre of town. Also a village.

Bosco: Wood.

Bovindo: Bay (or bow) window.

Breve periodo: Short period or term.

Buona posizione: Good position.

Buono stato: Good condition.

Cabina: Cabin.

Calce: Lime.

Caldaia: Boiler or water heater.

Camera: Room (two rooms/due camere, three rooms/tre camere).

Camera di commercio: Chamber of commerce.

Camera doppia: Double room with twin beds.

Camera matrimoniale: Double room with a double bed.

Camera singola: Single room.

Camera sul davanti/sul dietro: Front room/back room.

Cameretta: Small bedroom.

Camino: Chimney, fireplace.

Cantina: Cellar, wine cellar.

Capannone: Barn.

Caparra: Deposit.

Caratteristico: Typical, characteristic.

Carpentiere: Carpenter.

Carta bollata: An official paper with a tax stamp.

Carta d'Identità: Identity card.

Carta da parati: Wallpaper.

Casa: House.

Casa colonica: A farmhouse.

Casa canonica: Old church house.

Casa d'epoca: Period house.

Casa gemella: Semi-detached house.

Casa padronale: Country house.

Casa popolare: Public, low-rent accommodation that's rented to low-income families.

Casa di ringhiera: A traditional Milanese apartment block with apartment entrances off a long balcony above an internal courtyard.

Casa rurale: Rural property.

Casa signorile: Luxury home.

Casa urbana: Urban property. Note that many rural country properties are classified as urban.

Casale: Farmhouse.

Cascina: Farmstead.

Casetta: Small house.

Casette a schiera: A terrace of small workers' houses.

Cassone: Water storage tank.

Castello: Castle.

Catasto: Land registry.

Cemento (bianco): Cement (white).

Centralissimo: Central.

Centro: Centre.

Centro storico: Historic centre, old town.

Ceramica: Ceramic tiles.

Certificato di matrimonio: Marriage certificate.

Certificato di morte: Death certificate.

Certificato di nascita: Birth certificate.

Certificato di residenza: Residence permit.

Chiave: Key.

Cipollino: Onion marble with veins of green or white.

Circoscrizione: A subdivision of a *comune*, e.g. Rome is one *comune*, but it has 20 *circoscrizioni*.

Clausola (condizionale): Clause (conditional) in a contract.

Codice fiscale: Fiscal or tax number.

Colombaia: A pigeon house or dovecote.

Colonna: Column.

Colonnato: A row of columns placed at regular intervals, possibly carrying arches.

Coltivatore diretto: Farmer.

Commercialista: Accountant, one who does tax returns.

Comodissimo per i mezzi e negozi: Convenient for public transport and shops.

Complesso residenziale: Residential complex.

Compromesso (di vendita): Preliminary contract.

Comune: An administrative area, e.g. a self-governing town or city. Also a municipality or county, town or city council.

Concessione edlizia: Planning permission.

Concio d'angolo: The dressed stones at the corners of buildings.

Con gusto: Tastefully, e.g. furnished or decorated.

Condizionamento d'aria: Air-conditioning.

Condizione: Condition.

Condominio: Condominium or apartment. Also an apartment block.

Convivere: Sharing, e.g. an apartment or house.

Congelatore: Freezer.

Conguaglio: Adjustment. The term ENEL (electricity) and other utility companies use to refer to a bill (issued twice a year) based on actual rather than estimated consumption.

Consegna: Exchange of contracts.

Conservatorio: Conservatory.

Costruttore: Builder, developer.

Costruzione: Building.

Contatore: Meter (e.g. electricity).

Contenuto dell' abitazione: House contents, inventory.

Conto: Bill, account.

Conto estero: A foreign currency bank account.

Contrada: District.

Contraente: Contracting party.

Contratto: Contract.

Contratto di affitto: Rental lease.

Contratto preliminaire di vendita: Preliminary contract of sale.

Coppi: Roof tiles.

Coppi vecchi: Old roof tiles.

Corridoio: Hallway, corridor.

Corso: Main street, avenue or boulevard.

(in) Corso di costruzione: Being built, in the process of being constructed.

Corridoio: Hall, corridor.

Cortile: Galleried courtyard or cloisters.

Cotto: Terracotta.

Cucina: Kitchen or cooker.

Cucina abitabile: Eat-in kitchen.

Cucina a gas: Gas cooker.

Cucinotto: Small kitchen.

Cupola: Dome.

Decoratore: Decorator.

Denuncia: Legal or police statement.

Deposito: Deposit.

Deruralizzato: The process whereby a rural agricultural building (such as a barn) is legally converted into a dwelling.

Diritto di passaggio: Right of way.

Disdire: Cancel (a contract).

Disponibile: Available.

Doccia: Shower.

Dogana: Customs.

Domiciliazione: Direct debit payment (from a bank).

Domicilio: Address.

Doppi servizi: Two bathrooms.

Doppi vetri: Double glazing.

Doppio garage: Double garage.

Due piani: Two floors (like a duplex or maisonnette).

Edificio: Building, structure.

Edilizia: Builder's yard.

Elettricista: Electrician.

Emergenza: Emergency.

Ente Nazionale per l'Energia Electtrica (ENEL): The national electricity company.

Elettrodomestici: Appliances, white goods (cooker, washing machine, etc.).

Ente Nazionale Italiano per il Turismo (ENIT): The Italian state tourist office.

Entrata: Entrance.

Entroterra: Hinterland.

Equo canone: Fair rent or rent control.

Ettaro (ha): Hectare

Fabbricato: Building.

Fabbricato rurale: A rural or agricultural building which cannot be used as a dwelling until it has been 'deruralised'.

Facciata: façade.

Fai-da-te: Do-it-yourself (DIY).

Falegname: Carpenter.

Farmacia: Pharmacy, chemist.

Fattoria: Farm, farmhouse.

Ferramenta: Hardware store.

Ferrovia: Railway .

Ferrovie dello Stato (FS): The Italian state railway.

Finiture di lusso: Luxury finish.

Finestra: Window.

Fisco: Italian tax authorities.

Fiume: River.

Fondamenta: Foundation of a house or, in Venice, a street beside a canal.

Fontana: Fountain.

Fornello: Cooker.

Forno: Oven.

Forno a legna: Wood-burning oven.

Fossa settica: Septic tank.

Francobollo: Postage stamp.

Frigorifero: Refrigerator.

Fronte mare: Sea-facing, on the seafront.

Frontone: Gable.

Frutteto: Orchard.

Fusibli: Fuses.

Gabinetto: Toilet, WC.

Geometra: Surveyor.

Gesso: Plaster.

Gettone: Telephone token.

Ghiaia: Gravel.

Giardiniere: Gardener.

Giardino: Garden.

Gotico: Gothic. Delicate medieval architectural and ornamental style using pointed arches, high interior vaulting and flying buttresses to emphasise height.

Granaio: Barn.

Grande: Large.

Grattacielo: Skyscraper, tower block.

Grezzo: Uncut stone.

Grisaille: A style of painting on walls or ceilings in greyish tints in imitation of bas-reliefs.

Idraulico: Plumber.

Idromassaggio: Jacuzzi or massage bath.

Imbianchino: House painter. Also *pittore*.

Impianto: Fixtures

Imposta: Tax. Also a shutter on windows.

Imposta Comunale sugli Immobili (ICI): Property tax fixed by town (rates).

Imposta Comunale sull'Incremento di Valore degli Immobili (INVIM): Capital gains tax (now abolished).

Imposta Regionale sulle Attività Produttive (IRAP): Regional tax.

Imposta sul Reddito delle Persone Fisiche (IRPEF): Personal income tax.

Imposta sul Reddito delle Persone Guiridiche (IRPEG): Corporation tax that applies to companies and partnerships.

Imposta di registro: Stamp duty.

Imposta Servizio Comunale (ISCOM): Tax on communal services introduced in 1997.

Imposta sulle Successioni e Donazioni (ISD): Inheritance and gift tax.

Imposta sul Valore Aggiunto (IVA): Value added tax.

Indipendente: Detached.

Indirizzo: Address.

Ingegnere: Engineer.

Ingresso: Entrance hall.

Inquilino: Tenant.

Installatore: Electrician or one who installs.

Intarsio: Inlaid wood, marble or metal.

Interrato: Basement.

Intonacatore: Plasterer.

Intonaco: Plaster.

Inventario: Inventory.

Ipoteca: Mortgage.

Lago: Lake.

Lampadina: Light bulb.

Largo: Square.

Lavabo: Wash basin.

Lavanderia: Laundry.

Lavastoviglie: Dishwasher.

Lavatoio: Public washhouse.

Lavatrice: Washing machine.

Lavoro di idraulico: Plumbing.

Legname: Timber .

Legno: Wood.

Libero: Unoccupied, free.

Libretto di lavoro: Work booklet or permit.

Locanda: Inn, small hotel (usually cheaper than a pensione).

Loggia: A covered area on the side of a building. A gallery or balcony open on one or more sides, sometimes arcaded. It can also be a little garden house.

Luce: Electricity, lights.

Lungomare: Seafront road, promenade.

Lusso: Luxury.

Maniero: Manor.

Mansarda: Attic.

Manutenzione: Maintenance.

Marca da bollo: Tax stamp.

Mare: Sea.

Marmi: Marble.

Mattone: Brick.

Mensile: Monthly.

Merceria: Haberdashery shop.

Mercato: Market.

Metrature: Size.

Metri quadri (mq): Square metres.

Mezza pensione: Half board.

Mezzogiorno: A colloquial name for the southern part of Italy. Also means noon.

Millesimi: The term used to express the portion (in thousandths) of a condominium owned by each owner.

Misura: Size, measure.

Mobilio: Furniture.

Modernizzare: Modernisation.

Monolocale (con servizi): Studio or one room (with a kitchen and bathroom) apartment.

Monte: Mountain.

Moquette: Carpet.

Multiproprietà: Timeshare.

Municipio: Town hall.

Muratore: Mason or bricklayer.

Muratura: Stonework.

Muro: Wall.

Mutuo compreso: Mortgage included.

Mutuo per ristrutturazione: Loan for restoration.

Notaio: Notary.

Nuova: New.

Occasione: Bargain, offer.

Officina: Workshop.

Oliveto: Olive grove.

(in) Ordine: In order (good condition).

Originali: Original.

Ostello: Hostel.

Ottima posizione: Excellent (optimum) position.

Ottime condizioni/ottimo stato: Excellent condition.

Padrone/Padrona: Landlord/landlady.

Paese: Town, area, country village.

Paesino: Small village.

Pagamento: Payment.

(di) Paglia: Thatched.

Palazzo: Palace or mansion. Also a large building of any type, including an apartment block.

Parco: Park.

Parquet: Parquet (wooden) flooring.

(in) Parte ristrutturato: Partly restored.

Partita IVA: VAT registration number.

Parzialmente arredato: Partially furnished.

Pavimenti in cotto: Terracotta floors.

Pavimento: Floor.

Pazienza: Patience. Something you will need in abundance when dealing with Italian bureaucracy!

Pensione: Small hotel, often with board.

Perfette condizioni: Perfect condition.

Periferie: The suburbs (of a city).

Perito Agronomo: Land surveyor.

Permessi comunali: Planning permission (granted by comune or town).

Permesso di soggiorno: Permit to stay.

Piano: Floor (of a multi-storey building), e.g. primo (first), secondo (second), terzo (third) piano.

Piano nobile: Main floor of a palace, the first floor up.

Primo piano: First floor. Called the *Piano nobile* in a *palazzo*.

Piano regolatore: Zoning plan.

Piano terra: Ground floor (USA: first floor).

Piastrelle: Tiles.

Piastrellista: Tiler.

Piazza: Square. An urban space bounded by buildings.

Piazzale: Large open square.

Piccolo: Small.

Pietra/legno originale: Original stone/ wood.

Pietra serena: Soft, grey sandstone that's easily carved (common in Siena).

Piscina: Swimming pool.

Pitture: Paint.

Più spese: Plus expenses (e.g. utilities).

Poggiolo: Balcony.

Polizia: Police.

Ponte: Bridge.

Pontile: Wharf for boats.

Portico: Porch. Covered walkway, usually attached to the outside of a building. A roofed space, open or partly enclosed, forming the entrance and centrepiece to a façade.

Portiere: Porter, doorman or janitor in charge of an apartment block.

Portinaio/Portineria: Caretaker or concierge of an apartment block/porter's house.

Porta: Door

Porta blindata: Armoured door with a steel rod locking system.

Porto: Port.

Portone: Main entrance or door.

(a) Posto: Everything in order, good condition.

Posto auto/macchina: Parking space.

Pozzo: Well (for water).

Pozzo nero: Cesspit.

Pratica: File, Conveyancing.

Premio: Premium (e.g. insurance).

Prestito: Loan.

Preventivo: Estimate or quotation, e.g. for building work.

Prezzo: Price.

Prima casa: Principal home (as opposed to a second or holiday home) where you're resident.

Primo piano: First floor. (not ground floor)

Procura: Power of attorney.

Progetto approvato: Approved plans.

Pronta consegna: Ready to move in.

Proprietà: Property.

Questura: Police station.

Quotazione: Quotation.

Rabdomante: Water diviner.

Radiatori: Radiators.

Ragioniere(a): Accountant.

Referenziati: References required.

Regalomento di condominio: Regulations for an apartment (condominium) block.

Rendita catastale: Cadastral value of a property.

(da) Restaurare/Ristrutturare: To be restored.

Restaurato: Restored.

(da) Ricostruire: To be reconstructed.

Rilevamento: Land survey.

Rinascimento: Renaissance. The major school of Italian art, literature and philosophy in the fourteenth to sixteenth centuries that fused innovations in realism with the re-discovery of the great heritage of classical antiquity.

Rinnovamento: Renovation.

Riparazione: Repair.

Ripostiglio: Storage or junk room.

Riscaldamento: Heating.

Riscaldamento autonomo: Independent heating (which can be regulated or switched off by the tenant or apartment owners).

Riscaldamento centrale: Central heating. In an apartment block, this is provided centrally for all apartments, with the cost divided equally between them.

Rivo: Stream.

Rocca: Fortress.

Rococò: Rococo. Light, dainty eighteenth century art and architectural style created in reaction to heavy Baroque.

Rogito: Act or contract signed in front of notary.

Romanico: Romanesque. Architectural style of the eleventh and twelth centuries that reworked ancient Roman forms.

Rovina/Rudere: Ruin. Usually in historical sense.

Rustico: Rustic building. An old home requiring restoration or needs to be finished.

Sala: Room, hall.

Sala da pranzo: Dining room.

Salone: Sitting room, lounge. Hall

Salotto: Salon, sitting or lounge room.

Salvavita: Electricity circuit breaker or trip switch.

Sassi: Stones. Also houses in grottos in the town of Matera.

Scala/Scalinata: Stairway, staircase.

Scaldabagno/caldaie: Hot water heater or system (gas or electric).

(i) Servizi: Kitchen and bathroom. Excluded from the number of rooms quoted in an advertisement.

Scrittura privata: Privately produced conveyance document.

Scuderia: Stable.

Semi arredato: Semi-furnished.

Semicentro: The area just outside the centre of a city.

Seminterrato: Apartment on the basement level.

Senza: Without.

Serrande: Metal curtains or shutters on windows.

Servizi: Services or kitchen and bathroom.

Servizi allacciati: Services connected.

Servizi zonali: Neighbourhood services.

Servizio riscossione ruoli: Condominium or community fees for a property (e.g. an apartment) that shares building elements or services with other properties.

Sfratto: Eviction.

Sindaco: Mayor.

(da) Sistemare: To be put in order (needs some work).

Società: Building society.

Soffitta: Attic.

Soffitti a volta: Vaulted ceilings.

Soffitto: Ceiling.

Soggiorno: Sitting room.

Soggiorno pranzo: Living/dining room.

Sorgente: Spring.

Sottoportego: A street continuing under a building (like an archway) in Venice.

Spese: Expenses.

Spese agenzia: Agent's fees.

Spese del condominio: Condominium fees.

Spese condominiali comprese: Condominium expenses included.

Spiaggia: Beach.

Spiaggia libera/pubblica: Public beach.

Spiaggia privata: Private beach.

Stanza: Room.

Stanza da letto: Bedroom.

Stato: Condition.

Stato di famiglia: Family status documents.

Stazione: Station (e.g. railway).

Stima: Estimate or valuation.

Strada: Street, road.

Struttura: Structure.

Strutturalmente: Structurally.

Stucco: Plaster made from water, lime, sand and powdered marble, used for decorative work.

Studio: Study, den.

Suolo: Ground.

Supermercato: Supermarket.

Tapparelle: Metal or wooden shutters.

Tappeto: Carpet.

Tappeto erboso: Lawn.

Tassa communale dei rifiuti: Garbage tax.

Telefono: Telephone.

Termoautonomo: Independent and automatic heating system.

Terra: Ground floor.

Terrazza: Terrace.

Terreno: Land.

Terreno alberato: With trees.

Terreno boschivo: Wooded land.

Terreno coltivato: Cultivated land, farmland.

Testamento: Will.

Tetto: Roof.

Tinello: Small dining room or family room, den.

Titolo di Proprietà: Title deed.

Toiletta: Toilet, WC.

Torre: Tower.

Torrente: Stream.

Traghetto: Ferry.

Trattabile: Negotiable.

Travertino: Travertine. Light-coloured limestone widely used as a building material in both ancient and modern Rome.

Travi di legno/a vista: Wooden beams (exposed beams).

Ufficio Anagrafe: General registry office (e.g. in a *comune*) where records of residence, birth, death, etc. are kept.

Ufficio delle Imposte Dirette: Provincial tax office (also known as *Fisco*).

Ufficio postale: Post office.

Ultimo piano: Top floor.

Umidità dal basso: Rising damp.

Valore: Value.

Valore catastale: Cadastral (or fiscal) value. Assessment of a property's value for tax purposes.

Vani: Room.

Vasca: Artificial water basin or bath.

Vecchio: Old.

Vendesi: For sale.

Veranda: Porch.

Vetro: Glass.

Via: Street or Road (followed by the name).

Viale privato: Private road.

Vigili urbani: Local town police.

Vigneto: Vineyard.

Villa: Villa. A detached town or country house (usually a large estate). Also includes the park surrounding the house.

Villa Fattoria: The villa-farmhouse of a landowner.

Villaggio: Village.

Villino: Cottage, small detached house with a garden.

Vista: View.

Vista sul mare: Sea view.

Vista sul monte: Mountain view.

Vuoti: Empty, unfurnished.

Zona censuaria: The 'censor' zones into which large towns and cities are divided for registration tax purposes (small towns usually have only one zone).

Zona tranquilla: Quiet, peaceful area.

INDEX

SUGGESTIONS

Please write to us with any comments or suggestions you have regarding the contents of this book (preferably complimentary!). We are particularly interested in proposals for improvements that can be included in future editions. For example did you find any important subjects were omitted or weren't covered in sufficient detail? What difficulties or obstacles have you encountered which aren't covered here? What other subjects would you like to see included?

If your suggestions are used in the next edition of *Buying a Home in Italy*, you'll receive a small gift as a token of our appreciation.

NAME: _____

ADDRESS: _____

_____

_____

Send to: Survival Books, PO Box 146, Wetherby, West Yorks. LS23 6XZ, United Kingdom.

My suggestions are as follows (please use additional pages if necessary):

OTHER SURVIVAL BOOKS

There are other 'Buying a Home' books in this series including *Buying a Home Abroad* plus buying a home in Florida, France, Ireland, Portugal and Spain. We also publish a best-selling series of *Living and Working* books for America, Australia, Britain, France, New Zealand, Spain and Switzerland, which represent the most comprehensive and up-to-date source of practical information available about everyday life in these countries.

Survival Books are available from good bookshops throughout the world or direct from Survival Books. **Order your copies today by phone, fax, mail or e-mail from:** Survival Books, PO Box 146, Wetherby, West Yorks. LS23 6XZ, United Kingdom (tel/fax: 01937-843523, E-mail: survivalbooks@computronx.com Internet: computronx.com/survivalbooks. If you aren't entirely satisfied simply return them within 14 days for a full and unconditional refund.

BUYING A HOME IN . . .

Survival Book's 'Buying a Home' series of books are essential reading for anyone planning to purchase a home abroad and are designed to guide you through the jungle and make it a pleasant and rewarding experience. Most importantly, they are packed with valuable information to help you avoid the sort of disasters that can turn your dream home into a nightmare! Topics covered include:

- Homework & Avoiding Problems
- Choosing the Region
- Finding the Right Home & Location
- Real Estate Agents
- Finance, Mortgages & Taxes

- Home Security
- Utilities, Heating & Air-Conditioning
- Mving House & Settling In
- Renting & Letting
- Permits & Visas

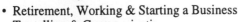

- Retirement, Working & Starting a Business
- Travelling & Communications
- Health & Insurance
- Renting a Car & Driving
- And Much, Much More!

Survival Books are the most comprehensive and up-to-date source of practical information available about buying a home abroad. Whether you're seeking a mansion, villa, farmhouse, townhouse or apartment, a holiday or permanent home, these books will help make your dreams come true. Buy them today and save yourself time, trouble <u>and</u> money?

ORDER FORM

Please rush me the following Survival Books:

Qty	Title	Price*			Total
		UK	Europe	World	
	Buying a Home Abroad	£11.45	£12.95	£14.95	
	Buying a Home in Britain (summer 1999)	£11.45	£12.95	£14.95	
	Buying a Home in Florida	£11.45	£12.95	£14.95	
	Buying a Home in France	£11.45	£12.95	£14.95	
	Buying a Home in Ireland	£11.45	£12.95	£14.95	
	Buying a Home in Italy	£11.45	£12.95	£14.95	
	Buying a Home in Portugal	£11.45	£12.95	£14.95	
	Buying a Home in Spain	£11.45	£12.95	£14.95	
	Living and Working in America	£14.95	£16.95	£20.45	
	Living and Working in Australia	£14.95	£16.95	£20.45	
	Living and Working in Britain	£14.95	£16.95	£20.45	
	Living and Working in Canada (summer 1999)	£14.95	£16.95	£20.45	
	Living and Working in France	£14.95	£16.95	£20.45	
	Living and Working in NZ	£14.95	£16.95	£20.45	
	Living and Working in Spain	£14.95	£16.95	£20.45	
	Living and Working in Switzerland	£14.95	£16.95	£20.45	
	The Alien's Guide to France (spring 1999)	£5.95	£6.95	£8.45	
				TOTAL	

Cheque enclosed/Please charge my Access/Delta/Mastercard/Switch/Visa* card,

Expiry date _____ No. __ __ __ __   __ __ __ __   __ __ __ __   __ __ __ __

Issue number (Switch only) _____ Signature: _____

* Delete as applicable (price for Europe/World includes airmail postage)

NAME: _____

ADDRESS: _____

_____

_____

Send to: Survival Books, PO Box 146, Wetherby, West Yorks. LS23 6XZ, United Kingdom **or tel/fax/e-mail credit card orders to 44-1937-843523.**